Guide for the Christian Perplexed

Guide for the Christian Perplexed

Edited by
Thomas P. Power

With Study Guide

☙PICKWICK *Publications* • Eugene, Oregon

GUIDE FOR THE CHRISTIAN PERPLEXED

Copyright © 2012 Wipf and Stock Publishers. All rights reserved. Except for brief quotations in critical publications or reviews, no part of this book may be reproduced in any manner without prior written permission from the publisher. Write: Permissions, Wipf and Stock Publishers, 199 W. 8th Ave., Suite 3, Eugene, OR 97401.

Pickwick Publications
An Imprint of Wipf and Stock Publishers
199 W. 8th Ave., Suite 3
Eugene, OR 97401

www.wipfandstock.com

ISBN 13: 978-1-61097-458-5

Cataloging-in-Publication data:

Guide for the Christian perplexed / Edited by Thomas P. Power.

xviii + 268 p.; 23 cm—Includes bibliographic references and illustrations.

ISBN 13: 978-1-61097-458-5

1. Theology—Miscellanea. 2. Christianity—Miscellanea. I. Power, Thomas P.

BR96 G80 2012

Revised Standard Version of the Bible, copyright 1952 [2nd edition, 1971] by the Division of Christian Education of the National Council of the Churches of Christ in the United States of America. Used by permission. All rights reserved.

New Revised Standard Version Bible, copyright 1989, Division of Christian Education of the National Council of the Churches of Christ in the United States of America. Used by permission. All rights reserved.

Manufactured in the USA

Contents

Contributors / vii
Acknowledgments / ix
Introduction by Alan Hayes and Thomas P. Power / xi

1. What Can We Know of Jesus? / 1
   Terence L. Donaldson

2. How Can the Wrathful God of the Old Testament Be Reconciled with the Gracious Lord of the New Testament? / 25
   J. Glen Taylor

3. The Challenge of Suffering / 44
   L. Ann Jervis

4. Signposts in a Strange Land: Doctrine, Memory, and Christian Life "on the Way" / 56
   Joseph L. Mangina

5. God Bless the Atheists: Faith and Antifaith Today / 69
   Ephraim Radner

6. Does God Condemn Non-Christians? / 87
   George Sumner

7. Why Evangelism? Being Caught Up in the Swoop of Grace / 98
   John P. Bowen

8. Who is My Neighbor? The Perplexities of International Development for Communities of Faith / 119
   David D. Kupp

9. Let's Talk about Sex / 154
   David A. Reed

- 10 Why Christian Spirituality? / 173
  Merv Mercer

- 11 Celtic Christianity and the Postmodern Spiritual Quest / 190
  Thomas P. Power

- 12 Is Worship a Waste of a Good Sunday Morning? / 201
  Annette Brownlee

- 13 Pastoral Perplexity / 221
  Paul Friesen

- 14 Pew Perplexity / 233
  Karen Stiller

- 15 Study Guide / 246
  J. Andrew Edwards

Bibliography / 261

Contributors

John P. Bowen is Associate Professor of Evangelism, Director of the Institute of Evangelism, Wycliffe College.

Annette Brownlee is Chaplain and Director, Centre for Lay Education, Wycliffe College.

Terence L. Donaldson is Lord and Lady Coggan Professor of New Testament Studies, Wycliffe College.

J. Andrew Edwards is a doctoral candidate in Systematic Theology, Wycliffe College, and Managing Editor, Parish Market, Liturgical Press.

Paul Friesen is Rector, St. Paul's Church, Halifax; Adjunct Lecturer, Atlantic School of Theology; Associate Fellow, King's College, Halifax; Scholar Associate, Wycliffe College.

Alan Hayes is Bishops Frederick and Heber Wilkinson Professor of Church History, Wycliffe College; Director, Toronto School of Theology.

L. Ann Jervis is Professor of New Testament, Advanced Degree Director, Wycliffe College.

David D. Kupp is Adjunct Faculty, Urban and International Development, Wycliffe College.

Joseph L. Mangina is Associate Professor of Systematic Theology, Wycliffe College.

Merv Mercer is Professor Emeritus of Anglican Formation, Wycliffe College.

Thomas P. Power is Theological Librarian, Adjunct Professor of Church History, Wycliffe College.

Ephraim Radner is Professor of Historical Theology, Wycliffe College.

David A. Reed is Professor Emeritus of Pastoral Theology, Wycliffe College.

Karen Stiller is a Member of the Board of Trustees, Wycliffe College and a freelance author.

George Sumner is Principal and Helliwell Professor of World Mission, Wycliffe College.

J. Glen Taylor is Associate Professor of Old Testament and Basic Degree Director, Wycliffe College.

Acknowledgments

THANKS TO HOPE PUBLISHING Company for permission to quote Sydney Carter's "Lord of the Dance" (© 1963 Stainer & Bell, Ltd. All rights reserved) in chapter seven.

For assistance in various ways I would like to acknowledge the following:

For acting as readers to papers: members of the faculty, Allan Loder, Wanda Malcolm, Christopher Schoon, Michael Knowles, Rev. Mike Michielin, and Rev. Dean Mercer. I want to thank Andy Edwards particularly. Not only did he act as editorial assistant to this project, but he also compiled a thoughtful study guide. I am grateful for his diligence and attention to detail.

For a grant in aid of publication I would like to thank The Leonard Foundation, and Rob Henderson of the Development Office, Wycliffe College for his good offices in respect of the same.

Introduction

Alan Hayes and Thomas P. Power

TWO OBSERVATIONS INITIALLY LED us to write this book. First, thoughtful Christians are legitimately perplexed by a number of issues of the church's belief and practice. They are perplexed partly because they recognize that the issues themselves are thorny and partly because they are not sure how to test the mutually inconsistent theories and explanations which are affirmed by diverse voices speaking with equal assurance. Second, most Christians find relatively little occasion or encouragement to address their perplexities with intellectual candor and integrity. If they dare to acknowledge their theological perplexities at all, they are too often told that these perplexities are unimportant or that they can be answered very simply or that they should be left to the experts.

Those who offer this book are professors at an Anglican theological college where our job is, in effect, to help students identify and address their theological perplexities. From our doing so with our students, it seemed a potentially worthwhile extension to do so with a wider constituency. We identified some key questions that many Christians today rightly find perplexing, and wrote chapter-length reflections on them. The result is this book.

We have called the book a guide. We are not advocating a particular theological position or presenting the manifesto of a school of thought. We are primarily hoping to introduce readers to some resources and perspectives that will help them reflect fruitfully on their Christian perplexities. This is not to say that we have pretended to remain theologically neutral and value-free. On the contrary, each of us has a point of view to offer on his or her particular topic. But in each case we have tried to recognize the legitimacy of other points of view, and we have tried to respect the reader's right to weigh the evidence freely. We have tried not to use rhetorical sleights-of-hand to cajole, bully, or flatter the reader into submitting to our own opinions. In fact, the authors themselves are not of a single mind on all issues; readers will notice a number of points where we disagree among ourselves. Our goal here is simply "to guide." In each case we present a perplexity, show what is at stake, suggest some pertinent considerations, note some of the alternative positions that have been adopted, and explain the approach that we would take ourselves. We imagine that few readers will agree with all the conclusions that are advanced here, but we hope and expect that most readers will find the content, approach, and style of the discussion helpful as they test or develop their own understanding of the "perplexing issues" identified in this book.

Although the book does indeed incorporate a certain diversity of perspectives, it is also fair to say that we agree on three common principles. First, we understand Christianity to be, like Judaism and Islam, a "religion of the book." We believe that those who think about and live the Christian faith need to be closely engaged with the Bible, understood as uniquely authoritative. This principle differentiates us from those who might consider the teaching of the Bible to be deeply tainted by the archaic thought-forms and primitive ethical norms of an ancient Middle Eastern culture, and therefore to require deconstruction and reconstitution according to the science and values of Western modernity.

Second, we understand the Bible to be an amazingly rich, diverse, and grace-filled set of documents, forever eluding human attempts to reduce it to elementary propositions and comfortable insights. Reading the Bible well therefore requires disciplined, critically aware, and discerning interpretation. This principle differentiates us from those whose reading of the Bible usually agrees with the common sense and personal piety which they bring to it.

Third, we are Anglicans, and we accept a principle which is characteristic of mainstream Anglicanism (though, of course, by no means exclusive to it): to do theology rightly requires an appropriate use of the academic tools of the humanities. These tools include the study of languages, the analysis of documentary texts and social contexts, history, logic, and clear writing.

It is on this basis, then, that we have addressed the perplexing questions identified in this book. We recognize that, in one form or another, each of these questions has been perplexing for many centuries. They have been the subject of controversy at the very least, and in some cases they have occasioned schism, inquisition, or religious warfare. Here, however, we have not emphasized past debates, but have preferred to focus on current discussions.

We begin with the question, "What can we know of Jesus?" Some say that our sources for Jesus's life are so ideologically driven that we cannot trust them at all; others affirm that the New Testament contains only divinely guaranteed historical truth, in spite of its incorporation, in several cases, of different versions of the same story. The thoughtful Christian will recognize a perplexity here, and will want to reflect on both the value and the limitations of the New Testament as an historical source for the life of Jesus. Terry Donaldson, professor of New Testament, and a specialist in the social milieu of first-century Judaism, presents a clear and systematic introduction to the New Testament evidence, laying an excellent foundation for the rest of the book.

If God has saved the world, why is there still affliction? Why would an all-powerful God who loves us permit us to face suffering? While it is barely possible to affirm either that the experience of suffering is entirely illusory or that God sends us suffering to serve larger cosmic purposes, few will be satisfied with either of these answers. Here, too, we confront a perplexing issue, and L. Ann Jervis, professor of New Testament, has made it a focus of her scholarly research for several years. She notes that the New Testament authors themselves struggled with it, and reports some of the ways they dealt with it. She shows, too, how readers today can appropriate their insights into their own faith.

Christian doctrine is perplexing because it can seem like a set of theological propositions handed down from on high by an ecclesiastical authority, hard to understand and little related to everyday life. Joseph Mangina, professor of systematic theology, acknowledges that doctrine in this perspective is certainly perplexing, but argues that it might better be understood as "faithful memory" that allows us to receive and pass on the community's knowledge of Jesus. Doctrine does not "explain" God, but it allows us to speak of God with integrity. When its proper function in the life of the church is recognized, it can be seen as very practical indeed.

The Old Testament is perplexing to many Christians partly because it seems to belong primarily to another religion, Judaism, and partly because it depicts a God who does a great many unpleasant things, such as destroying young men who make fun of Elisha the prophet, and entertaining prayers to bash in the heads of babies. Some Christians, including the second-century Marcion of Pontus and, more recently, some German Christians of the Nazi era, have been particularly negative about the Old Testament. Today, although few Christian preachers might attack it outright, many simply avoid preaching on it. J. Glen Taylor, professor of Old Testament, shows why the Old Testament is essential for an understanding of Christ, and urges us to note how sometimes our resistance to it exposes some soft spots in our own spirituality.

In our multi-cultural society, many Christians are particularly perplexed by passages in scripture and by doctrinal teachings that restrict salvation to followers of Christ. This kind of exclusivism seems embarrassingly intolerant, but if the alternatives are either that religion does not matter at all, or that all religions say the same thing, then perplexities arise there, too. George Sumner, Helliwell professor of world mission, directly addresses the relation of Christianity to other religions. He avoids huge generalizations, recognizing that Christianity comes in many forms and varieties, as indeed do Judaism, Islam, and other world religions. Nevertheless, it is clear that there are indeed some resemblances between, say, the biblical doctrine of creation and the Islamic *sharia;* both teach right order and virtue. But it is also clear that there is uniqueness in Christian claims for the importance of Jesus Christ.

World religions apart, atheism has had a resurgence in our time and this has presented new challenges to people of faith. In untangling the different threads of neo-atheism, Ephraim Radner, professor of historical theology, presents it as a modern western phenomenon containing two branches, philosophical and moral, that have coalesced by virtue of popular writing and debate. While atheists point to evil, suffering and catastrophe in the world as evidence of the absence of a caring God, Christians look to belief in God as the primary point of reference to which all else is subsidiary. When we know God we do not allow tragedy, discomfort, or trial to subvert that reality. This allows us to love and forgive. The Bible reveals the purpose of God for humanity, a purpose that culminates in Jesus Christ.

Many Christians feel perplexed over the issue of how best to share their faith with others. While they are convinced and enthusiastic about their faith, they are often tongue-tied, awkward, and feel intrusive when it comes to talking about it with other people. In considering this issue, John Bowen, professor of evangelism, using the image of the dance, lays out for us the "what," the "why," and the "how" of evangelism. From it, it becomes clear that people come to faith in a variety of ways and in different contexts, and Bowen invites us to be sensitive and aware of this potential in our everyday interactions with people.

A perennial question for Christians is to understand fully how to respond to the question, "Who is my neighbor?" both in its local and international development contexts. The question has particular relevance today in our global world. A significant part of the problem is to understand the perplexities of development, how development relates to Christian faith, and what our response should be. In his analysis, David Kupp, who teaches in our MTS (Development) program, provides a close critique of the range of issues particularly in an urban context but also offers clear pointers about how the church should proceed in this area. In preference to an all-too-ready tendency among church members to believe that action on their part will solve the problems of the world, he proposes instead an approach of deep engagement with the issues of society.

Worship over the generations has been another source of perplexity for people. Annette Brownlee, chaplain to Wycliffe College, provides us with a new and refreshing understanding of the rich spiritual life that can flow from our worship. Foundational is that God provides us with the opportunity to worship and it us our decision to respond. We must remember, however, that worship is not about us. Instead, Brownlee, reminds us that "Worship is about the action God took in light of the mess we have made of the life God gave us." It should come naturally to believers to participate in this public, shared, and visible act. Ultimately, worship is our response in gratitude, love, and humble acknowledgement for what God has done (and continues to do) for us as sinners.

Sexual issues have never been easy for the church, but David Reed, professor emeritus of pastoral theology, writes that the sexual revolution of the 1960s made sex an exceptionally complex social reality. One result is that the relatively simple official teachings and categories which satisfied many churchgoers in earlier generations are of little use today. On the other hand, it is not that the church is required to bless all contemporary patterns of sexuality, since, clearly, "all is not well in post-1960s sexland." One problem is that sexual experiment corrodes community; another is that it victimizes children. A Christian perspective will begin with the recognition that sex is not a matter of biology alone; it is profoundly spiritual, too.

What is most conspicuously perplexing about Christian spirituality is that some of its recent forms have lost their meaning. Merv Mercer, emeritus professor of Anglican formation, begins his essay with a vivid description of the sinking *Titanic*, and then strikingly compares the great but tragic ship to the institutionalized Western church. So much of our recent Christian spirituality has been linked to a twentieth-century vision of modernity that, as the latter has begun losing its force, so has the former. But our response should be not discouragement, but the hope that, as T. S. Eliot wrote, "The Church must be forever building, and always decaying, and always being restored." Mercer outlines some of the essential features of an authentic Christian spirituality in a postmodern age.

Recently a Celtic festival in southern Ontario attracted an estimated 13,000 people. One of them was Thomas Power, theological librarian and an historian of Irish Christianity. Perhaps many came to the festival simply because they liked Irish music and Irish crafts; but Power also takes note of a broad contemporary flowering of interest in Celtic spirituality, both pagan and Christian. A Celtic spirituality is characterized, among other things, by a pre-modern stress on community, image, creativity, and nature. Why are so many in our postmodern culture attracted to Celtic spirituality? And what can the church today learn from it?

Subjoined to the main essays are the reflections of a pastor, Rev. Dr. Paul Friesen, who provides some directives for pastors, preachers, and parish priests on how the *Guide* might assist in their ministries; and a contribution from Karen Stiller who gives the perspective of a layperson in the pew. Also we have appended a study guide, compiled by Andy Edwards, a doctoral student in systematic theology at Wycliffe College. We believe that this study guide will be useful for personal study or for use by study groups in churches. Either way the intention is that it can be used as a tool to extend reflection on the essays in this volume. We encourage its wide use.

A final word of counsel. These perplexities, though real and important, are subordinate. The fundamental Christian perplexity is of a different order; it is the mystery of God's love which, transcending our comprehension, claims our hearts and minds, and which, penetrating our humanity, shapes and directs our lives, and indeed all of human history. The real purpose of a book like this, and perhaps of any Christian book, is, we think, to put the subordinate perplexities in their subordinate place, so that the first and final mystery is at the center. We would like to think that we have succeeded in this; but our readers can decide for themselves. The topics addressed in this book—our knowledge of Jesus, the meaning of suffering, the function of doctrine, the understanding of scripture, the place of other religions, the challenge of atheism, the pleasures and complications of sexual differentiation, the nature of worship, the way to evangelize, understanding who our neighbor is locally and globally, and the diversities of spirituality—all point to the heart of the mystery of God, "in knowledge of whom standeth our eternal life, whose service is perfect freedom."

1

What Can We Know of Jesus?

Terence L. Donaldson

INTRODUCTION

PRONOUNCEMENTS BY COMMITTEES OF academic scholars do not usually become media events, but this is precisely what has happened in the past few years with the Jesus Seminar. Its twin volumes, *The Five Gospels* and *The Acts of Jesus*,[1] have captured public imagination, partly because of a continuing fascination with Jesus in North American society and partly because of the media savvy of the Seminar's co-chairpersons, Robert Funk and Dominic Crossan. The questions addressed by the Seminar—concerning the reliability of the New Testament gospels and the authenticity of the deeds and sayings attributed to Jesus—while by no means new, have usually been discussed in sober lecture halls and learned academic tomes. But the Seminar's way of addressing these questions has been more academic street theatre than ivory-tower discourse. Their procedure of voting with different-colored beads—red for things that Jesus undoubtedly did or said, black for actions or sayings that he undoubtedly did not, with shades of pink and grey in between—and their publication of a correspondingly color-coded version of the gospels (a clever takeoff on traditional red-letter editions) have

---

1. Funk et al., *The Five Gospels*; Funk and the Jesus Seminar, *The Acts of Jesus*.

been shrewdly devised to capture the attention of a sound-bite, photo-op culture.

Public interest in the Jesus Seminar has been further heightened, however, by the fact that in its version of the gospels there is precious little red ink to be found at all; in other words, the total number of sayings and deeds considered to be certainly authentic is strikingly small. (There is probably little red ink in the publisher's balance sheets for these volumes as well, but that is another matter!) The only red (i.e., certainly authentic) segment of the Lord's Prayer, for example, is the opening "Our Father"; no red appears in the Beatitudes whatsoever!

This brings us to the question posed in the title of this chapter. The question of what we can know of Jesus has been raised by intelligent outsiders at least since the time of the second-century writer Celsus and, since the Enlightenment, increasingly by scholars within the Christian tradition. While the Jesus Seminar tends to occupy the more skeptical end of the scholarly spectrum, what is new about it is not so much the answer it tends to favor as the way in which it has aroused public interest in the question.

Faced with this question, Christians of a traditional sort might want to respond that the answer is obvious—what we can know about Jesus has been reliably preserved for us in the gospels—and might react with some annoyance that the Jesus Seminar has been able to gain such a hearing among a credulous public. But matters are not quite so simple. The gospels are complicated documents; the issues that dominate the modern study of Jesus have been generated not solely by the unwarranted skepticism of publicity-seeking scholars but at least partly by the nature of the gospels themselves. To take one small example, was the last supper a Passover meal, as Mark and the other Synoptic Gospels indicate (see Mark 14:12),[2] or did it take place the night before Passover, as John's gospel has it (John 13:1; 18:28)? Or, within the Synoptics themselves, how exactly did the disciples respond to the incident where Jesus came to them walking on the water—by worshiping him and acclaiming him as Son of God (Matt 14:33) or with lack of comprehension because "their hearts were hardened" (Mark 6:52)? Again, where did the encounters with the risen Jesus take place? Only in and around Jerusalem, as in

---

2. The Synoptic Gospels are Matthew, Mark, and Luke, so named because they tend to share a common viewpoint on the story of Jesus, especially when compared with John's gospel.

Luke-Acts (the disciples are actually commanded by the risen Jesus to remain in Jerusalem until Pentecost; Luke 24:49)? Or in Galilee, as in Matthew and Mark? As these examples indicate, the question of what we can know about Jesus is a live one, and the answer cannot simply be read off from the New Testament as if it were an answer sheet at the back of a textbook. Still, scholarly skepticism—unwarranted varieties included—is present in large doses in the Jesus Seminar and its spinoffs, and the answer is not to be read off from its productions either.[3]

EVIDENCE AND INTERPRETATION

There are several dimensions to our question, which we will have to address in due course. One has been highlighted by the Jesus Seminar, and has to do with the evidence at our disposal. To put it in the most general terms: What solid information do we have, from the gospels and elsewhere, about the life, teaching and activity of Jesus? Contained within this general question are some more specific ones: What evidence is there for Jesus outside the New Testament? With respect to the New Testament itself, how reliable is the material in the gospels? Are there indeed sayings or events that should be in black type, to pose the question in terms of the Seminar's color scheme? To the extent that the answer to this question is yes, what considerations might be put into play in order to differentiate between "red" and "black" material?

But this is only part of what is contained in the question, "What can we know of Jesus?" For the knowledge of Jesus that is being sought here is not simply a catalogue of reliable information. What we are interested in knowing is what the information adds up to, what overall portrait emerges of the person of Jesus, his agenda and his significance, what structure is to be built with the raw evidential material. Here is where matters get confusing. For while modern reconstructions of the life and ministry of Jesus tend to agree in general terms about the most reliable items of information concerning Jesus,[4] the resultant portraits are bewildering in their variety. An apocalyptic prophet of the end times, a maverick rabbi, a Galilean holy man, a wandering sage, a politically oriented champion of the underclass,

---

3. In addition to the books produced by the Seminar as a whole, see Crossan, *The Historical Jesus*; Funk, *Honest to Jesus*.

4. I am oversimplifying to make a point.

a Zealot revolutionary, an itinerant Cynic gadfly—the recent spate of Jesus books has included all of these "takes" on the story and more. While some of these are incongruent with the traditional portraits found in the gospels, most of them at least bring aspects of the gospel accounts into fresh new light. The question of what we can know of Jesus, then, involves the identification not only of reliable information about him but also of the most appropriate interpretive model within which this information is to be understood and made meaningful.

JESUS OF HISTORY, CHRIST OF FAITH

Before tackling our question directly, it will be helpful to stand back and consider a preliminary question about the question, one having to do with the potential significance of whatever might emerge at the end of the process. Why might it be important to identify what can be known about the person, aims and achievement of Jesus of Nazareth? Who might want to know, and why? The sheer variety of the Jesuses that have been proposed suggests that the personal predispositions brought to the task by interpreters have at least some impact on the profile of Jesus that is produced. This book is addressed generally to those with some interest in how the Christian gospel might be understood in the contemporary context. Thus the question has to do with the ongoing religious significance of the earthly Jesus himself.

As a way of bringing the question into focus, it will be helpful to start where the Jesus Seminar's *The Five Gospels* starts—with the Apostles' Creed. With roots going back to the second century, this creed, traditionally used in the context of baptism, reflects one of the earliest Christian attempts to articulate the core beliefs of the church. It is instructive to come at this creed from the perspective of the question, "What is the ongoing religious significance of Jesus of Nazareth?" The relevant portion of the creed is brief enough to be cited in full:

> I believe in Jesus Christ, his [God's] only Son, our Lord,
> who was conceived by the Holy Spirit,
> born of the Virgin Mary,
> suffered under Pontius Pilate,
> was crucified, died and was buried;
> He descended to the dead.
> On the third day he rose again . . .

What is striking about this (and any other traditional) creed is the absence of any article concerning the earthly Jesus himself. The creed jumps over the events of his life, moving straight from his birth to his death and resurrection. The implication seems to be that the events of Jesus's active ministry—teaching, preaching, gathering disciples, healing, conflict with the religious authorities and so on, are of minor importance in any Christian assessment of Jesus's significance. The Apostles' Creed seems to suggest that what we might be able to find out about the earthly Jesus does not really help us to get at his ongoing religious significance at all.

This distinction between the "Jesus of history"—the human person, with his own particular agenda, self-understanding and accomplishments—and the "Christ of faith"—the "only Son of God" who "for us and for our salvation came down from heaven," as the Nicene Creed puts it—is one of the basic assumptions underlying the activity of the Jesus Seminar and other scholarly quests for the historical Jesus. The distinction can be exaggerated (on which more in a moment), but it is nevertheless real. One cannot read through Luke-Acts, for example, without being struck by the difference between the message proclaimed *by* Jesus in the Gospel of Luke (centered on the coming reign or kingdom of God and its present implications) and that proclaimed *about* Jesus by the early Christians in the Acts of the Apostles (centered on the saving significance of Jesus's death and resurrection as Messiah and Lord). A similar distinction is apparent between Paul's summary of what he calls the "gospel" in 1 Cor 15:3–8 ("Christ died for our sins in accordance with the scriptures . . .") and the Lord's prayer in Matt 6:9–13 (where the focus is on God and God's reign, with Jesus's own person and role not mentioned at all).

The Jesus Seminar represents an approach in which the distinction between the earthly Jesus and the gospel Christ tends to be seen as a mutually exclusive either/or. *The Five Gospels*, for example, describes the Apostles' Creed as a text in which "Jesus is *displaced* by the Christ" (my emphasis). Or again: "Once the discrepancy between the Jesus of history and the Christ of faith emerged from under the smothering cloud of the historic creeds, it was only a matter of time before scholars sought to disengage the Jesus of history from the Christ of the church's faith."[5]

---

5. Funk et al., *The Five Gospels*, 7.

The assumption appears to be that the real earthly Jesus has been so obscured by a mythical Christ foisted on the Christian movement by the apostle Paul and those of his ilk, that Jesus can be restored to view only by means of heroic reconstructive work carried out by scholars who have been able to free themselves "from the dark ages of theological tyranny."[6]

This approach is, I believe, exaggerated. The gospels themselves combine an interest in the earthly Jesus with a commitment to the gospel Christ. As their name suggests, the gospels represent a narrative version of the gospel, an attempt to narrate the events in Jesus's active ministry according to a plotline discernible in condensed form in such texts as 1 Cor 15:3–8 and the Apostles' Creed. But while the distinction is not to be exaggerated, it is at the same time not to be denied. The pre-Easter message of Jesus is not simply to be equated with the post-Easter message about him, as if the only thing on Jesus's mind was how to get Pilate to crucify him so that they could both get their names into the Apostles' Creed. Jesus's own message seems to have centered on the reign of God, its nearness and the need for Israel to prepare for its appearance. While this message and the preaching of the early church are not mutually exclusive—indeed, I will argue for an important element of continuity between them—neither are they identical. The statements "I was sent only to the lost sheep of the house of Israel" (Matt 15:24) and "in Christ God was reconciling the world to himself" (2 Cor 5:19), for example, express quite different conceptions of Jesus's task and achievement. They are not to be changed one into the other by some interpretive sleight of hand, no matter how well intentioned. The Jesus Seminar is quite right in making a distinction between Jesus's own understanding of his calling and mission and the church's understanding of his achievement and lasting significance, even if Seminar members are prone to exaggerate the difference.

EASTER

Standing between these two understandings of Jesus's mission, of course, and precipitating the transition from one to the other, is the Easter experience. From all accounts, the events of what the church has come to call "Good Friday" were shattering for the disciples of Jesus. They had

---

6. The phrase appears in ibid., 8.

accompanied him to Jerusalem, in growing expectation and hope "that he was the one to redeem Israel" (Luke 24:21). In the original Greek form of the statement just quoted, the emphasis falls on "he," which, I believe, captures very nicely the mood of the disciples as they sought to come to terms with Jesus's death. "We had hoped that *he* was the one to redeem Israel," they lamented, but evidently he was not: messiahs by definition do not suffer at the hands of Israel's enemies; they triumph over them.

But then, unexpectedly, on the day after the sabbath, the disciples began to have experiences (however we might understand them) that convinced them that death was not the final event in the story, but that God had raised Jesus from death into the new life of the age to come. This had several immediate ramifications. First, since Jesus had been executed as a messianic pretender, resurrection must be God's reversal of that verdict, God's own vindication of Jesus's messianic status. In other words, the resurrection convinced the disciples that Jesus was, despite the unexpected event of the crucifixion, the long-awaited Messiah of Israel. But secondly, if death and resurrection were an integral part of Jesus's role as Messiah, then it was necessary for them to rethink a lot of things—including both their inherited tradition concerning the nature and task of the Messiah and their previous perceptions of Jesus's life and ministry. Their new belief that it was "in accordance with the scriptures" that the Messiah should suffer, die and be raised (cf. 1 Cor 15:3-4) provided them with a whole new frame of reference for reading Israel's scriptures and for understanding the life and ministry of Jesus.

Two points of clarification are needed before we move on. First, it is necessary to acknowledge that as early Christians engaged in the process of unpacking the significance of all this, they did so with a considerable degree of diversity and variety. Paul and Matthew have quite different understandings of the place of Israel's Law in the new, Christ-centered scheme of things; Paul and James have equally diverse perspectives on the relationship between "faith" and "works." Still it can be argued with considerable justification that the main Christian movement shared a basic commitment to the core set of convictions that Paul describes in 1 Cor 15:3-8 as the "gospel."

Second, my description of the new, post-Easter framework and its role in early Christian reinterpretation of things does not depend in any way on the reality of the resurrection itself. Early Christianity (including the New Testament) was produced by a dynamic combustion between the disciples' experience of the earthly Jesus himself and their subsequent belief that he had been raised. The only thing that needs to be assumed at this point is the disciples' belief in the resurrection. Even if John Allegro were right in his outrageous suggestion that belief in the resurrection was the outcome of a session with hallucinogenic mushrooms,[7] the subsequent "combustion" could be understood in (more or less) the same way.

But however this new belief emerged—hallucination or (as Christians have always believed) mighty act of God—it has definite consequences for the question of what we can know of Jesus himself. Our most significant accounts of Jesus's life and activity (I will address extracanonical material presently) have been produced by communities whose "take" on Jesus has been significantly altered by this new belief that emerged at a point after his earthly life and activity had come to an end. In the canonical gospels, their recollections of Jesus's preaching, teaching and activity have been filtered through what they had later come to believe, namely, "that the Messiah is to suffer and to rise from the dead on the third day, and that repentance and forgiveness of sins is to be proclaimed in his name to all nations, beginning from Jerusalem" (Luke 24:46–47). By contrast, the two disciples on the road to Emmaus, whose deep disappointment at Jesus's death (Luke 24:21) was noted above, would have produced quite a different account of Jesus's life and activity, if they had had occasion to do so at this point in their experience when the story seemed to have reached a termination point in his death.

This has definite implications for the nature of the gospels as sources for the pre-Easter Jesus. The gospels were produced not as archives of Jesus's life but as proclamations of the gospel, documents whose purpose was to elicit and confirm faith in Jesus as Messiah and savior. The post-Easter perspective on Jesus's true character and significance, then, has had a defining effect on the way Jesus is remembered and portrayed in the gospels. At the very least it has functioned as a filter in the sense both of determining which elements would be preserved and presented (on the analogy of a water filter) and (as with a lens filter) of casting a particular hue over the whole field of vision. In some cases it may even

---

7. Allegro, *The Sacred Mushroom and the Cross*.

have had a more generative effect, resulting in the actual production of gospel material.

SEQUENCE AND ORDER

Let us look at some examples. At the least problematic level, there is the matter of order. The Synoptic Gospels in particular contain many of the same incidents but in quite different sequential order, suggesting that the sequences of their narratives were determined more by thematic concerns than by any desire to preserve any actual historical order. Both Matthew and Luke, for example, contain the account of the would-be disciples who are confronted with the true costs of discipleship (Matt 8:19-22; Luke 9:57-62). In Matthew, the incident takes place prior to the account of the stilling of the storm, just as Jesus was heading for the boat. Luke also has the stilling of the storm incident, but places this in the previous chapter (8:22-25). The would-be disciples, by contrast, approach Jesus in Luke's version shortly after his departure for Jerusalem (9:51), an event that in Matthew's Gospel takes place eleven chapters later (19:1). Further, Mark also recounts the stilling of the storm, but here it takes place just after the parable of the sower (and related parables in 4:1-33). Matthew, by contrast, places these parables in chapter 13, five chapters after the stilling of the storm. Not that agreement in sequence is totally absent; all four gospels, for example, link the beginning of Jesus's ministry with that of John the Baptist and bring the story to an end with the events in Jerusalem (last supper, arrest, trial, crucifixion, burial, resurrection). But in between, the sequence of narration varies considerably, apparently having been determined by thematic concerns, i.e., by the needs of the gospel message that is being proclaimed in the gospel story rather than by any desire to record sequential history.

But the goals and perspective of the gospel writers are not limited in their effect to the matter of order alone. Returning to an example cited above, in their accounts of the incident concerning Jesus's walking on the water (Matt 14:28-33; Mark 6:47-52), Matthew and Mark conclude in strikingly different ways: Matthew states, "those in the boat worshiped him, saying, 'Truly you are the Son of God'" (Matt 14:33), where Mark writes, "they were utterly astounded, for they did not understand about the loaves, but their hearts were hardened" (Mark 6:51-52). It is possible to split the difference and to say that the reaction of the disciples was mixed with Matthew recording the more positive assessment and Mark the more dubious. But this fails to do justice to either account, neither of which portrays a mixed response. Moreover, each account is consistent with the broader portrayal of the disciples' response in the respective gospels as a whole. While Mark tends to portray the disciples as somewhat dimwitted, incapable of perceiving Jesus correctly prior to the resurrection, Matthew presents the disciples as already possessing an accurate perception of Jesus even before the final events in Jerusalem. If we are forced to choose (and a choice of some kind seems to be called for), it seems more likely that Mark's portrayal is closer to the truth and that Matthew has seen this event through a post-Easter filter, ascribing to the disciples a perception and a response that was more in keeping with the post-Easter situation. It is not surprising that the Jesus Seminar has given this aspect of Matthew's gospel a "black" (i.e., inauthentic) rating.

The post-Easter perspective is even more pronounced in John's gospel. While the narratives in John might supplement our information from the Synoptics about the events in Jesus's ministry, the lengthy discourses attributed to Jesus are so unlike the speech of Jesus as we hear it in the Synoptics, so similar to the language of the author himself (it is difficult to know sometimes where Jesus's speech ends and the author's commentary begins; e.g., 3:11–21; cf. 3:31–36), and so characteristic of a post-Easter perception of Jesus's person and mission that it is hard to hear in them the same voice that we hear in, say, the Sermon on the Mount. Indeed, many scholars see Jesus's discourses in John's gospel as a paraphrase of the deeper meaning of Jesus's life and activity as perceived by the author and his community at a later date, rather than as anything like a transcript of the actual speech of Jesus. Not that the emphases in John (the identity of Jesus as the divine Son of the Father, come down from heaven to bring eternal life to those who believe in him) are completely without parallel in the Synoptic Gospels (e.g., Matt 11:25–27). But the author of the Fourth Gospel seems to have picked up these weak signals and amplified them considerably, perhaps in accordance with the principle enunciated in John 16:12–15.

OTHER SOURCES

When scholars pose the question, "What can we know about Jesus?" then, they usually mean, "What can we know about the activity, teaching, aims and self-conception of the earthly Jesus, as these would have been perceived by those close to him prior to the events that brought this earthly ministry to an end?" To use the gospels in this quest means finding some way to counteract the effect of their post-Easter perspective on Jesus—bracketing it, eliminating it, or at least taking it into account in some appropriate way. Before seeing how this might be done, however, it is appropriate to consider the possibility of other source material. For if there was evidence for Jesus that was not subject to this post-Easter filter—or better (since we all view reality through one filter or another), evidence that perceived Jesus through some different filter or framework—we might be able to gain some perspective in our assessment of the gospels.

While such evidence exists, it is unfortunately not plentiful enough to supplement the gospels in any substantial way. Still, some mention should be made of it.[8] Curiously enough, the most significant of these sources might be found within the gospels themselves. Most scholars are convinced that embedded in Matthew and Luke is a source, usually dubbed "Q," that Matthew and Luke have independently incorporated into their own work. In order to say something about Q, it is necessary to provide a brief description of how scholars think the Synoptics came to be written.

In addition to the kind of differences outlined above, the first three gospels also contain striking similarities in content and wording, similarities extensive enough to suggest some sort of literary relationship among the gospels. Some of these similarities are in reported speech. Matt 3:7–10 and Luke 3:7–9, for example, contain almost identical versions of John's preaching; similar agreements in the sayings of Jesus are frequently encountered (e.g., Matt 6:24 and Luke 16:13; Matt 16:24–28, Mark 8:34–9:1, and Luke 9:23–27). At first glance, such similarity in wording is not surprising; it might simply be attributed to accurate reporting. But at second glance it is quite significant. Jesus and John almost certainly spoke in their native Aramaic, but the gospels were written in Greek. Similarities in wording, then, cannot be attributed

---

8. For a full description and assessment, see Meier, *A Marginal Jew*, 1:56–166.

simply to accurate reporting; their presence in Greek must be due to some literary linkage over and above simple dependence on a common Aramaic speech or speech record. In other words, the gospel writers must have been depending on a common written source, or one or other of them has used one (or more) of the already existing gospels as source material. (It needs to be noted that our concepts of plagiarism and intellectual property would have been foreign to the ancients.) In addition to speech, the gospels also contain striking similarities in narrative description (e.g., Matt 14:36 and Mark 6:56), summarizing comments (Matt 7:28-29, Mark 1:22, and Luke 4:32), and the like.

To cut to the end of a long and complicated story, most scholars are convinced that in composing their gospels, the writers made use of already existing written sources (Luke says as much in Luke 1:1-4). Specifically, it is believed that Mark was the first gospel to be written and that it in turn was used by Matthew and Luke as the basic framework for their expanded, second-generation gospels.[9] Their reason for producing such gospels, presumably, was that they had access to additional material pertaining to Jesus that was worth preserving. In particular, it is believed that Matthew and Luke had access to a written collection (in Greek) of Jesus's sayings. This hypothetical document has, in the course of scholarly discussion, come to be known as Q (from the German *Quelle*, or "source").

If such a document existed, it has several points of relevance to our question. For present purposes, however, the most pertinent point is that Q apparently contained no account of Jesus's death and resurrection. Some scholars infer from this that Q provides evidence of a different early perspective on Jesus, one that saw his significance in his teaching and preaching rather than his death and resurrection. This position has the decided disadvantage of a double burden of proof, since it consists of a hypothetical perspective posited on the basis of a hypothetical document. What gives it some credence, however, is the existence of the *Gospel of Thomas*.

The *Gospel of Thomas* is one of the documents discovered at Nag Hammadi in Egypt, evidently part of a library of Gnostic Christians. In form, *Thomas* is similar to what scholars have envisaged for Q; that is, it consists entirely of discourses—a total of 114 separate sayings or

---

9. There is considerable debate and uncertainty about the identity of the writers of the gospels. The gospels themselves are anonymous; the names of their supposed authors were supplied later in church tradition.

parables—with no narrative element at all. In particular, like the hypothetical Q document it contains no account of the suffering, death and resurrection of Jesus. Where the *Gospel of Thomas* sayings overlap with the Synoptic Gospels (e.g., the parable of the Banquet [*Gos. Thom.* 64; Matt 22:1–14; Luke 14:15–24]; the parable of the Wheat and the Weeds [*Gos. Thom.* 57; Matt 13:24–30), they do not seem to be dependent on the Synoptics; that is, they seem to reflect an independent preservation of the saying rather than being simply a reworked version of the synoptic account. Now there is no evidence that the *Gospel of Thomas* is related to Q in any direct way. Its relevance for the present point is that, like Q, it represents a "take" on Jesus that is not filtered through the experience of the resurrection. It should be noted in passing, however, that apart from this possible indirect literary evidence, there is no direct evidence for a form of Christianity that located the significance of Jesus solely in his teaching with no reference to his resurrection and personal identity.

Outside the New Testament, the most important reference to Jesus is found in the writings of the first-century Jewish historian Josephus. His *Antiquities of the Jews* contains two references to Jesus. The second, in *Antiquities* 20.200, is found in a section describing the death of James (the brother of Jesus and leader of the Jerusalem church). Josephus mentions in passing that James was "the brother of Jesus who was called the Christ." The statement seems to assume that the readers of the account will be familiar with Jesus, an observation that becomes pertinent when we consider the earlier reference (Josephus, *Antiquities* 18.116–19). As it stands, this earlier statement about Jesus is highly suspect, in that it could only have been written by a Christian. Josephus, disenchanted with messianic figures generally and certainly not a Christian, could not have written that Jesus "was the Messiah" who "on the third day [after the crucifixion] appeared to them restored to life." Since the writings of Josephus were preserved by Christian monks and scholars, it is most probably the case that the passage as it stands is the work of Christian revisers. But it is unlikely that the passage was created out of whole cloth. As was observed above, the subsequent passage concerning James seems to presuppose an earlier mention of Jesus. Most scholars feel that Josephus had said something about Jesus at this point, indicating at least that he was a teacher and miracle worker who had been crucified by Pontius Pilate at the instigation of Jewish leaders. Still, there is nothing in the passage to suggest that Josephus had access to indirect information about Jesus. His knowledge of Jesus and his activity may simply have been provided by Christians themselves.

Similar conclusions are to be drawn about the references to Jesus and early Christianity in three late first- and early second-century Roman writers: Suetonius (*Claudius* 25.4), Tacitus (*Annals* 15.44) and Pliny the Younger (*Letter* 10.96). That is, while they are of great interest for what they tell us about developing Roman awareness of Christianity, they contain no independent evidence about Jesus. Jewish rabbinic references to Jesus emerge only later, and are likewise secondary.

In one respect, then, material from outside the Christian tradition is of very little help in reconstructing the figure of Jesus. But in another respect, it plays an absolutely crucial role. If we know anything at all about Jesus, we know that he was a Jewish preacher, teacher and miracle worker who came into conflict with the religious and political establishment in Judea and was executed as a messianic pretender by the Romans. For a reconstruction of Jesus's agenda and activity to be successful, then, it must be able to account for these basic facts. That is, it must be able to fit Jesus plausibly into the context of first-century, Roman-occupied Judea and to account for his execution at the hands of the occupying powers.

Fortunately, we have been blessed with a great quantity of literary and material evidence for the Greco-Roman world in general and the Jewish world in particular. This is not the place to attempt even a partial list of this material. It ranges from the writings of Josephus, with its full (though hardly impartial) account of the history of Judea; to the Dead Sea Scrolls, which open a window onto a fervent Jewish sect; to first-century archaeological remains, including the ankle bone of a crucified man in Jerusalem and a small fishing boat in the Sea of Galilee. Taken in total it allows us to reconceive in considerable detail the social, religious and political environment in which Jesus is to be sought and understood. The resultant understanding of this environment provides us both with illumination of the gospel material at many points and with a kind of control mechanism—that is, any portrait of Jesus needs to be plausible in this environment.

DIRECT EVIDENCE

Such portraits, however, are drawn on the basis of the more direct evidence, to which we now turn. Any modern reconstruction of the person and program of Jesus tends to be built up on the basis of at least three constituent elements: (1) the determination of a set of fixed points, i.e., basic data that are beyond refute and are foundational for any reconstruction; (2) a decision about how the rest of the tradition is to be used; and (3) an overarching interpretive model. Each requires some elaborative discussion.

Over the course of the modern discussion, scholars have developed several "criteria of authenticity," that is, criteria for determining indisputable facts about Jesus's teaching and activity. I will not attempt anything like a complete description here, but I will mention two that are particularly pertinent. One is the "criterion of dissimilarity," which attempts to identify material that is so dissimilar to the interests and concerns of the church that it must go back to Jesus. Put differently, what is being sought here is gospel material that even on the most skeptical of assumptions could not have been created by the early church. One example, i.e. the baptism by John the Baptist, will have to suffice. A glance at Matthew's account of the baptism (Matt 3:13–17) will illustrate the fact that the story raised some difficulties for early Christians. Why should the sinless savior have submitted to a "baptism of repentance for the forgiveness of sins" (Mark 1:4)? Even the most skeptical scholar needs to recognize that the church would not have invented a story like this. Jesus's identification with the person and program of John the Baptist needs to be seen as one of the set of foundational points on which any reconstruction of Jesus's own person and program needs to rest.

The second criterion to be mentioned here is the "criterion of multiple attestation." Greater reliability can be attributed to elements of Jesus's teaching or characteristic activity that are found in most or all of the sources or strands of gospel material. The proclamation of the kingdom or reign of God, for example, is not restricted to Mark or to Q or to just the special material found in Matthew or Luke. The fact that it is found in all these bodies of material (and thus is "multiply attested") means that no one can doubt the presence of the kingdom theme as a key element in Jesus's preaching.

On the basis of criteria such as these, scholars identify a set of authentic elements that usually include such things as the following:

identification with John the Baptist; the proclamation of the kingdom; popularity with the common people; association with "sinners"; teaching in parables; engaging in acts of healing; gathering of disciples; addressing God in prayer as "Abba" (Father); conflict with the religious and political establishment; and execution as a messianic pretender.

The second element in any reconstruction of Jesus's person and program involves an assumption or a decision about what to do with the large quantity of gospel material that can be identified neither as certainly authentic nor as so reflective of post-Easter perspectives that it needs to be seen as a product of later development. Here one finds quite a spectrum of approaches. At one end are minimalist approaches that assume that if authenticity cannot be demonstrated according to criteria such as those described above, then the material is inauthentic, i.e., seen as the later invention of the church.[10] Such radical skepticism, however, seems to be clearly unwarranted. If the church was prepared to retain material that was embarrassing (e.g., baptism by John the Baptist) and refrained from creating material that might be relevant to their own post-Easter context (e.g., narratives having to do with whether uncircumcised Gentiles could become disciples), then there seems to be little reason to be skeptical of the mass of material that is at least consistent with the certainly authentic core. At the other end of the spectrum we find more inclusive approaches that attempt to incorporate as much additional material as possible.[11]

While scholars often attempt to construct rational justification for their approach to this material and their position along this minimalist/maximalist axis, it seems to me that this is often a justification after the fact. That is, the choice of material is often determined more by the shape and requirements of the portrait of Jesus that the scholar wants to emerge at the end of the process than by some criteria determined independently at the outset. Which brings us to the third element present in most reconstructions—an overarching hypothesis about Jesus's person and program; in other words, an interpretive model.

Most reconstructions of Jesus's life and ministry tend to posit or to argue towards some overall interpretive framework within which Jesus is to be understood. Some of these are based on identifiable models from Jesus's own context—a prophet of the end times, for example, or

---

10. E.g., Bultmann, *Jesus and the Word*.
11. E.g., Wright, *Jesus and the Victory of God*.

a Galilean sage. Others are based on more generalized themes, or on a composite of several different models and themes. Interpretive models play an integral and decisive role in any research project, whether it be in science, history, or biblical studies. In the case of Jesus research, more attention needs to be paid to such interpretive frameworks than is often the case.

NECESSARY CRITERIA

An assumption frequently at work in current scholarly treatments of Jesus is that there is a radical disjunction between the beliefs and message of the early church and those of Jesus himself. As was mentioned above, I want to maintain a distinction between the two. But all too often the existence of this distinction is taken to imply that the beliefs of the early church are of no relevance whatsoever to the quest for Jesus himself and thus must be resolutely bracketed out and excluded from the investigation. But why should this be so? Why should the pre-Easter Jesus, who on any account was an original and creative thinker who had a powerful impact on his followers, have had no impact at all on their post-Easter thought and activity? Why should we exclude at the outset the possibility that the post-Easter estimation of Jesus can be of no help whatsoever in discovering his own characteristic themes and agenda?

Now to allay any suspicions (or, perhaps, to dash any hopes) that I am trying to smuggle a traditional, pre-critical reading of the gospels across the Easter border, I need to reaffirm my belief that the Easter experience precipitated a radical reorientation in the disciples' estimation of who Jesus was and what God was doing through him. But the reorientation, I argue, is a reworking, not a replacement, of their earlier experience of Jesus, and cannot be understood without it.

What I am proposing as an interpretive model, then, is a kind of algebraic equation in which Jesus's activity and agenda is the X to be discovered, on the basis of its relationship to other, more certainly known quantities. I see the post-Easter faith of the disciples as the result of a dynamic interaction between two factors—(1) the disciples' experience of Jesus's message and ministry (i.e., the X to be discovered), and (2) the subsequent Easter experience, which convinced them that God had raised Jesus from the dead. Solving for X, then, the question to be answered is this: What sort of person and program must the disciples have experienced as they followed Jesus around Galilee and Judea that, when combined with the new experience of the resurrected Jesus, would have produced the kind of Christianity that we discern at the earliest stages of the New Testament tradition?

To help us answer this question, we can note from our earlier discussion that our unknown quantity X is part of three other algebraic equations, or, to put it another way, has to satisfy two boundary conditions. First, the resultant portrait of Jesus needs to account for and be consistent with the set of details that emerge from a judicious application of the various criteria of authenticity. Our X is not a completely unknown quantity; its core elements can be discerned by means of these criteria. While there is no reason to limit the authentic material to this set of details, any portrait of Jesus needs to account for them in a full and convincing way.

Second, the resultant portrait of Jesus needs to fit comfortably into the religious, social and political environment of first-century Judaism. This is not to eliminate distinctive or unique features at the outset; anyone who gathers a following and creates an impact must stand out from his or her contemporaries in some way. But by the same token, to be able to gather a following and have an impact, Jesus's person and program must have reflected and resonated with the convictions and concerns of his cultural environment. So we are looking for an X that is at home in a first-century Galilean and Judean environment.

Third, the resultant portrait of Jesus needs to account for the crucifixion. Jesus was executed as a messianic pretender by the occupying Roman government; this outcome sets some conditions that need to be fulfilled by any reconstruction. We are looking for an X that might, in the right circumstances, evoke enough hostility that Pilate would execute him as a messianic pretender.

JESUS'S SELF-AWARENESS

Before leaving this general discussion of interpretive frameworks, there is one additional issue that needs to be recognized, having to do with Jesus's own consciousness and self-awareness. Subsequent Christian thinking, both within the New Testament and beyond, has attributed a unique, elevated identity to Jesus. Somehow (and centuries of theological wrangling and creedal formulation have attempted to express just how), God's very essence (it has been asserted) was fully and uniquely present in the human person, Jesus of Nazareth. Most modern Jesus scholarship, by contrast, has tended to operate on the assumption that the Jesus reflected in the gospels, especially the Synoptics, is able to be understood in more human terms. That is, while he may well have been aware of a unique calling and an intimate relationship with God, he did not walk around Galilee with the secret knowledge that he really was the second person of the Trinity, "true God of true God, begotten not made, of one being with the Father." Because of this, Jesus research has often been perceived by orthodox Christians of a traditional sort to represent an undermining of the faith.

This raises issues that would require a chapter of its own (and probably a different author). Here I will simply make two clarifying distinctions. First, what we are searching for here has to do primarily with the perception of Jesus by others rather than Jesus's own self-consciousness. This is not to deny that there is a connection between the two, nor is it to suggest that it is somehow illegitimate to inquire into the "aims and intentions of Jesus." However, the material that has come to us provides us with much more evidence for the impressions that Jesus made on those around him and much less—and even then only indirect—evidence for his own self-consciousness and self-understanding. In asking what we can *know* about the Jesus of history we need to begin with the more solid and direct evidence, which has to do with the perceptions and memories of others.

Of course, indirect evidence does have evidential value, and so it is not inappropriate to ask what we might be able to discern from the impressions Jesus made on those around him about his own self-consciousness. This brings me to the second distinction, having to do with the content of the creeds and Jesus's own self-consciousness. It is quite possible to affirm the creeds without necessarily understanding them as statements of Jesus's own self-consciousness. While the later creedal formulations speak of the exalted nature of Jesus as the pre-existent Son of God, they also speak of his incarnation and full humanity. If his full humanity is to be taken with any seriousness at all, this may well suggest that the assertion of Jesus's divine nature cannot be used as a theological trump card to exempt him from the characteristic particularities and limitations of contextualized human existence.

Given a statement about Christ's self-emptying such as we find in Phil 2:7, it is not necessary to assume, in the name of orthodoxy, that the truth of the Nicene Creed depends on it being a description of how the earthly Jesus understood his own identity and role. It is not necessary to assume, for example, out of a misguided loyalty to orthodox tradition, that it was part of Jesus's self-conscious agenda to generate a church that would endure for centuries after his death and resurrection, founded on the belief that he himself was "true God from true God, begotten not made, of one being with the Father," the one through whom "all things were made." It is possible to understand Jesus as engaged in a mission directed primarily to Israel, centered on the proclamation of the imminent appearance of the reign of God and the need for Israel to prepare itself in advance of the crisis that would usher in God's reign. At the same time, of course, we do not need to avoid, out of a misguided loyalty to critical scholarship, the possibility that Jesus understood his person and mission in ways that might, under the influence of the Easter experience, have produced the kind of faith that is presupposed by the New Testament accounts as a whole.

THE GENTILES

To clarify what I mean, here, let us explore this example a little more. What sort of algebraic equation can we deduce in which the earliest Christian understanding of itself as the "church" is the product of Jesus's mission to Israel, as the disciples perceived it, *plus* the impact of the resurrection experience? To explore this in its entirety would require a whole book in itself. But let me pick up several aspects of it.

One aspect is the inclusion of the Gentiles. Within a very few years of the crucifixion the early Christians were not only opening their doors to Gentile members but actively recruiting them. This attitude seems to stand in considerable contrast to that of Jesus. "I was sent only to the lost sheep of the house of Israel," Jesus is reported to have said in Matt 15:24 (cf. Matt 10:5–6). While such explicit statements of an ethnically restricted mission are found only in Matthew (and thus do not satisfy the criterion of multiple attestation), they are nevertheless confirmed by a number of additional considerations.

(1) *Jesus's baptism.* John's mission was patently Israel-centered; according to both the gospels and Josephus (*Antiquities* 18.117) he was concerned to call forth a repentant remnant within Israel in advance of the kingdom of God. Jesus's baptism by John indicates that he identified with such an Israel-centered mission as well (though this does not imply that his vision was identical to or constrained by that of John).

(2) *The parameters of Jesus's activity.* The general pattern of Jesus's travels and activity suggests that he directed his mission primarily to Israel. While Gentiles occasionally sought him out (and were commended for their faith, a point to which I will return), it is primarily Jewish crowds, locales and concerns that fill the horizon of the gospels.

(3) *The crucifixion.* The fact that Jesus was executed as a messianic pretender also underscores the Israel-focus of his mission.

(4) *The circumcision controversy.* While the early church quickly began to open its membership to Gentiles, there was considerable controversy over the precise terms on which they were to be admitted and the degree of conformity to the Jewish law that would be required of them. This would not have been the case if Jesus had already established clear precedents.

At the same time, however, Gentiles enter the horizon of Jesus's mission in significant ways. As was mentioned above, there are several accounts in which Gentiles petition Jesus (Matt 8:5–13; Mark 7:24–30), who in turn praises them for their faith.

Further, he apparently anticipates that when the kingdom arrives in its fullness, Gentiles will come to share the kingdom banquet with Abraham, Isaac and Jacob (Matt 8:11). This statement can be illuminated considerably by contemporary Jewish patterns of thought. In Jesus's day there was a widespread belief within Judaism that when the kingdom arrived—when God intervened in a dramatic way to vindicate Israel, to subjugate Israel's enemies, to eradicate evil and to gather the dispersed—then the Gentiles would recognize the folly of their idolatry, turn to the God of Israel and be invited to share in the blessings of the kingdom (e.g., Isa 2:2–4; Zech 8:20–23; Tob 14:5–6; and so forth). In all probability Jesus shared this view; while the priority for the present was to prepare Israel for the kingdom, in the future—when the kingdom arrived—the Gentiles would be invited to share in the blessings of salvation.

It is easy to see how a belief in the resurrection of Jesus could have combined with such an attitude towards Israel and the Gentiles on Jesus's part to produce the situation that we actually do find in the early church. The experience of the resurrection convinced the disciples that the age of the kingdom was breaking into the present in a dramatic way and was about to arrive in all its fullness (e.g., Acts 1:6; 1 Cor 10:11; Heb 6:5). This in turn could readily have led them to believe that the time to invite the Gentiles had also arrived. The fact that Jesus himself had challenged traditional interpretation of the law in significant ways would at least have left open the question of the terms on which Gentiles should be admitted into the church. While the argument could be articulated in more detail, the fact that we can construct a coherent alignment of these three terms—the situation in the early church, the impact of the resurrection, and elements in the gospels that can be supported by certainly authentic material—provides solid confirmation of this aspect of gospel tradition.

THE DEATH OF JESUS

As a second example, let us consider the idea of Jesus's death as a saving event—the early Christian belief that "Christ died for us." This one is considerably trickier, in that the saving significance of Jesus's death was a central element of early Christian belief and thus a major factor in the post-Easter filter through which the ministry of Jesus is viewed in the gospels. One can, therefore, understand the hesitancy with which many scholars approach texts in the gospels in which Jesus attributes significance to his own death (e.g., Mark 10:45) or uses crucifixion language with respect to the life of discipleship (e.g., Mark 8:34).

Again, however, it is not necessary to assume that this aspect of early Christian belief was totally the product of the post-Easter church, with no raw material drawn from Jesus himself. For one thing, it takes no great leap of faith to believe that Jesus anticipated the possibility of his own death. After all, it was readily apparent that anyone who went about proclaiming the reign of God in territory that was firmly under the reign of Caesar, and who gathered crowds and provoked controversy in the process, was courting danger. The fate of John the Baptist provided a vivid case in point, one which Jesus must have pondered deeply. Further, the demonstration in the temple (Mark 11:15-18) indicates that it was not a matter of Jesus simply being aware of the risks he was running; at this crucial point at least, he almost went out of his way to provoke them. For the period of Passover was a time when the city was teeming with excitable visitors and when the political authorities, therefore, would have been in a state of high alert, wanting to nip any disturbance in the bud. Such a deliberately provocative gesture, then, suggests not only that Jesus anticipated the possibility of his death but also that he was willing to take actions that made such an outcome almost inevitable. This in turn implies that he may well have given some consideration to the implications of suffering and death for his ministry.

THE SON OF MAN

What sense might we be able to make of this? This is not an easy question, and I cannot enter into a full discussion here. Nevertheless, I would like to make one suggestion of how past-Easter thinking about Jesus's death may have been stimulated in part by his own self-understanding. The suggestion has to do with the enigmatic term, Son of Man, which clearly was Jesus's own preferred way of referring to himself. The scholarly debate about the meaning of this term as it appears in the gospels has been particularly intense and complex, and we cannot even begin to sketch the complexity here. Still, a strong case can be made that the most pertinent background for the term is to be found in the figure of "one like a son of man" in Dan 7:13 (RSV).

At this point in Daniel's vision the seer has just seen four successive world empires, each symbolized by a grotesque beast of one kind or another. At the climax of the vision these are replaced by God's kingdom, symbolized not by a beastly figure but by "one like a son of man"—i.e., a human figure. Two things are of particular interest in the passage. One is that this human figure is closely associated with the people of Israel as a whole. In verse 14, the "dominion and glory and kingship" are given to this "one like a son of man"; but in a parallel passage a few verses later the "kingdom and dominion and the greatness of the kingdoms under the whole heaven" are given "to the people of the holy ones of the most high" (Dan 7:27). The "son of man," therefore, somehow represents, symbolizes or is identified with the people as a whole. The other pertinent feature of the passage is that the people receive sovereignty only after a period of intense suffering at the hands of the fourth beast (Dan 7:23–24). This suffering is brought to an end only with God's intervention to overthrow the beast and to vindicate the people.

It is at least possible, then, that lying behind Jesus's use of the term "son of man" is a representative self-understanding. Jesus may well have understood his own particular calling to identify fully with the "people of the saints of the Most High," sharing their oppression and judgment at the hands of the Roman power, in anticipation of vindication in the soon-arriving kingdom of God. The experience of the resurrection could readily have led the disciples to transform this model of identification into the more generalized notion of Christ's death "for us."

CONCLUSION

In my discussion of the question "What can we know of Jesus?" I have chosen to put the emphasis on the second word rather than the first— that is, on the question of how we can arrive at an accurate and coherent portrait of Jesus rather than on the portrait itself.

The previous two examples will have to suffice as illustration of how we might move back behind the powerful experience of the resurrection to discern the person and program of the earthly Jesus as perceived by the disciples. If there were space to develop this in more detail, I would do so under four headings: (1) kingdom, (2) community, (3) cross, (4) Christ.

Perhaps the best way to bring the present discussion to an end is to return to the question "who wants to know, and why?" For the figure of Jesus, as we encounter him in the gospels, continues to confront us at a deep and personal level. If one poses with any seriousness the historical question "What can we know of Jesus?" one sooner or later comes face to face with a question that is much more existential: "Who do *you* say that I am?" (cf. Mark 8:29). A great deal is at stake in how one responds.

How Can the Wrathful God of the Old Testament Be Reconciled with the Gracious Lord of the New Testament?

J. Glen Taylor

FEW PEOPLE TODAY ARE familiar with a Christian named Marcion who lived in the second century AD. However, many people today share the views for which he became both famous and notorious in the early church. A wealthy shipbuilder from Pontus by the Mediterranean Sea, Marcion preached a certain understanding of the Bible that seemed attractive to many, but which was condemned as heresy.

What was it that Marcion believed? He taught that the wrathful God we read about in the Old Testament bore no relation to the loving God and Father of Jesus Christ about whom we read in the New Testament. True, Jesus was the Son of God—but, added Marcion, he was not the Son of that angry god of the Old Testament.

Unlike Marcion, most Christians link Jesus with the God of the Old Testament. But like Marcion, most Christians, at one time or another, have felt some measure of discontinuity between the Old Testament God of wrath and the one whom Jesus taught his disciples to call Abba, "Papa." It is difficult to deny; certain parts of the Old Testament do seem to paint a picture of God that is hard to reconcile with Jesus and the "good news" of the New Testament. Take, for example, God's command to annihilate the Canaanites or the psalms in which a "pious" person prays for the heads of his enemies' babies to be bashed on a rock. How are statements like these to be reconciled with the teaching of Jesus that we should love and pray for our enemies? Or take the action of God who destroyed a group of young men for mocking his prophet Elisha? How can we equate this God with Jesus who took little children on his lap and blessed them? Small wonder, some might say, that the seeds of Marcion's heresy still take root in the minds of many Christians today.

Why does it matter that so simple and understandable a view as Marcion's lives on? What, after all, is the problem with a few private convictions about which Testament is to be preferred? Who in our culture of tolerance, not to say also of evolving ideas, minds a little discord such as we imagine between the Old and New Testaments? Does it not make sense in a way that the "Old" Testament reflects more primitive ideas and is thus somewhat obsolete and that the "New" Testament has more charitable, progressive ideas and is thus more relevant for today? Does not the very idea of a person's view being judged by the church as "heresy" smack of a judgmental attitude that is no longer in vogue today?

As good as these objections to being too hard on Marcion may sound, there are in fact good reasons to oppose them still today. For one thing, so harsh a view of the Old Testament and its God is dangerously close to (or is) anti-Semitism. To deride the Hebrew Bible (our Old Testament) and its God is to cast aspersion on the cornerstone upon which Jewish identity is built. For another thing, so harsh a view of the Old Testament is to dissociate Jesus and Christianity from the historical and religious context in which it is set and which gives it its meaning. Without his vital connection to the Old Testament and its God, Jesus appears out of nowhere, uninvited and unexpected, to fulfill a mission that is completely unintelligible and thus meaningless. Let Marcion have his way and we have as much hope of understanding Jesus's love for humankind as of understanding Romeo's love for Juliet, if a thief had stolen Shakespeare's script of this famous play, along with the stage and its props, and all the attending characters. But, no thanks to Marcion, we do have the full story and the context, including in Jesus's case his appearance on the stage of real history. Just as we owe to Shakespeare's famous play why Romeo drank poison, so we owe to the Old Testament via the witness of the New why Jesus died on the cross. A Jew in the line of King David, and the fulfillment of a promise made in Second Samuel 7, Jesus appeared on a stage that was set to receive a long-expected kingly messiah. As the theologian Reinhold Niebuhr put it: "No Christ could validate himself as the disclosure of a hidden divine sovereignty over history or as a vindication of the meaningfulness of history, if a Christ were not expected."[1]

As important as background and context are, if that were the only role of the Old Testament, Marcion could still be right to some degree. After all, one could still claim that the background and props provided by the Old Testament are a dark and ugly foil against which Jesus shines all the more brightly. But the Old Testament is far more than mere background. It is no snakeskin to be sloughed off or chaff to be let fly once the grain has appeared. Rather, for Jesus himself, the God of the Old Testament was his own father, whose name, as the Lord's Prayer reminds us, was to be "hallowed" by his followers. The Jesus of grace and love affirmed that the Old Testament contained the very words of God, from which were set aside no dot from a single "i" and no cross from a single "t." In truth the Old Testament became *more*, not less, scrutinized and appreciated as scripture in light of the ministry of Jesus, a ministry to which, so he claimed, the Old Testament pointed and through which it was fulfilled. Taking its cue from Jesus, the church has never questioned the authority of the Old Testament. The question rather was which books pertaining to Jesus and the apostles were rightly to be discerned as standing *en par* with it. Once the business of discerning the Christian canon was over, the Old Testament still made up *three-quarters* of the *Christian* Bible.[2] (Does the practice of our church reflect this truth today? I suggest not and that Marcion has been allowed to have his way!)

The importance of the Old Testament for the church can also be appreciated by considering how much the New Testament, in its imagery, assumptions and references echoes and builds upon the Old. Among recent writers perhaps no one has shown better this indebtedness of the New Testament to the Old than Elizabeth Achtemeier. She reminds us that we owe to the Old Testament our understanding of the nature of the church (the new covenant people), of ourselves (made in the image of God, loved by but also alienated from God), of the world (a good

---

1. Niebuhr, *The Nature and Destiny of Man*, 2:15.
2. Note how unintelligibly the New Testament begins without the Old being understood as coming before (Matthew 1): "A record of the genealogy of Jesus Christ, the son of David, the son of Abraham. Abraham was the father of Isaac, Isaac was the father of Jacob, and Jacob the father of Judah and his brothers," and so forth.

thing created by God), and of God.³ Note how often the contents of the Old Testament receive mention in her discussion below, which is limited only to the earthly ministry of Jesus:

> For those New Testament writers who told the story of Jesus' earthly life and death, Jesus was described as a new Moses (Matthew), or as the prophet like Moses, who was to come (John; Acts); of as the Suffering Servant who gave his life as a ransom for many (Mark). He was the one who freed Israel from her final slavery (Galatians); the one who instituted the new Sinai covenant of the prophets in his blood (1 Corinthians; Hebrews); who made the perfect sacrifice for sin once for all (Hebrews). He was Psalm 118's stone that the builders rejected, which had become the head of the corner (1 Peter). He was Isaiah 8's rock of stumbling for the Jews and foolishness for the Gentiles (1 Corinthians). He was the ideal righteous man of the psalms, suffering and praising his father from the cross (Passion stories). In short, the traditions of the exodus, Passover, and Sinai, the Hexateuchal and prophetic traditions and the Psalter, and . . . the Wisdom writings, all found their goal in Jesus Christ, and that plan that God began with his first release of people from Egypt was, according to the New Testament writers, brought to completion in the story of the crucifixion and resurrection.⁴

With all these points in common between the New Testament and the Old, and with the Old Testament receiving the full endorsement it did from Jesus, the early church had good reasons for thinking that Marcion was chopping away at the trunk of the tree and not simply at some old branch that he regarded as ugly and distasteful.

In what follows I want to promote an understanding of the Old Testament as a wonder-filled and perpetually inspiring part of Christian scripture that is not simply background to the "good news" of the gospel, but that is an integral part of the gospel story itself.

---

3. Achtemeier, *Preaching from the Old Testament*, 21–26.

4. Ibid., 24, offering a summary of her earlier *The Old Testament and the Proclamation of the Gospel*.

OWNING UP TO DIFFICULTIES

Let us be honest. Some parts of the Old Testament are difficult, even distressing, to read. I believe that a good place to begin is with an honest admission of this very fact.

Why is it important to come clean about our discomfort? First, there is no point in pretending that things are otherwise. Second, and more importantly, we must acknowledge and face these passages if we ever hope to learn from them. What are their lessons? They vary to be sure, but a common thread that runs through many is that they can teach us about the very issue I am raising, that of honesty. By acknowledging some distaste for what we read in the Old Testament, we enter into the very spirit of the Old Testament itself. This is so because what we often find distasteful in the Old Testament reflects or mirrors those things that we find distasteful about ourselves and about God, things we might otherwise choose to ignore or hide. In other words, many of these passages force us to a level of openness and honesty with ourselves, with others, and (most troubling perhaps) with God that we find discomforting by reason of what they tell us of our true feeling towards ourselves, others, and God.

There is a dynamic role to these so-called troublesome passages such that what one person finds distasteful another does not, depending on the attitudes and level of self-awareness and honesty displayed by that individual. For example, a self-righteous person might take particular offense at a passage that implies humans are steeped in sin and stand guilty before a righteous God, whereas a person with a higher sense of personal guilt would not. Or again, for example, a deeply pious person with a high view of God's perfection and holiness might take offense at a passage in which Job or a psalm writer openly and overtly expresses anger or frustration towards God on the grounds of his alleged abandonment, persecution or the like. This dynamic quality to what we find offensive can often serve as a kind of guide to an area under which the word of God might be bringing us under judgment for the very attitudes that we hold that cause the offense. In this way, then, our honesty and openness becomes a gateway through which we move beyond mere offense to such things as self-examination, confession of sin, or some disposition towards God, or attitude about him, to which he is open but we are not. In short, my appeal is for honesty about the Old Testament, which will, in turn, invite and inform our own honesty.

I have alluded briefly to ways in which the Old Testament not only invites our honesty but informs or judges it as well. A specific example taken from Ecclesiastes will help to illustrate this. I sometimes hear Christians say that Ecclesiastes seems so skeptical and pessimistic that they find it hard if not impossible to reconcile with the more upbeat tone of other books or even the good news of Jesus itself. Ironically, however, some of these same Christians experience an incongruity in their own lives between their own cynical or pessimistic attitudes, on the one hand, and their affirmation of the victory of God through the gospel on the other hand. The irony of course is this, that the very book (Ecclesiastes) that proves so troublesome to some Christians for its sour, downbeat perspective has the unique potential to mirror, address and expose similar attitudes of pessimism or doubt that many Christians, despite being people of "the good news," often genuinely experience. A difficult book like Ecclesiastes, then, can be seen to challenge the very Christians so troubled by it towards a whole new level of honesty and openness towards themselves, God and others.

A final point on honesty moves in a slightly different direction. I refer to the observation made long ago by Joseph Butler and, before him, by Origen who put it as well as any: "he who believes the Scripture to have proceeded from him who is the Author of Nature, may well expect to find the same sort of difficulties in it, as are found in the constitution of Nature."[5] The English biblical scholar David Wenham makes this same point when he writes:

> Now if the same sort of difficulties that we find in the Bible are also to be found in Providence, it follows that attempts to make the Bible acceptable to the modern palate by deleting all that appears "savage" and "blood-thirsty" will land us in insuperable difficulties over the question of Providence. We can see for our own eyes that God allows war, famine, disease, torture and misery—and that on a colossal scale. Though it is profoundly difficult to understand, it is thoroughly consistent with what we see in the Bible. It is in fact easier to accept the God of the Bible than it is to accept a liberalized God whose character has ceased to be terrible. The God of liberal theology is not only out of touch with the Bible, but also with the world as we find it.[6]

---

5. I owe the relevance of Butler's and Origen's work to Wenham, *The Goodness of God*, 25.

6. Ibid., 26.

Two important points follow from this. First, many of the difficulties we see in the Old Testament are similar to the ones we see in the realm of nature, both of which are spawned by God. Second, if we are able to acknowledge the general goodness and beauty of nature despite the occasional instance of brutality or horror we find in it, we should be able to have a similar appreciation of the Old Testament despite the occasional passage or episode that seems brutal or otherwise troublesome.

In sum, it is important to admit to whatever feelings of discomfort we may have towards the Old Testament and that through the honesty that such admission requires one finds a clue to appreciating a goodly portion of the Old Testament itself. This is so because the Old Testament conveys and invites a stark honesty that is true to nature and experience. This is so also because many of the passages that we find troubling are laden with power, power to judge our naiveté about the reality of human sin or about the sheer complexity of life, even when lived for God. Ultimately there is often a catharsis brought about by these passages if, instead of dismissing them, we allow them to bring us into conformity with the God of a complex, often harsh and disturbing world.

A NOTORIOUSLY DIFFICULT PASSAGE

In Psalm 137:9 the psalmist prays the following regarding his enemies: "Happy shall they be who take your little ones and dash them against the rock!" There is perhaps no more troubling passage for Christian readers than this one. What follows is a list of several considerations, none original to me, that serves to illustrate that even a difficult passage such as this warrants reverent attention as part of the canon of Christian scripture:

- Like it or not, the passage reflects real and true feelings that people can and do have; none of us is beyond the hatred underlying it. (Here then is another good example of the brutal honesty discussed previously.)
- There is nothing to suggest that the psalmist's words are recorded with approval, but only as a true indication of how he felt before God. (After all, what thought of ours, if genuinely felt, is God not willing to hear?)

- The psalmist is not taking matters into his own hands by doing as he wishes; rather he is unburdening his vengeful thoughts before God.

- Unlike many parts of the Western world today, ancient Israel was often a place where unspeakably vicious crimes of war and barbarism were inflicted upon innocent civilians. The mindset of the psalmist is thus better judged today in the context, say, of a Tutsi in Rwanda during the genocide of the 1990s than in the context of upper-middle-class North America where the experience of senseless bloodshed may involve as little as the prick of a finger. (Although the experience of 9/11 and terrorism gives pause for caution in this respect.)

- We ourselves may not be praying all that differently, only less concretely and more generally, when we say, for example, "deliver us from evil" in the Lord's Prayer. The answer to this prayer could have no less devastating consequences for the wicked.

- The psalmist *may* be doing little more than praying that there might not be another generation of those who wantonly shed innocent blood.

- The psalmists had an underdeveloped understanding of the afterlife compared to ours. From their down-to-earth, more limited perspective, if justice was not served in this life, it was not served at all. This in turn led to a problem even more pressing than a single case where justice was miscarried: *it seemed to imply that God was not just*. This of course constituted an enormous theological problem in the Hebrew understanding of God. In other words, from the psalmist's perspective it seemed that where God's justice was concerned, it was either now (in this life) or never.

I am not suggesting that all the difficulties with this passage are resolved in light of these points. I hope nevertheless that these notes above help to support my claim that no part of Scripture should be dismissed without consideration. As a student and later scholar of the Old Testament I have found *no* passage that refuses, upon careful consideration, to speak the mind of the Spirit in a way that is helpful to the faithful seeker and in turn the broader community of faith.

REVELING IN TWO NARRATIVE PASSAGES OF THE OLD TESTAMENT

The saying is well known that the best defense is a good offense, and in light of this two different Old Testament texts illustrate the value of taking the Old Testament seriously as scripture for the church. One passage comes from the Torah (Pentateuch), and the other from the Prophets (including Joshua through Kings). Moreover, each passage underscores a different aspect of the richness of the Old Testament. The first is a narrative passage from Genesis that serves to illustrate the point that, despite what we may have been taught about the law being *opposed to the gospel*, the law in the broadest sense of Torah *is gospel*.

A Torah Passage (Genesis 31–33)

Here the passage is the well-known story of Jacob fleeing the wrath of his uncle Laban only to encounter what he believes is the inevitable, imminent wrath of his brother, Esau, whose blessing he had stolen many years before.

An important key for understanding the story, as has been suggested by several scholars, is that Esau plays a role in the narrative as both himself and, in a literary sense, as a symbol or figure of God. This notion of understanding Esau on two levels, as human and God-like, can be seen most clearly in Genesis 33:10 where Jacob, upon meeting his brother Esau, says to him: "to see your face is like seeing the face of God—since you have received me with such favor." Evidence of this dual role for Esau also comes from the famous wrestling match Jacob endured the previous night with a being described both as a "man" and as "God" (Gen 32:22–32).[7] My point is that we are to read the narrative not only as the suspense-filled story of whether and how Jacob was

---

7. Elsewhere I have argued that this dual role for Esau is made clear even earlier in the narrative through the fact that Esau is described as coming from the land of Seir with a host of men (Jacob presumes soldiers) with him (Gen 32:3–6). The correspondence between this description of Esau and the following description of God elsewhere in the Torah was likely not lost on readers: "The Lord came from Sinai, He dawned forth from Seir; He shone forth from Paran. With him were myriads of holy ones; at his right hand a host of his own" (Deut 33:2). In other words, in Esau's coming from Seir to meet Jacob with an army of four hundred men, we are reminded of the ancient tradition of God also coming from Seir on Jacob's behalf, and with an army or host accompanying him.

reconciled to his brother, but also as the story of whether and how Jacob was reconciled *to God*.

At an earlier point in the story, Genesis 32:1–21, the text takes much delight in exploring the circumstances of Jacob's reconciliation. Here too the theme of double meanings is important, but this time to tease out, among other things, the different possible means by which Jacob will be reconciled to Esau (along with, as we have seen, to God). The different options are artfully laid out by means of different ways in which the expression "two camps" can be understood.

The first mention of two camps is in 32:1–3 where a camp of angelic messengers visits Jacob and his camp, in light of which the meeting place is called *Machanaim*, which means "Two Camps." This impromptu encounter with angelic messengers serves to remind Jacob of God's presence and promise of provision as he reenters the promised land.[8] On this reading, the two camps are clearly Jacob's human camp, on the one hand, and God's angelic camp on the other hand.

The second mention of two camps occurs in 32:8 where, upon hearing that Esau and a band of four hundred men are coming to meet him, Jacob divides his own camp of family and herds in two. Jacob does this so that if Esau should wipe out the one camp, the other camp would escape as a remnant. On this different reading of two camps, a reading invited by the writer as an alternative to the previous camp of Jacob of and God, the two camps are the ones Jacob divides into two from his own original single camp.

If we take stock of the significance of two camps at this point, the reader has two choices: in the first case, Jacob's camp and God's camp, and in the second case, the two camps of Jacob into which he had split his original single camp. Given the text's own intended ambiguity over the referent of "two camps," the biblical writer is inviting us to ponder: on which set of double camps is Jacob relying? Is it the one that includes the angelic camp of God, in addition to that of Jacob? Or is it the one that consists merely of his two camps? On the issue of whether Jacob will trust in God's help and mercy or in his own schemes, the text suggests that Jacob is, quite literally, "divided" on the matter! Will his plans to be reconciled to God (as well as to Esau) include reliance on the grace

---

8 As several scholars have noted, the passage is reminiscent of the earlier occasion when, upon departing from the land, Jacob was similarly attended by "messengers of God" (Gen 28:10–18).

of God and his promise? Or will he rely entirely on his own skill and cunning demonstrated by his strategy to cut his losses against Esau by dividing his own camp in two?

To this point we have noted the importance of double meanings in the story. In order to determine how Jacob will be reconciled to his brother Esau (who, recall, also symbolizes God), we need to notice another case of pairing. This time it is a play on the similar sound of two different Hebrew words, the word for "camp" (*machne* in Hebrew), and the word for "gift" (*mincha* in Hebrew). This will prove important as we proceed.

Having said his prayer that night, Jacob decides the next morning to send a "gift" (*mincha*) to Esau, a gift consisting of a generous amount of livestock. The word "gift" occurs twice more in the following context, one in v. 18 where Jacob tells his men to explain that the livestock Esau sees are a "gift" for him, and the other in v. 20 where the narrator tells us that Jacob will appease Esau with a "gift" in the hope of being accepted by his brother.

Finally, the writer brilliantly introduces our wordplay that brings together the discussion of camp and gift: "And so the *mincha* ["gift"] went on ahead of him, while he himself lodged that night in the *machne* ["camp"]" (32:21, author's translation). It is important to notice here that it is only when the "gift" through which Jacob seeks to pacify his brother (alias God) has been separated from him that the angelic figure encounters him near his camp. The stage is now set for the marvelous story of Jacob wrestling with the angel, where Jacob's reconciliation with God is played out and where, at the same time, his reconciliation with Esau the next day is foreshadowed.

The well-known account of the wrestling match between Jacob and the angelic figure follows. Although Jacob is wounded in the struggle, God vindicates him. The passage continues to insist that we understand Jacob's opponent both on the two levels of the human, on the one hand, and the divine on the other. Jacob's wrestling partner is thus called a "man" but at the same time is clearly an agent of God.

After Jacob's wrestling match, the narrative continues in chapter 33 with Jacob finally meeting Esau. True to his character, and with Esau approaching presently, Jacob divides his family into groups with the wives and children he favors most at the rear and himself at the front. But none of what Jacob has done to appease Esau or to plan for his wrath through the offering of a gift matter. Esau's actions speak for themselves: "Esau ran to meet him, and he embraced him, and fell upon his neck and kissed him, and they wept" (Gen 33:4). Finally, the dialogue between Jacob and Esau underscores the means by which Jacob was reconciled to his brother (and to God). Picking up one last time on the link between *machne* ("camp") and *mincha* ("gift"), the text has Esau say to Jacob: "What do you mean by all this *machne* ["camp"] that I have met?" To which Jacob soon replies: "No, please. If I have found favor in your eyes take my *mincha* ["gift"] from my hand," and then continues with a brilliant bringing together of the themes of human and divine reconciliation, "for to see your face is like seeing the face of God now that you have received me favorably" (33:8–10, author's translation).

Now it is clear from the story of Jacob's wrestling with the god-like man figure that we should not dismiss entirely as a means of winning God's favor Jacob's own machinations and scheming ("for you have striven with God and with humans, and have prevailed" [Gen 32:28]). From the broader narrative it is nonetheless clear that Jacob was reconciled to his brother and to God not on the basis of his peace offerings, nor ultimately on the basis of his reliance on his own self-devised alternative camp, but solely on the basis of the blessing that the camp of God chose freely to bestow upon him. The narrator is at pains to place Jacob's appeasing "gift" as far away from the "camp" where God blesses as possible.

I hope that my point is clear by now. I make it with my Hebrew class when we study this passage by beginning with prayer, and then by reading Eph 2:8–9: "For by grace you have been saved through faith, and this is not your own doing; it is the gift of God—not the result of works, so that no one may boast." Once my students have gotten the point that a key theme in this text resonates clearly with Paul's notion of salvation by grace, I remind them that Christians often claim that the Old Testament is all law whereas the New Testament is all gospel. Yet here, of course, we find the gospel right in one of the five "law" books of Moses! My hope is that they admit the view is mistaken and that the Old Testament is really an integral precursor to the later fuller gospel message with which it is consistent. When correctly understood, there is no passage that is clearer about God's salvation of his people Israel (including us) by grace apart from works than the broad narrative framework of this, a passage contained in the Torah, "law," of the Old Testament.

A Passage from the Prophets (1 Kings 22)

In the section on the Torah, above, I examined a passage that, although typically linked with the law and the connotations Christians often bring to it, clearly expounds Jacob's justification before God, as well as before his brother Esau, on the basis of grace and not works, a theme that to many will sound more like Paul than the writer of Genesis.

The passage here from the Prophets (which in the Hebrew canon includes our historical books Samuel through Kings) at first appears confused and warlike, yet it bears an important and timely message for the church. My purpose here is not to highlight consistency between the gospel teaching of the two testaments, as with the passage above, but to highlight a way in which the Old Testament can and should be used as an authoritative basis for reflection on a contemporary issue.

As a story, the tale of the true prophet Micaiah's clash with the four hundred false prophets of Israel is well told, engaging and at points intentionally humorous. In a manner reminiscent of the Gulf War of 1991 in which the United States sought coalition partners to force Saddam Hussein to retreat from Kuwait, which he had recently occupied, the rulers of Israel and Judah discuss becoming coalition partners to displace the king of Syria from Jabesh-Gilead, a disputed territory that this king had recently occupied. A wonderful story unfolds that turns on the problem the kings encounter as they seek God's will by consulting various prophets. The one coalition partner, the king of Judah, presses his prospective partner, the king of Israel, to consult one more prophet in addition to the four hundred whom they have consulted already. The king of Israel is nevertheless reluctant because there remains only the prophet Micaiah, who is notorious for prophesying bad things about the king. Micaiah proves true to his reputation and prophesies disaster, but, surprisingly only after he has parroted the same favorable prediction as did the four hundred prophets. In an ironic twist it is the wicked king of Israel who rebukes Micaiah for not telling the truth in the name of the Lord. Only then does Micaiah come clean by predicting a disastrous outcome to the proposed campaign. The king of Israel then turns to the king of Judah (and humorously to reader as well) and says, "I hate him, for he never prophesies anything favorable about me, but only disaster" (1 Kgs 22:8). The king of Israel nevertheless decides to tempt fate by going disguised into battle only to be killed by a fluke shot from an archer who was supposed to be aiming solely for the one dressed as king. So it is that the wicked king Ahab of Israel dies, just as Micaiah had prophesied.

Despite the flow and fun of the story, there are nonetheless points at which one is surprised, puzzled or both. Why, for example, as we have noted, does the true prophet swear to tell the truth in the name of the Lord only, at first, to lie and then, after the evil king of Israel cajoles him, only then tell the truth? Indeed, it strikes the careful reader as odd that such jarring twists should arise in so artfully crafted a narrative with, among other things, an absolutely perfect sense of timing where humor, suspense, plot development, and resolution of conflict are concerned.

As with all of scripture, the story must be read carefully, meditatively and with a mind open to the writer's agenda, not the reader's. Careful reading first paid off for me when I asked why King Jehoshaphat of Judah says, after hearing from no less than four hundred prophets of Israel, "Is there not yet a prophet of the Lord of whom we may inquire?" (1 Kgs 22:7, author's translation). Most translations gloss over the problem by translating, "Is there *no other* prophet of the Lord of whom we may inquire?" But this misses the point entirely. By looking back and asking where else we might encounter four hundred prophets of Ahab we recall that in the famous contest between Elijah and the false prophets, there were 450 prophets of Baal who were killed, but there is also mention of four hundred prophets of the goddess Asherah, the fate of whom remains unspecified. Following a suggestion first made by the biblical scholar David Noel Freedman, I believe that these four hundred prophets of Asherah are the same prophets called in by the king of Israel and about whom Jehoshaphat is rightly dubious when he asks for an opinion from a prophet of the Lord.[9] In short, when the king of Judah asks if there is still not a prophet of the Lord of whom we may inquire, it is not the writer who has made a mistake but the reader who has missed the point if he does not make the connection. These four hundred prophets were in effect double agents: to the wicked king of Israel, husband of the notoriously idolater Jezebel, these are *so-called* prophets

---

9. Archaeological evidence that has come to light in the past twenty-five years has made it clear that Yahweh was closely linked with the goddess Asherah by Israelites unfamiliar with, or defiant of, more normative traditions reflected in the Bible. The historian is aware of the link and allows the prophets of Asherah to be regarded by the king of Israel as prophets of the Lord (this, after all, is Ahab the husband of queen Jezebel) as he likely did, but not in the eyes of the king of Judah, nor, by this subtle textual clue, by the historian himself.

of the Lord, but to the spiritually discerning king of Judah these were in reality the dubious prophets of Asherah hauled into service in the king's court along with the prophets of Baal who had since been killed.[10]

If careful reading pays off, so too does not imposing upon the meaning of the text one's own questions and concerns. If we were to stop with the observation that the four hundred prophets were pagan, we might be tempted to slip into something like a moralizing sermon on the importance of distinguishing true prophets from false ones, but to do so would miss the point entirely. A remaining key lies in wrestling honestly with a problem in the text, that of falsehood, not just on the part of the "true" prophet Micaiah, but also on the part of the Lord when the text implicates him in a plan to send "a lying spirit in the mouth of all his prophets" (1 Kgs 22:22).

Brevard Childs observed that conservative Christian scholars had produced few truly good commentaries on Jonah in the twentieth century. To Childs these scholars were so preoccupied with defending the claim that a big fish had swallowed a man that they did not reckon well with the actual message of the story. We are in danger of making the same mistake with the story of Micaiah if we rush to the Bible's defense by making Micaiah into a sarcastic prophet or by somehow "explaining away" the Lord's evident complacency in the plot to bring about the downfall of the wicked king Ahab by allowing a lying spirit to deceive him. My point is not that it is impossible to do this, but rather that to do so would be to miss the point, as is clear from other evidence.[11] The confusion that exists in the text between truth and falsehood is itself an important part of the message of the text.

---

10. Asherah is the name of a goddess mentioned in the Old Testament. Recent archaeological studies, including those undertaken by the author, have confirmed that—whether out of ignorance or defiance is not clear—some Israelites considered Asherah to be related to Yahweh as a sort of consort.

11. I refer to the fact that in addition to having surprising cases of association with lying by both the Lord and the true prophet, we have the bad guy (king Ahab) rebuking the good prophet for not telling the Lord's truth (1 Kgs 22:16). Note also how much of the story, despite its good telling, pits prophets side by side, inviting us thereby to participate in the problem. Note too that the story also effectively rehearses for readers various ways and means by which to distinguish a true prophet from a false one. After all this, frustration is added to frustration in that the king of Israel disregards advice he recognizes is true, acts deceptively, but is killed nonetheless.

If the passage seeks to highlight the problems and complexities of distinguishing true prophecy from false, where is the solution? To find the answer we must read carefully one more time.

Special attention should here be paid to Micaiah's parting words: "Mark my words, all you peoples" (1 Kgs 22:28, author's translation). It is a curious fact that these are the exact same words with which the later prophetic Micah begins, as has often been noted by scholars. Most scholars, however, regard the link as an error on the part of some later biblical editor who, by putting the same words in the mouth of each prophet, foolishly equated the two prophets because of the similarity of their names, and this despite the roughly 150 years of difference.[12] The link should be taken far more seriously and, although it may be the work of a later hand, that later editor understood the meaning of 1 Kings 22 perfectly and with this allusion pointed to a solution to the problem of confusion, prevalent at that time, over how to distinguish false prophecy from true prophecy.[13] Like the story, the editor is picking up on a growing realization reflected in texts like Jeremiah 28 that there is no foolproof way of distinguishing true from false prophecy. (A popular example of the problem is in fact Jonah; technically even he was a false prophet because what he said about the imminent destruction of Nineveh did not come true! It was perhaps the knowledge that God's mercy would inadvertently make him a false prophet that led him to run on board a ship going the other way.) Here in 1 Kings 22 the editor suggests that the true word of the Lord can be identified indisputably only when it comes to be part of the *written scriptural books* such as in Micah. In other words, when Micaiah leaves the scene in 1 Kings 22 saying, "Mark my words, all you people," readers are invited to resolve the difficulty raised by the story, of distinguishing true prophecy from false, by making the verbatim link that these parting words have with a written, *scriptural* prophet of the same name. In other words, Micaiah is launching a sort of arrow with a message on it that provides the answer to the problem of how to decide which prophet is in the right.

---

12. The difference in Hebrew between "Micah" and "Micaiah" is negligible.

13. Despite the fact that there were well-established criteria, such as whether or not the prophecy came true, the late time at which the true prophecy became evident, and other circumstances, made distinguishing true prophecy from false an enormous challenge.

The answer to the problem does not lie in the message itself, which reads "Mark my words all you people," but in where the note finds its target. Directed in its flight by the arrow whose radar is "locked on" to any other Bible passage bearing the same words as on the note, the arrow lands on the introduction to the written canonical Micah, Micaiah's later namesake, in order to suggest that the answer to the problem is marked by the target where the arrow has landed, with prophecy that is now codified in a written scriptural book. The message is thus that the only way to distinguish true prophecy from false prophecy is by recourse to the written words of prophecy that the community, under the direction of the Spirit, has embraced as God's written word in the form of canonical scripture.

Shortly after studying this passage I was approached for some advice by the rector of a well-known Anglican parish in the Toronto area. He explained that a member of his church gave a prophetic utterance quite a long while previously at a charismatic type of evening service. He went on to explain that many people in the church had found the prophetic word to be deeply relevant to their situation and so timely and true as to warrant greater recognition as a word from the Lord. In light of the significance of this utterance, some members of the congregation had asked the rector (who was now asking me) if it would be acceptable to have the word written in a binder and kept in a prominent place at the back of the church along with the Bibles and prayerbooks. Partly in light of this allegedly confused passage, I quickly responded that I thought it best if prophetic utterances like this not be recorded in such a way as to be attributed a status akin to the once-for-all-given written Word of God. This matched the rector's own sense of what was appropriate, and so he declined the request.

For my purposes here it is not important whether the advice was right or wrong. My point is that a passage such as 1 Kings 22 can and should be drawn upon by Christians as an authoritative reference point in a similar manner to the way in which they would draw upon the New Testament. This is consistent with the practice of the New Testament writers themselves and finds expression in it as well, for it is there we read the following: "All Scripture is inspired by God and is useful for teaching, for reproof, for correction, and for training in righteousness" (2 Tim 3:16).

In the second Scripture text above, an attempt was made to show the relevance of a passage that appeared at first to be of little relevance and in fact troubling where the matter of truth telling was concerned. My aim was to demonstrate from a seemingly unlikely source—a warlike, confusing Old Testament narrative—how the Old Testament can and should be used within the church. My aim also was to encourage a slow and careful reading of Scripture that seeks to follow the text's own concerns and trajectory rather than issues or problems with the text, including the desire we might have to rescue it morally (as if the Holy Spirit needed our help!).

From both passages studied above a slow, thoughtful reading of the text can reward us with fresh, important insight that is enlightening and helpful to the individual Christian and to the church. From the earlier sections in this essay we have seen that many passages that we find at first challenging or difficult are in many cases the ones that have the most to teach us; challenging passages often present their own challenges—to us! Even in the case of a notoriously vindictive psalm we have seen how a slow, sympathetic, and thoughtful reflection can change our initial distress to a measure of understanding.

CONCLUSION

Lesser known than Marcion's problem with the Old Testament is his similar problem with the New Testament. Tellingly, Marcion excised from his Scriptures not only the entire Old Testament but much of the New Testament as well! Thus he rejected all of the gospels except for Luke (which he even abbreviated) and the rest of the New Testament except for ten of Paul's epistles (which he also edited). Evidently the problem experienced by consistent Marcionites could not help but spill over into the New Testament as well. On further reflection this is not surprising. There are, after all, some pretty disturbing parts of the New Testament. (Recall, for example, what John the Baptist says of the Messiah: "His winnowing fork is in his hand, and he will clear the threshing floor and will gather his wheat into the granary; but the chaff he will burn with unquenchable fire" [Matt 3:12].) Besides, too, the two testaments have a lot of themes in common, are part of the same Christian Bible, and were written ultimately by the same author, the God and Father of our Lord

Jesus Christ. At least that is what I hope you will be able to affirm now with greater conviction than before.

Basing itself on the authority and example of Jesus and the apostles, the early church *rightly* confirmed afresh that the Old Testament contains the very oracles of the God. This God is none other than the Father of our Lord, Jesus Christ. May Marcion rest in peace.

3

The Challenge of Suffering

L. Ann Jervis

SUFFERING CHALLENGES CHRISTIAN BELIEVERS. It challenges us because it seems not to fit with what we believe about God: God is all powerful and entirely good and loving. The question we ask in the face of suffering is: why does a good and omnipotent God permit the pain we witness and experience? Suffering also challenges us because we believe that in Jesus Christ God has conquered death and demonstrated God's commitment to healing the pain of the world. The existence of suffering challenges every human being, but it particularly challenges those for whom it creates cognitive dissonance: if we believe that God has saved the world through Jesus Christ, why is affliction so rampant in the world?

This is a large topic, a topic too large for one chapter of a book. Also, in all its complexities it is too large for this author. Let me address one question that can be asked in the context of this topic: what do the earliest writers about the Christian faith say about suffering? In order to answer this question I will focus on the parts of the New Testament that are in all likelihood the earliest to have been written: the gospel of Mark, the letters of Paul and passages from Matthew and Luke commonly regarded as from Q.[1]

---

1. Q is the designation scholars of the Bible use to indicate passages that Matthew and Luke share in common and that appear to have been in existence prior to the writing of Matthew and Luke.

What we discover when we read the early New Testament is that the authors speak of at least two kinds of sufferings. They speak of the suffering that all human beings know: disease, loss, social exclusion, death. They also, shockingly enough, discuss suffering that is promised to those who choose to follow Jesus.

THE SUFFERINGS THAT ALL HUMANS KNOW

The early New Testament writings (Mark, Paul, and Q) address the issue of general human suffering. Since these writings are written from the perspective of faith in Jesus Christ and are also written to nourish faith in Jesus Christ, it goes without saying that they do not address the problem of suffering as a philosophical puzzle. These texts are convinced that, subsequent to the birth, death and resurrection of Jesus Christ, the whole world must be viewed through the lens of Christ's work. Although, as we will see, they have slightly different understandings of general human suffering, it would be fair to say that for Mark, Paul and Q, general human suffering (such as disease, loneliness, and death) is thought of as now being *healed* through Jesus Christ. That is, these texts believe and affirm that God in Christ is healing the pain that is and they promise—indeed, they guarantee—that there will be a time when there will no more weeping, no more sorrow. On account of God's action in Christ, the earliest Christian writers believe in a time when there will be only joy and well-being and life.

For instance, the source (Q) that Matthew and Luke used in creating their gospels affirms that Jesus's presence means that the sick are healed, the poor know good news, and the dead are raised. When John the Baptist sends his disciples to Jesus to inquire whether Jesus is the one Israel has been waiting for, that is, the one who would bring in God's kingdom, the one who would inaugurate a time of peace and prosperity and well-being and perhaps even of everlasting life, Jesus answers: "Go and tell John what you have seen and heard: the blind receive their sight, the lame walk, the lepers are cleansed, the deaf hear, the dead are raised, the poor have good news brought to them" (Luke 7:22; a part of Luke that is generally considered to be from Q). Here we see that general human suffering is thought of as now being healed with the presence of Jesus. Furthermore, in Q, Jesus's disciples participate in his healing.

Jesus sends his disciples out to heal. This is clear from Jesus's instructions to his disciples: they are to give peace, to cure the sick, and to announce the good news that the reign of God has come. Jesus directs his disciples: "Carry no purse, no bag, no sandals; and greet no one on the road. Whatever house you enter, first say, 'Peace to this house!' And if anyone is there who shares in peace, your peace will rest on that person; but if not, it will return to you. Remain in the same house, eating and drinking whatever they provide, for the laborer deserves to be paid. Do not move about from house to house. Whenever you enter a town and its people welcome you, eat what is set before you; cure the sick who are there, and say to them, 'The kingdom of God has come near to you.'" (Luke [Q] 10:4–9). The message of the kingdom and the gift of healing is given freely. There is no requirement on the part of those who are healed except to welcome the gift. Those who ask receive, those who search find, those who knock will have the door opened to them (Luke [Q]11:10). God gives good things to those who ask (Luke [Q] 11:13). Q, in other words, is convinced that human suffering is healed by the presence of Jesus.

Paul, on the other hand, attends to the fact that suffering continues even after the resurrection of Jesus. Of course, this was a big issue for early Christian thinkers to sort through. If, as they believed, Jesus was the one God had sent to bring in the time of eternal life and joy, and if his resurrection proved that he was the one who had conquered death, then how could it be that, after Christ's resurrection, suffering and death should continue. Paul's way of making peace with this dilemma is to say that currently the creation "groans" but that there is hope for an end to this groaning (Rom 8:18–23). In other words, Paul acknowledges the problem: even after God's work in Christ, suffering remains. In response to this problem Paul offers the hope that there will be an end to suffering—an end that is dependent on present believers.

The end to suffering will finally come when the children of God are revealed. Paul is convinced that all who believe in Jesus are children of God. Children of God are those who wait in hope for the redemption of their bodies (Rom 8:23), that is, they wait for liberation from the decay that haunts the current situation. Paul makes sense of the fact that pain and death continue after Christ's resurrection by trusting that the children of God, i.e., believers in Jesus Christ, are signs of the liberty from affliction that is to come.

Unlike Q, Paul grapples with the failure of the coming of Christ to immediately heal the pain of the world. Q is exceptionally optimistic. One of the reasons, in fact, for thinking that Q is very early is precisely because of its remarkable enthusiasm about the power of Christ to make all things better now. Q believes that Jesus and the disciples of Jesus are capable in this time of curing sickness, redressing social inequities and raising the dead. Paul, on the other hand, recognizes and struggles with the continued affront of suffering and death.

The gospel of Mark shares both Q's optimism and Paul's realism. Mark presents Jesus as a healer who addresses humanity's afflictions. At the beginning of the gospel we read about Jesus healing everyone, from a man with a withered hand, to a woman who had been bleeding for years, to a girl who has died. There is no requirement to be a disciple of Jesus in order to receive this healing. In fact, Jesus often discourages those whom he heals from becoming disciples. For instance, in the first chapter of the gospel Jesus heals a leper but does not allow the leper to follow him. In Mark, Jesus dispenses free healing, and his disciples do the same. Mark writes that Jesus' disciples cast out demons and healed the sick (Mark 6:13). At the same time, however, Jesus in Mark recognizes that in this time there will still be pain. For instance, poverty will remain. The remarkable interchange between Jesus and some of his followers when a woman anoints his head with expensive ointment includes the challenge by his followers: "Why was the ointment wasted in this way? [It] could have been sold for [a large sum] and the money given to the poor" (Mark 14:4–5). When the followers harangue the woman, Jesus responds, "Let her alone; why do you trouble her? She has performed a good service for me. For you always have the poor with you, and you can show kindness to them whenever you wish" (Mark 14:6–7). In Mark we see the confident belief that Jesus is the healer of humanity's sufferings—he exorcises demons, heals diseases, and raises the dead. But we also see a sort of realism—poverty continues even though Jesus has come.

The earliest Christian writers, then, wrestled with the continued presence of suffering. All three of the biblical writings we have examined face up to the fact that humanity's pains remain, even though God, in Jesus, has begun to heal them. There is a range of opinion about how complete and immediate is the solution to suffering brought by Jesus. The writer(s) of Q proclaim that Jesus and his disciples have power to heal the sick, remedy the situation of the poor and raise the dead. In other words, Q proclaims the belief that humanity's sufferings may *now* be overcome through the presence of Jesus and those who follow him. Paul, on the other hand, wrestles with the continued presence of pain, loss and death. He acknowledges humanity's sufferings, yet affirms his belief that because of Jesus Christ there is a firm hope for glorious liberty (Rom 8:21) of all travail. The gospel of Mark shares both Q's conviction that Jesus and his followers can immediately cure pain and distress, and Paul's recognition that suffering continues after Jesus's death and resurrection.

This range of opinion in the earliest New Testament indicates both faith that God in Christ is healing the world, and a capacity to look human pain squarely in the face. Among the first Christian writers were those who did not pretend that all was now fine; they were realists who at the same time believed that current suffering is, and will be, transformed by the God who raised Jesus from the dead.

SUFFERING THAT ACCOMPANIES BELIEF IN JESUS

One of the more shocking and sobering aspects of the New Testament is the conviction that suffering is promised to those who follow Jesus. The New Testament texts claim that while God heals human suffering through Jesus Christ, those who follow Jesus take on a burden of suffering. The world's suffering is healed not only through God's activity in sending Jesus, allowing him to die, and raising him, but also through the activity of those willing to give their lives to Jesus. This is not a feature of the Christian life that is advertised in our churches. In some manifestations of Christianity it is not just ignored, it is, in my view, perverted. For instance, some forms of Christianity promise that faith in Jesus means a life full only of good things. The basic assumption in this form of Christianity is that, if one is saved by Jesus, one's life should be prosperous and peaceful; if we truly believe we will not suffer.

The early New Testament, however, regularly promises not prosperity or comfort to Jesus's disciples, but rather hardship. Both Jesus and his disciples are to proclaim good news to the poor. This proclamation will result not in material wealth for either Jesus or his disciples. In fact, Jesus says, "How hard it will be for those who have wealth to enter the kingdom of God!" (Mark 10:23). Disciples of Jesus are portrayed as those without homes, having only the clothes on their backs, and as those who have to rely daily on God for bread (Luke [Q] 11:3). The result of preaching good news to the poor is that disciples are often shunned (Luke [Q] 10:10) and persecuted (Luke [Q] 6:22).

The early New Testament promises affliction to those who would follow Jesus. In Mark, Jesus makes it plain that, even though he is the Messiah—the one Israel has been waiting for to put an end to struggles and injustices—nevertheless he must die. While his death will not be the end, for he will be raised from the dead, he must nevertheless go through suffering and death. Jesus warns his disciples that if they want to follow him, they will have to endure the same things: "If any want to become my followers, let them deny themselves and take up their cross and follow me" (Mark 8:34). Jesus tells his disciples that they must be last of all and servants of all (Mark 9:35). There is a promise attached to such self-denial and self-giving—those who do this will then be first. But, of course, they will be first in a society of others who are willing to be servants. In other words, the society of those who follow Jesus does not provide for social ladder climbing, with all of its material and ego benefits. Jesus sends out his disciples with nothing except the bare minimum. They cannot even have two coats, only one. They are to be vulnerable in the world, taking with them no bread, no purse, and no money (Mark 6:8).

In Mark, Jesus promises that his disciples will know persecutions, even though they have done the incredibly difficult thing of leaving their homes, their family and their livelihood for him. Thus he tells them: "Truly, I tell you, there is no one who has left house or brothers or sisters or mother or father or children or fields, for my sake and for the sake of the good news, who will not receive a hundredfold now in this age—houses, brothers and sisters, mothers and children, and fields *with persecutions*" (Mark 10:29–30, emphasis added). Jesus promises his disciples that they will drink the cup that he drinks and that they will be baptized with the baptism that he is baptized with (Mark 10:39), that is, they will share Jesus's suffering.

Following Jesus in Mark means walking the road that Jesus walked. Jesus lived on the margins economically and socially—even Jesus's family in Mark thinks he is crazy (Mark 3:21). Jesus's mission to dispense healing and to preach the good news that God is now establishing God's will on earth meant that Jesus was a servant of all, and suffered and was killed by the respectable people in his culture—the chief priests and elders. Suffering, of course, is not all that is promised to Jesus, or to his disciples. After death comes resurrection, after the hardship of a life of discipleship comes the promise of eternal life. The strange saying about receiving in this time houses, brothers and sisters and mothers and children and fields, with persecutions concludes with this phrase: "and in the age to come eternal life" (Mark 10:30). Mark does, however, emphasize that the joy and bliss of eternal life is won only after going through what Jesus went through. Mark makes it plain that the mission of Jesus—a mission of bringing in the kingdom of God, which means defeating disease, poverty and death—is achieved only through suffering. Jesus's mission is accomplished through the cross of Jesus and the cross that his disciples bear. The suffering of the world is healed through the voluntary suffering of Jesus and his disciples.

For Paul, believing in Jesus means participating in the drama of Jesus's life and being "in Christ." This is somewhat different from Mark's understanding. Mark calls disciples of Jesus to follow in Jesus's footsteps; it is as if Jesus breaks the trail, and Jesus's followers place their feet in Jesus's own footprints. For Paul, on the other hand, believers in Jesus Christ are *in* Jesus Christ. Believers live "in Christ" and so participate in the ongoing activity of Jesus's life, death and resurrection. For Paul, our faith is the faith of Christ. Paul writes: "we believed in Christ Jesus, so that we are justified by Christ's faith" (Gal 2:16).[2] Our life of faith is constituted by having died with Christ, by having been crucified with Christ, and by having been buried with Christ. Paul writes: "Do you not know that all of us who have been baptized into Christ Jesus were baptized into his death? Therefore we have been buried with him by baptism into death" (Rom 6:3–4). Paul also writes: "I have been crucified [co-crucified] with Christ; and it is no longer I who live, but it is Christ who lives in me" (Gal 2:19–20).

Believers may participate not only in Christ's faithful life and his death, but also in his resurrection: "Therefore we have been buried with him by baptism into death, so that, just as Christ was raised from the dead by the glory of the Father, so we too might walk in newness of life" (Rom 6:4). However, the promise of newness of life, the promise of resurrection depends, in Paul, on suffering with Christ. In Romans,

---

2. Note that this is a different translation of the Greek than may be found in most Bibles, although see the note for this translation in the NRSV.

Paul writes that believers in Jesus are heirs of God and fellow heirs with Christ, "if, in fact, we suffer with him so that we may also be glorified with him" (Rom 8:17). Affliction, tribulation and suffering are facts of life for those in Christ. Paul advises: "Rejoice in hope, be patient in suffering, persevere in prayer" (Rom 12:12). Tribulation is one of the activities of the Christian. For Paul, Christians *will* suffer and their suffering is the suffering of Christ. Believers suffer with Christ and are in the death he died.

The character of such suffering is that it attunes believers to the current circumstances in the whole of creation. Through the Spirit believers groan, as does the creation, because of the suffering of the present time. The passage in Romans to which reference was made earlier makes this point: "I consider that the sufferings of this present time are not worth comparing with the glory about to be revealed to us. For the creation waits with eager longing for the revealing of the children of God; for the creation was subjected to futility . . . We know that the whole creation has been groaning in labor pains until now; and not only the creation, but we ourselves, who have the first fruits of the Spirit, groan inwardly while we wait for adoption, the redemption of our bodies. For in hope we were saved" (Rom 8:18-24). I take this passage to mean that those who are "in Christ," those who are Christian believers, groan along with the groaning of creation. We share in the sufferings of the world.

Through sharing in the sufferings of the world, by being "in Christ," hope is produced. Paul writes: "we rejoice in our sufferings, knowing that suffering produces endurance, and endurance produces character, and character produces hope" (Rom 5:3-4, RSV). Christian suffering is productive and is part of the way God is healing the world.

Finally, in Q, Jesus repeatedly tells those who would follow him that they will suffer various things—loss of family, rejection, marginalization, and persecution: "Whoever comes to me and does not hate father and mother, wife and children, brothers and sisters, yes, and even life itself, cannot be my disciple. Whoever does not carry the cross and follow me cannot be my disciple" (Luke 14:26-27). "Blessed are you when people revile you and persecute you and utter all kinds of evil against you falsely on my account" (Matt 5:11). To a person who would follow him Jesus says, "Follow me." But the person said, "Lord, first let me go and bury my father." But Jesus said to him, "Follow me, and let the dead bury their own dead" (Matt 8:21-22). Jesus says, "I am sending you out like sheep into the midst of wolves" (Matt 10:16). Jesus says, "Do not fear those who kill the body " (Matt 10:28).

The reason that disciples of Jesus suffer is because they, like him, are proclaimers of the kingdom of God. In Q, being a disciple of Jesus means having enemies and living on the margins. Loyalty to Jesus is at the same time disloyalty to many of society's most dearly held values. In Q, allegiance to Jesus clashes with society's most treasured ideals: the stability of a home, being loyal to family above all else, being accepted in community, living peacefully, and preserving one's life. According to Q, following Jesus means forfeiting all of these things. In Q, discipleship suffering results from the clash between the status quo and the reign of God which Jesus brings. Disciples, as people giving their fealty to the one demonstrating the reign of God, and as people who work for that reign, are caught in the crossfire between the coming reign of God and society's values. They suffer as frontline workers establishing new boundaries for God's reign. Their suffering is productive and purposeful. The suffering required of those who follow Jesus does not require them to become victims and the character of their suffering is neither self-destructive nor depressive. Followers of Jesus suffer in order to expand the reign of God.

One of the last century's most influential thinkers about the suffering of the Christian was Simone Weil. In the course of thinking about the love of God and affliction, Weil wrote that affliction is characterized by hardness and discouragement, so that the afflicted person turns inward and is unable to help others: "at the very best he who is branded by affliction will only keep half his soul . . . afflicted people are in no state to help anyone at all and ...are almost incapable of wishing to do so."[3] This is not the kind of affliction Q describes. The suffering Q portrays has a victorious quality, for it comes in the course of participating in establishing God's reign.

SUFFERING AND THE REIGN OF GOD

The cause of suffering in Q is allegiance to Jesus. The character of this suffering is, then, that it is for another. The suffering of disciples is acutely other-centered. It is based in having given one's life to another; it is rooted in having given one's life away. Q's understanding of discipleship

---

3. Weil, "The Love of God and Affliction," 441.

suffering leaves no room for preoccupation with self, thinking that through suffering one may attain standing in the eyes of others, even of God. Q's presentation of suffering is that it represents loyalty to another—to Jesus—not concern for one's own sanctity.

In Q, disciples suffer not *as* Jesus, but *because* of Jesus and the reign of God that he brings. There is in Q no hint of what we found in Paul—that we suffer because we are "in Christ." In Q, suffering is simply part of the job description of disciples. Disciples have various activities: healing the sick, offering peace, declaring the presence of the kingdom, and suffering. Speaking realistically, even shrewdly, Q's description of following Jesus includes living as social outcasts, hating family, taking up one's cross, knowing persecution, and knowing fear. The nature of the business of being Jesus's follower includes suffering.

Discipleship suffering serves the purpose of bringing in the reign of God. It is not a ticket to heaven, nor is it a challenging exercise leading to personal sanctification; it is simply part of what is for those who would extend the boundaries of God's reign. Suffering is the inevitable accompaniment to the task of extending the reign of God, for the world as it is resists God's reign.

The reign of God present in Jesus extends to those incapable of putting themselves forward, or even of saving their lives. The reign of God manifested in Jesus, in which Jesus's disciples live and for which they work, includes the weak, and so it disturbs society's definition of security. Q challenges followers of Jesus to take up their crosses, for, as Q sees it, the cross is the only instrument strong enough to heal the world.

CONCLUSION

We see in what the early New Testament says about suffering, two important points made over and over again. First, God is now mending the world's suffering through Christ, and second, those who are Christians will suffer in the process of God's healing the world.

We may be much more comfortable with the first point than the second. We may resist the second; we might not want to think that we sign up for suffering by being part of the church. Or we may acknowledge the second point and, in fact, we may have experienced ways in which this is the case. If we have experienced suffering as a result of following Jesus we may also know the dangers in recognizing that fact. After all, thinking of ourselves as sufferers has its own intrinsic dangers. We might think of suffering as a means to an end, as in "the more I suffer, the better Christian I am." Or we might be tempted to feel victimized by our lives, as in "Oh, I am going through a hard time because I am supposed to, there is nothing I can do about it, this is my lot."

In my view, these responses are not consistent with the suffering of believers represented by Q, Paul, and Mark. These texts do not present discipleship suffering as a means to increase one's rank as a Christian (if such were even possible). Neither do they present the suffering accompanying belief as producing a sense of victimization or depression. Rather, suffering as disciples is done with a sense of hope, productivity, and purpose. This does not mean, of course, that there are not moments of despair. For instance, Paul's statement in the face of affliction, "we do not lose heart" (2 Cor 4:16), acknowledges the possibility of despair. Nevertheless, since the suffering which believers in Jesus know is the result of being focused on Jesus and on others, it resists the possibility of being self-focused and depressive.

Another possible response to the recognition that Christians will suffer in the process of participating in God's healing of the world is that we may feel embarrassed by the health and happiness we know. We may wonder why we are not suffering more. Does this mean that we are not being faithful? Should our whole lives be clouded with suffering if we are to be faithful Christians?

Distinguishing between accepting and benefiting from the healing God makes available to believers in Christ (forgiveness of sins, physical, emotional and social healing), and accepting and participating in the suffering ministry that brings healing to others, is a challenge that must be undertaken by each Christian believer and church community. There are times when we may confuse the two. We may, for instance, be so involved in suffering with the world that we do not recognize that God wants us to receive some sort of healing. On the other hand, we can become so focused on our own well-being and on how God might provide even greater comfort and satisfaction in our lives that we neglect God's call to bear our crosses for the sake of the world.

We have seen that these texts speak not just about the challenge *of* suffering but about the challenge *to* suffer. The challenge *to* suffer asks of each Christian believer and each church community a remarkable degree of discernment. The challenge to suffer emphasizes the necessity of prayer, in which we come to discern what kind of suffering God calls us to be part of. The challenge to suffer also underscores the necessity of Christian community, in which we test and refine our understandings of the arenas in which God asks us to bear our crosses.

It may be relatively easy to see how the sacrifice involved in giving time, money and energy to serving the needy is an aspect of discipleship suffering. It is not so easy to know how to understand personal pains such as disease, the breakdown of relationships, the loss of a job, and so forth. That is, sufferings that come to Christians that are not ostensibly related to serving God are more difficult to process. The wisdom to know how to understand these sufferings in the context of Christian discipleship requires prayer and community. It may be that a particular loss is meant to be taken as a challenge to trust that God does, in fact, heal and redeem; a challenge to believe in God's goodness and power. It may be, in other words, that our pain is meant to be salved, and in the process our faith purified and strengthened. On the other hand, it may be that our individual suffering is not assuaged, but that in our coming to terms with it we grow more into the likeness of Christ. When our suffering is not directly related to serving God it can be difficult to know how our particular pains relate to our life of discipleship. Nevertheless, through handling in faith an experience of pain and loss we may, in fact, be being conformed to the image of Christ. Again, prayer and Christian community provide invaluable assistance.

What is clear from the earliest Christian writings is that a life of following Jesus is a rich and full life, a life which promises the extremes of human existence. Believers in Jesus will know glory and eternal life, provided, as Paul says, "we suffer with him" (Rom 8:17).[4]

---

4. For additional material by L. Ann Jervis on the topic of suffering see Jervis, *At the Heart of the Gospel*; Jervis, "Accepting Affliction: Paul's Preaching on Suffering"; and Jervis, "Suffering in the Reign of God." See the bibliography for details.

4

Signposts in a Strange Land

Doctrine, Memory, and Christian Life "on the Way"

Joseph L. Mangina

DOCTRINE CONTESTED

Christianity is a religion, if not *of* doctrines, at least marked by them in significant ways. Examples that leap to mind are the doctrine of the Trinity, hammered out at the Council of Nicea in 325 AD; the teaching on Christ's divine and human natures, affirmed by the Council of Chalcedon in 451; and the doctrine of original sin, traceable to the writings of the great North African theologian Augustine of Hippo. Some doctrines are well known, like the Reformation doctrine of justification by faith alone or the Roman Catholic teaching on Christ's real presence in the Eucharist (transubstantiation). Others are more obscure. How many Western Christians are aware that in 787, bishops assembled at the Second Council of Nicea endorsed the veneration of icons of Christ, Mary, and the saints? This is one of the signal dogmas of Eastern Christianity, yet it does not bear nearly the same weight in the Western church, nor does it command the same widespread awareness.

Nowadays, that Christianity is indelibly marked by doctrines does not seem to count very much in its favor. The reasons for this are many. The late modern era is an age of suspicion, in which truths handed down by "authorities" are viewed as a form of tyranny over the mind of the individual. A high-culture form of this view is Immanuel Kant's slogan *sapere aude*, "dare to know," or as we might say "think for yourself." This motto is emblazoned over the front entrance to Massey College, just down the street from where I teach in Toronto. It is in fact the perfect creed for the modern research university. A popular expression of the same view may be seen on bumper stickers that loudly proclaim: "Question Authority."

To be sure, criticizing the Enlightenment myth of the lonely, individual knower has become something of a cottage industry among postmodern philosophers. Thinkers such as Wittgenstein, Derrida, Foucault, and Rorty have all emphasized that there is no knowledge that is not "situated" in language and history.[1] Our knowing is inevitably shaped by the narratives and communities we inhabit. If this is the case, it is not hard to imagine that doctrines or dogmas might not also play a constructive role in our knowledge. A doctrine, we might say, is simply an authoritative teaching held by a community. As the philosopher of religion, William Christian, wrote, "The doctrines a community brings with it into the world are mainly doctrines about the setting of human life and the conduct of life in this setting. These are the doctrines the community exists to promote and to nurture in the lives of its members."[2]

When doctrines are viewed in this light, two things quickly become apparent. First, that doctrine—communally authoritative teaching about what is true—is a ubiquitous feature of human life. It is not only Christians who have such teachings. Muslims teach that there is but God and Mohammed is his Prophet; Latter-Day Saints teach that the Book of Mormon was given to Joseph Smith by the angel Moroni; and Buddhists teach that Nirvana, a state beyond all suffering and desire, can be attained by following the excellent Eightfold Path. Nor do we have to limit ourselves to "religious" examples. The tradition that is modern capitalism may be said to adhere to the doctrine or dogma of the free market, whose invisible, beneficent "hand" may be said to require as much faith as anything in the Nicene Creed. A utilitarian ethics philosopher like Peter Singer may be said to embrace the dogma "minimize suffering," a variant on the "maximize happiness" of his nineteenth-century prede-

---

1. Still useful as a guide to the philosophical terrain is Placher, *Unapologetic Theology*.

2. Christian, *Doctrines of Religious Communities*, 1.

cessors Jeremy Bentham and J. S. Mill. To escape doctrine altogether you would have to escape human life in community, an ideal as unattainable as it is unattractive.

The other thing we can quickly see about doctrines (religious or otherwise) is that they are not ends in themselves. In each of the cases mentioned above, the doctrine conveys something essential about what this particular tradition holds to be most important in human life, indeed in the entire cosmos. Doctrines are, on the one hand, held to be true—this is how the world just *is*—while on the other hand they are subservient to practice. As an academic student of Buddhism, I may know all sorts of facts about the character of Nirvana, perhaps even many things of which the average Buddhist is ignorant. But unless I myself enter into the way of life known as the Eightfold Path, I am no Buddhist.

Christian teachings, too, are about both truth and practice. The ultimate truth to which Christian doctrine points is (not surprisingly) God. This God, moreover, is not deity in general—whatever we might mean by that phrase—but a very particular God, namely the God who created the world and everything in it; who chose and dwelled in glory among his people Israel; and who became incarnate among us in his Son, Jesus Christ. Jews worship this God under the name YHWH, the name revealed to Moses at the burning bush, while Christians confess him as the Father, the Son, and the Holy Spirit, the holy and blessed Trinity. According to Jesus himself, the greatest of all the commandments is, "you shall love the Lord your God with all your heart, and with all your soul, and with all your mind, and with all your strength," and, as a corollary to this, that "You shall love your neighbor as yourself" (Mark 12:30–31). The love of God and neighbor—this is the practice or way of life that goes with the confession of God as Trinity.

Now God is a rather odd and mysterious "person" to know and love, just as the stories that tell of this God are weird and wonderful. Karl Barth called it "the strange new world of the Bible."[3] Christian doctrine may be thought of as a series of signposts erected on this disorienting landscape.[4] They are not God, obviously, though they do

---

3. See Barth, "The Strange New World Within the Bible." In fact, Barth wrote simply *die neue Welt in der Bibel*; the English word *strange* was the addition of the translator.

4. I borrow this image, and the title of this essay, from Walker Percy, *Signposts in a Strange Land*. The title of this posthumous work is taken from Percy's remarkable essay "Notes for a Novel about the End of the World," where he writes that unlike a realistic novelist (such as Jane Austen), who describes a familiar and stable world of

bear witness to God. Nor are they a substitute for the actual living of a Christian life. But doctrine does play a crucial, subordinate role in helping to orient us rightly, preventing the taking of wrong turns, keeping us on the right path. In this regard, it is worth recalling that one of the more ancient names for Christianity is simply "the way" (cf. Acts 9:2; 18:26; 19:4, 23; 22:4; 24:14, 22). Of course, in John's gospel Christ is himself called *the* Way, and this provides us with another way of thinking about doctrine: they are a set of guides or reminders the church has put in place, directing us in all things to the one who is the "way" to the Father (John 14:4–6).

In the remainder of this essay, I will explore Christian doctrine from three angles. First, we will explore how doctrines assist in the church's task of memory, helping each generation of believers to hand on faithfully what they have received. The church needs some assurance that it is preaching the gospel of Jesus Christ and not some "other gospel" (Gal 1:6). Second, we will see how doctrines help articulate the reason or pattern at work in Christian beliefs about God. Finally, I will offer a few thoughts on the practical function of doctrine in shaping and guiding the Christian life. As "signposts in a strange land," doctrines help to orient Christians on the extraordinary adventure in which they are engaged.

FAITHFUL MEMORY: DOCTRINE HANDED DOWN

The roots of Christian doctrine may be found in Israel's worship of YHWH (in English Bibles, the divine Name is generally rendered as "the LORD"). The prayer known as the Shema Israel begins like this: "Hear, O Israel: the LORD our God, the LORD alone" (Deut 6:4). Judaism is often grouped together with Christianity and Islam as a form of "monotheism." This expression is, if anything, much too weak. The point about the biblical deity is not just that he is unique—a cosmic principle might also be unique, but you would not necessarily worship it. Rather, the Lord is one in that he is a particular Person, a God with name and a history, a lover who tolerates no rivals: "I am the LORD your God, who

---

social relations, the contemporary postapocalyptic novelist "set[s] forth with a stranger in a strange land where the signposts are enigmatic but which he sets out to explore nevertheless" (102).

brought you out of the land of Egypt . . . you shall have no other gods before me" (Exod 20:2–3). Like partners in a stormy marriage, YHWH and Israel share a complicated history. Much of Judaism consists in recalling this history, giving thanks for God's steadfast love despite Israel's sin and disobedience.

The early Christians carried over the Jewish faith in the one Creator God, who led Israel out of Egypt and gave the Law to Moses. But they also believed this same God had done a new and astonishing thing. Sending Jesus of Nazareth as Israel's Messiah, God allowed him to die a humiliating death on a cross—a seeming defeat; but then God raised him from the dead on the third day. In light of the resurrection, the cross appeared in a new light: as a victory of apocalyptic proportions, in which Christ had vanquished the powers of sin, death, and the devil that menaced God's good creation. Jesus was not merely Israel's Messiah but "Lord of all" (Acts 10:35), exalted "far above all rule and authority and power and dominion" (Eph 1:21).

Given this faith in a "cosmic Christ," it would have been very easy for Christians to lose sight of Jesus as a particular, historical person. They might easily have proclaimed a generic savior, at the same time both Everyman and no man in particular. It is of the greatest consequence for later Christianity that this did not happen. In the New Testament, the divine Son of God is none other than Jesus, the wandering rabbi from Nazareth. The Word who was with God from the beginning "became flesh" in the womb of a human mother. He ate, drank, wept, was moved to anger, fed hungry crowds, and provided the wine for a village wedding feast. He told vivid parables that made God's coming kingdom seem vivid and real. At the last he suffered and died. This historical figure, Christians say, is none other than the life-giving Word himself, the eternal Son of the Father.

Such claims were no doubt as problematic to many people in the first century as they continue to be today. Surely God, we are tempted to say, is a purely transcendent or spiritual reality, standing aloof from the messy events and accidents of history? Surely the "historical Jesus" who lived and died in the first century is one thing, the eternal "Christ of faith" quite another? Would it not be easier to keep these in separate compartments, saying that Jesus is a particular revelation *of* "the Christ" (leaving room, perhaps, for other and perhaps better such revelations) rather than that he *is* the Christ.

Nonetheless, there was something in the faith of the early church that stubbornly resisted such easy solutions. Jesus, the first Christians believed, was not merely a teacher who spoke in a compelling way about God. He was not even a convenient receptacle in which a divine being, the Son of God, dwelt during his brief time on earth. No, Jesus was the Son of God, born to a particular woman named Mary, condemned by a Roman official named Pontius Pilate, and nailed to a cross for claiming to be "king of the Jews." Metaphysics and history are here inseparable (if not identical). As the nineteenth-century philosopher Søren Kierkegaard pointed out, all this makes Jesus quite different from a revered human teacher like Socrates or Confucius.[5] When disciples of Socrates have learned the lessons he has to offer, they can leave Socrates behind with good conscience; the good teacher is precisely the one who makes himself dispensable. The Buddha's path to enlightenment can in principle be arrived at by anyone, even if it was the Buddha who first happened to announce them. By contrast, Christians receive something from Jesus that they could never have attained on their own. Nor do they ever "graduate" from him to a higher level of wisdom. He is no mere teacher, but the Son of God who forgives sins and bestows life, who *is* life and love itself. If Jesus (in the passage from John cited above) is "the way, the truth, and the life," it is also true that in this case the way is itself the goal.

One consequence of the Christian stress on Jesus's specific, nonsubstitutable identity is that Christianity, no less than Judaism, is irreducibly a religion of memory. This explains the importance the New Testament sets on getting the story straight, including the value of eyewitness testimony. A famous passage from Paul's first letter to the church in Corinth offers a good example:

> Now I would remind you, brothers and sisters, of the good news that I proclaimed to you, which you in turn received, in which also you stand, through which also you are being saved, if you hold firmly to the message that I proclaimed to you—unless you have come to believe in vain. For I handed on to you as of first importance what I in turn had received: that Christ died for our sins in accordance with the scriptures, and that he was buried, and that he was raised on the third day in accordance with the scriptures, and that he appeared to Cephas, then to the twelve.

---

5. See Kierkegaard, *Philosophical Fragments*.

> Then he appeared to more than five hundred brothers and sisters at one time, most of whom are still alive, though some have died. Then he appeared to James, then to all the apostles. Last of all, as to one untimely born, he appeared also to me. (1 Cor 15:1–8)

The Greek word Paul employs when he says he "delivered" the story about Jesus to the Corinthians is *paradidonai*, meaning "to hand over" or "to transmit"; the corresponding noun is *paradosis*, or "tradition." Human tradition viewed in the abstract is ambivalent. Some traditions are benign, others beneficial but time-conditioned and dispensable, while others we view in retrospect as simply repugnant. Thus the fact that the Jim Crow laws in the American South were "tradition," constitutive of a certain way of life for white Southerners, does not make them right. The gospels often show Jesus opposing bad traditions—usually those that involve barricading oneself behind a secure wall of religious practice. Thus he calls the scribes and Pharisees to account for clinging to the traditions of their ancestors rather than obeying the word of God (see Mark 7:1–13).

Tradition, then, is not always a good thing. Yet the early church had the task of remembering and bearing witness to a very particular Lord—for better or worse, that put it in the tradition business. It became a matter of sorting out the true traditions about Jesus from false and distorting ones. The test for distinguishing the two was whether a tradition could be deemed *apostolic*, that is, in accord with the teaching of the apostles. To be sure, Christians confessed that the Lord was present with them even now by the power of his Spirit (Matt 18:20). The issue was not whether Jesus was present, however, but precisely who this "Jesus" is. For that, the church was dependent on the testimony of the apostles, the original "eyewitnesses and ministers of the Word" to whom Jesus appeared after his resurrection (Luke 1:2; Acts 1:22). Genuine tradition in the church is apostolic tradition. We affirm the importance of this tradition whenever we confess faith in "one, holy, catholic, and apostolic church."

Here, at last, we can return to the notion of doctrine or authoritative teaching. *A Christian doctrine is nothing other than a teaching that preserves, or at least claims to preserve, some aspect of the apostolic tradition concerning Jesus.* Doctrines do not play this role in isolation. They jog the community's memory in concert with other, more basic forms of that memory, most notably scripture and the church's practice of worship in the name of Jesus. To conclude this first part of our discussion, we will briefly examine the relation between doctrine and these other aspects of apostolic tradition.

Christian doctrine is answerable, first of all, to the testimony of scripture. Where else is apostolic tradition to be found, other than in the writing of the apostles? The New Testament has always served as the most basic touchstone of genuinely apostolic teaching. This is not because the New Testament was actually written by apostles—this would be true of few, if any, of the twenty-seven books in the collection—but because these books carry what might be called the "apostolic seal of approval." Christians believe that under the Spirit's guidance, the church has selected those writings that faithfully convey the apostolic witness concerning Jesus. But, of course, the New Testament itself cannot be understood apart from the scriptures of Israel, the books Christians call the Old Testament. For the earliest Christians, these scriptures were the only "holy books" available, as the New Testament was still in process of being written and collected. In one of its most fateful decisions, the church acknowledged that its story must be seen in basic continuity with Israel's story, and that the Old Testament was, therefore, indispensable. To know what is apostolic, we must search *all* the scriptures (cf. Luke 24:27), not just the apostolic writings between Matthew and Revelation.

The other basic form of apostolic tradition, and therefore a basic touchstone of doctrine, is the church's practice of worship in the name of Jesus. Recall Jesus's words to his apostles at the last supper: "Do this in remembrance of me" (Luke 22:19; 1 Cor 11:24–25). The community's gathering to give thanks and praise to God in Jesus's name is itself a remembering, a recalling of the gracious acts of the triune God. The church's historic pattern of worship is the context of memory. This forbids the fundamentalist effort to derive a system of "pure doctrine" directly from the Bible, as if the latter consisted in isolated empirical statements, just as it forbids inflated claims on behalf of the church. In its worship, the church is constituted as a community that is fundamentally receptive. It is a eucharistic community, living by "giving thanks" (Greek: *eucharistia*). The apostolic tradition must be sought, rather, in the context of doing what the apostles did, namely, giving thanks to the Father through Jesus in the communion of the Spirit. It was when the disciples on the Emmaus road sat down and broke bread with Jesus that "their eyes were opened, and they recognized him" (Luke 24:31). The Lord himself opens their eyes, in the breaking of bread.

It should be stressed that insisting on worship as a form of apostolic tradition by no means implies downplaying the role of scripture. This is quite impossible, given that worship itself drinks deeply at the wells of scripture and constantly sends us back to search and examine the biblical witness to Christ. It is simply to say that scripture is not primarily a textbook of facts or beliefs that can simply be read off the text by individuals, but must be read and interpreted within the church. Saint Luke tells us that the Christian community in Jerusalem "devoted themselves to the apostles' teaching and fellowship, to the breaking of bread and the prayers" (Acts 2:42). Teaching—doctrine—is one important element in the church's life. But it makes sense only in a context marked by fellowship, prayer, and sharing enacted in Jesus's name.

THE RULE OF FAITH: DOCTRINE AS PATTERN

The most common form in which ordinary Christians are likely to encounter doctrine are the ancient creeds.[6] Many churches employ the Apostles' Creed in the context of baptism, just as many recite the Nicene Creed as part of the liturgy of the Eucharist or Lord's Supper. The Nicene Creed in particular can seem dauntingly abstract, filled with complex terminology: "begotten not made, of one being with the Father." Yet beneath the complexities one can discern a common basic pattern, a design woven into the whole fabric of the church's worshiping, praying, and believing. Church fathers like Tertullian and Irenaeus referred to this pattern as the *regula fidei* (Latin for "rule of faith" or "rule of *the* faith"). In its beginnings, the rule was not identical with any one theological formulation or doctrinal litmus test. Its roots were in scripture and the church's liturgy, particularly in the rite of baptism, where it was obviously important to be as clear as possible about the responsibilities new converts were assuming, both in terms of doctrinal confession and way of life.

As proposed by the church fathers, the rule of faith had three major aspects. First, the rule of faith stressed the centrality of Jesus Christ himself, crucified for our sake and raised to new life by the Father. Paul states

---

6. On this topic, see most recently Jenson, *Canon and Creed*.

the church's message in its most basic form: "that Christ died for our sins in accordance with the Scriptures, and that he was buried, and that he was raised on the third day in accordance with the scriptures" (1 Cor 15:3–4). The gospel message thus directs our attention on the concrete *person* of Jesus of Nazareth. There is no way to make sense of this message if Jesus were a mere religious "symbol" or generic savior figure. Nor can he be understood primarily in terms of his teachings, important as these are for his followers. One cannot separate the creedal affirmation of Christ as Son of God from the Sermon on the Mount, or the way of the cross. Yet the church holds that Jesus's teaching is important first of all because of *who* he is—the Messiah of Israel and Son of God, the One "born of the Virgin Mary" and who "suffered under Pontius Pilate." In the face of strong temptations to the contrary, the church resisted abandoning faith in the Jesus described in the gospel narratives. Had it done, it would have had to stop being the church.

Second, the rule of faith implied clear convictions about the God who had sent Jesus. The church fathers said that when Christians confess their faith in "God," they intend to speak of none other than the God of Israel, the Creator who fashioned all things and pronounced them good. Whatever else Christianity might be, it could not be a rejection of Israel's faith in YHWH. Nor could it have anything to do with a hatred of this world (a common feature of Gnosticism and other early heresies). Evil exists and must be combated, but the creation itself is not evil, indeed a major component of Christian worship is giving thanks for the good gifts of the earth. To understand Jesus, in other words, one needs to see him within the larger purposes of the One he called Father, the almighty "Maker of heaven and earth."

A third aspect of the rule of faith has to do with the community that proclaims the gospel message. Jesus's followers believed that following his ascension, God poured out the Holy Spirit to gather and sanctify a renewed people of God. ("We believe in the Holy Spirit," to cite the words of the Apostles' Creed.) This community of the end times was no obscure sect, but a universal assembly gathered from earth's farthest corners ("the holy catholic church"). It was knit together as a holy people sharing holy things ("the communion of saints"), who through baptism into Christ's death look forward to an eternal life with him ("the forgiveness of sins, the resurrection of the body, and the life everlasting").

We can see, then, how the rule of faith expands the church's basic confession of Jesus Christ by reminding us *what else* we need to affirm if we would speak of him with integrity. If Jesus is Israel's Messiah, then we must speak of YHWH and the gift of creation. If Jesus is the bringer of God's kingdom, then we must speak of the Spirit's gathering a people to be a sign and foretaste of that kingdom. Faith in the Creator and in the Spirit's work is part of what it means to confess and follow the Jesus Christ. So it is that the rule of faith sets the stage for the church's doctrine of the Trinity. It does so by, as it were, tracing the pattern woven deep in the fabric of scripture and the church's worship. Prior to what theologians have said about the Trinity, prior even to the formulation of the Creed itself, is the Christian community's instinctive naming of Christ and the Spirit in the same breath with God, often in the context of prayer and praise. To take an example almost at random: "pray in the Holy Spirit; keep yourselves in the love of God; look forward to the mercy of our Lord Jesus Christ" (Jude 1:20–21; see also 2 Cor 1:21–22, 13:14; Eph 5:18–20; Rev 1:4–5).

Viewed in this light, it should be clear that the doctrine of the Trinity does not, as is often charged, purport to "explain" the mystery of God's triune reality as Father, Son, and Holy Spirit. The doctrine grows out of prayer and returns to prayer; and in prayer we do not try to explain God, but we speak to him. Rather, the doctrine functions as a sort of reminder, pointing the church back to the peculiar shape and contours that make the mystery of the Word made flesh the particular mystery it is, indeed *the* mystery, this strange reality that powerfully draws us into itself, that we cannot take our eyes off of. The doctrine of the Trinity does indeed tell us something true about God, but not by explaining God away. The Catholic philosopher Gabriel Marcel made a famous distinction between problems and mysteries, the difference between the two being that problems can (in principle anyway) be solved, whereas a true mystery only becomes deeper the longer one ponders it. Problems are to be overcome, mysteries entered into.

I should hasten to add that to speak of God as mystery does not mean our knowledge of God is vague or uncertain, much less that nothing can be known of God at all. Such agnosticism would go entirely against the grain of the early church's life and witness. In confessing faith in the Trinity, Christians really do make claims about "the way things really are": that there is but one God, that this God created the universe, that the things of this world are good, that God entered our history with saving power in Jesus of Nazareth. These are but some of the more important truth claims made by Christians. In Luther's classic work the *Small Catechism*, each article of belief concludes with the words "This is most certainly true." There would be little point in praying if we did not think such prayers are heard, by a God who wills our good, often despite our blind and misguided perceptions of what would, in fact, be good for us.

THE DRAMA IN THE DOGMA: DOCTRINE LIVED

Christians do, then, use doctrines to assert that God is the deepest truth about the world we inhabit. Precisely as such, they are not to be thought of primarily as abstract "beliefs," to be pondered behind a desk or studied in a laboratory. Recall that the church's teachings concerning creation, Christ, and the Trinity emerged as Christians reflected on the apostolic witness in light of worship and proclamation (witnessing the gospel in the world). The proper home of doctrines is in the actual living of Christian life in community. To recall the image I offered earlier, they are markers on the highway, signposts in a strange land, witnesses to the Lord who accompanies us on the way and is the Way himself.

It is in the context of this shared journey—for like all good adventure stories, from *Huckleberry Finn* to *The Lord of the Rings* to Harry Potter, the Christian adventure is best undertaken with companions—that doctrines may begin to make a kind of sense.[7] Thus doctrines about Jesus point us to the one who, in his becoming flesh for our salvation, embodies the reality of "God with us." Soteriological (that is, to do with salvation) doctrines remind us that there is no seeking of God that is not a response to God's seeking, and finding, us in Christ. Doctrines about the church remind us that we are not the first ones to have set out on this journey, but that it is lived in the company known as "the communion of saints." And the doctrine of the Trinity, finally, is the great reminder that the God Christians worship is no lonely, isolated deity, but the God whose very life is a kind of communion, and who seeks to establish communion with his lost creatures.

---

7. See Hauerwas, "Christianity: It's Not a Religion, It's an Adventure."

"It is the dogma that is the drama," wrote Dorothy L. Sayers, the great English detective writer and Christian apologist.[8] She meant by this claim to counter the superficiality of much modern religion, the kind that exalts feeling and personal relationship over God and truth. I think Sayers had it half right. The dogma is not, in and of itself, the drama. As I hope I have shown in this essay, doctrine is but a kind of commentary on the apostolic tradition embedded in scripture, liturgy, and the church's life of prayer. Yet Sayers was right in so far as doctrine or dogma helps situate us within the great drama of God's purposes with his creation. Stretching from Genesis to Apocalypse, from the beginning of all things to their end in the New Jerusalem, this drama not only describes the world's deepest truth; it is a story in which God calls us to be involved.

A familiar bit of wisdom says that the proof of the pudding is in the eating. The proof of Christian doctrine, one might say, is in the lives that bear witness to the God of whom the doctrines speak. Doctrine invites us not to become experts in doctrine (though the church needs even a few of those!), but to engage in those practices of worship, prayer, and the patient reading of scripture that are essential to Christians on their common journey. Doctrines provide but a map of the territory, imperfect no doubt, constantly subject to clarification in light of the scriptural witness, yet indispensable if we are to live lives faithful to our calling.

There are important questions about doctrine I have not been able to address in this chapter. Does the church's teaching develop across time? Are some doctrines permanent and irreformable—that is, have they become so integral to the church's identity that the church could not dispose of them without fatal detriment to herself and her message? What is the relation between scripture, tradition, and worship as sources of authority? And not least, what role is properly played by a magisterial teaching office, called to intervene in cases where doctrine is doubtful or contested?

These are contentious questions, not easily answered; but I hope that the current chapter has at least provided a framework in which we might begin to think about them. Doctrines matter in the end, because they help us see more clearly that in Jesus Christ the triune God has come among us, the Creator who wills good for his creatures. "This is most certainly true."

---

8. Sayers, *Creed or Chaos?*, 3.

5

God Bless the Atheists

Faith and Antifaith Today

Ephraim Radner

NOT THAT LONG AGO, large advertisements appeared on the sides of London buses. One advertisement said this: "There's Probably No God. Now Stop Worrying and Enjoy Yourself."[1] (One could add here that this advertisement strikes the ears as especially hollow in the face of things like the horrors of Port-au-Prince, Haiti, or Baghdad in recent years. Maybe there is no God, but "stop worrying and *enjoy yourself*"?) Anyway, similar so-called atheist bus campaigns have been launched in other countries, with either the same slogan or alternative ones, like "Why Believe in a God? Just be good for goodness' sake!" (Washington, DC) and "The bad news is that God does not exist; the good news is that you don't need him" (Genoa, Italy). The campaign itself was the idea of a British comic and ardent secularist, Ariane Sherine, and originally funded by the British Humanist Association. But part of its energy derives from a relatively new and activist promotion of atheism that has grown up over the last ten years, led by some very visible and, at least if one were to judge by book sales, popular writers. Indeed, the British Atheist Bus Campaign received quite an initial boost when one of these prominent writers, Richard Dawkins, agreed to match some of the funds raised.

---

1. http://www.atheistbus.org.uk.

What is this new public muscle flexing by atheists all about? Indeed, one hears the phrase, "the New Atheism," as if it is marks a revolutionary movement, rising up amid the rubble of reactive and irrational religiosity. Strictly speaking, however, the phrase has been used in relation really to just four bestselling authors, who have recently gained a wide public profile by attacking the rationality and morality of religious belief, and especially Christian belief. The four authors are the British evolutionary biologist Richard Dawkins, whose money went into the bus campaign, and especially his book *The God Delusion*; the Harvard philosopher Daniel Dennett, whose book *Breaking the Spell* also topped the lists; there's also Sam Harris, a previously unknown neuroscience graduate student (he now has his doctorate) who made publishing headlines with *The End of Faith* and *Letter to a Christian Nation*. Finally, there is Christopher Hitchens, a cultural critic with provocative conservative credentials, who came out with *God Is Not Great: How Religion Poisons Everything*.[2]

You can find out far more about these authors and the purported "movement" they have spawned by browsing the Internet, for these are the cyber-corridors they haunt. It really is a kind of modern information-culture phenomenon. Although people *buy* books, they often do not read them. The real motor to the "New Atheism" has been online and on television, with articles, debates, interviews, online conferences, websites, profiles, and more, all spewed out at an astonishing pace. On the one hand, I am going to give but a little background, lay out some typical arguments, and then offer my own defense of religious and Christian rationality. On the other hand, I am also going to try to show why atheism, from a Christian perspective anyway, is not silly at all, but is a challenging and perhaps necessary element of our world and our hearts.

I will be addressing the concept of reason a good bit, because *rationality* and *reason* are the watchwords of the New Atheists. To believe in God and to order one's life according to such a belief, these atheists say, is not only irrational; it is actually *evil*. The New Atheism website, which is devoted to these four authors, groups they are associated with, and other writers, lists as the New Atheist credo the following: "Intolerance of ignorance, myth and superstition; disregard for the tolerance of reli-

---

2. Dawkins, *The God Delusion*; Dennett, *Breaking the Spell*; Harris, *The End of Faith*; and Harris, *Letter to a Christian Nation*; Hitchens, *God Is Not Great*.

gion. Indoctrination of logic, reason and the advancement of a naturalistic worldview."[3] Where did such a view come from?

THE RISE OF ATHEISM

Atheism is a modern, Western phenomenon. That should be warning enough. Its origins are in the sixteenth century in the midst of Christendom's breakup, and the notion that "there is no God" engaged a more generalized sense of despair over religious violence amid a dislocating world.[4] On the whole, the scattered atheistic views we find openly expressed in this era for the first time were marginal and held with a certain "outsider" swagger. Atheism's more socially accepted foundations do not arise until a bit later, in the eighteenth century Enlightenment.

On the whole, we can see two strands that emerge from this period. First, there is British philosophical atheism, epitomized in someone like David Hume, which stresses the *irrationality* of religious belief. Its own impetus lay in the post–English Civil War reaction against religious fervor, especially such "fanatical" energies as one might find among sectarian "enthusiasts," as they were called (and religious "enthusiasm," an event the enthusiasts believed, was a bad thing).[5] Secondly, there is French political atheism, which stresses the *moral* evils arising out of religious belief, especially in the form of an oppressive Catholic Church. Voltaire's famous exhortation in a letter that was later published—*écrasez l'infame* ("crush this wickedness")—referred to the wickedness of all persecuting superstition; but it was aimed especially at the organized religion of the Catholic Church. The French Revolution eventually prohibited Christian practice altogether and imposed by law a "religion of reason." They did this on the basis of a range of arguments explicitly marshaled against Christianity's purported evils as an antihuman and immoral movement, bound by superstitions and injustices.[6]

These two strands of early modern atheism set the tone for much contemporary atheism. Subsequent nineteenth century attacks on

3. Online: http://www.newatheism.org.

4. The classic volume is Febvre, *The Problem of Unbelief in the Sixteenth Century*; likewise Popkin, *The History of Scepticism*; more recently, Israel, *Radical Enlightenment*.

5. Berman, *A History of Atheism in Britain*.

6. Cf. the history, sympathetic to revolutionary "dechristianization," by Michel Vovelle, *The Revolution against the Church*.

Christian theism in particular followed in due course, as Christianity is the main form of religious belief Western atheism has ever really been concerned with until recently.[7] (Islam is now a favorite target, although usually summoned up as a proxy for Christian evangelicals. One often hears easy segues from the Taliban to Rick Warren, for instance.)

On the one hand, there is the "moral" argument against theism that moves, for instance, from Marx to Nietzsche and beyond, i.e. that Christianity is oppressive and unjust.[8] There is the philosophical trajectory that is concerned with the irrationality of Christianity. This last strand—what we can call English philosophical atheism—garnered new energy in the wake of scientific arguments from evolution to physics, and neo-empiricist and analytical philosophy from Bertrand Russell to A. J. Ayer and others carried on a vigorous attack against religious claims based mainly on their purported illogical, unprovable, and antiscientific grounds.[9] But the two streams of atheism—philosophical and moral—have now merged in many of the most popular instances: scientists predominate among the bestsellers. Thus Dawkins is an evolutionary biologist, Harris a fledgling neuroscientist (waylaid by his bestselling fame), Steven Weinberg a Nobel Prize-winning physicist; nonetheless Dennett is a philosopher of mind, Michel Onfray (author of *Atheist Manifesto*) is a populist philosopher, Hitchens was a conservative cultural critic, and so on.[10]

We will return presently to the motive of the New Atheism. But what are their main arguments? Let me use an accessible example, that is, an online exchange of letters between Sam Harris and Andrew Sullivan, "Is Religion Built upon Lies?" Sullivan is a well-known conservative political journalist and a rather traditional Roman Catholic, except for one feature, which is his public and extensive defense, as a gay man, of gay marriage. This confluence of characteristics would be enough to get him attention; but Sullivan is also a highly articulate and fluent writer, and his willingness to be an interlocutor for Harris was eye catching. The exchange of letters took place over several months on the

---

7. On this period, see the overview in Alistair McGrath, *The Twilight of Atheism*.

8. See Hart, *Atheist Delusions,* with Nietzsche hovering in the background.

9. Cf. the classic 1966 volume *God and Philosophy* by Anthony Flew, reissued in 2005 by the author with a reassessment of his original views.

10. Onfray, *Atheist Manifesto*.

well-visited religion site *Beliefnet* in 2007, drawing literally thousands of reader comments.[11]

Harris's arguments go all over the place. But they derive generally from the New Atheist commitment to "logic" and "naturalism," that is, a materialistic worldview that can and must somehow, according to their ethics, be "verified." Harris wants empirically testable truth and cannot find it in the Christian faith. But he also views the irrational *insistence* of religious believers in the face of rationality as a large contributory factor to human evil; and so, like Voltaire, he argues that religious belief needs to be "crushed." Indeed, Harris in one of his books goes so far as to argue that "some propositions are so dangerous that it may even be ethical to kill people for believing them."[12] In this case, he is thinking not only of the "deranged" Muslim horde, but of more fanatical Christians as well.

On the philosophical side, Harris argues that all the talk about God's existence and nature being somehow "special" and "beyond" normal empirical criteria of testability that we hold for the rest of our lives, is a form of "ontological fancy footwork" and "all that business about God being 'definitionally' the creator of the universe, outside of space and time, etc. just doesn't wash. The 'marzipan at the center of the sun' is definitionally at the center of the sun. Does this mean there *is* marzipan at the center of the sun?"[13] He is withering in his insistence that "God-talk" is simple gibberish, repeated by the stubbornly deluded.

Further, Harris asserts that there is just no way to provide evidence for religious claims. Miracles, maybe? Unless you are willing to believe the miracles and then the claims based on miracles made by Indian holy people, storefront hustlers, Muslim Sufis and the rest, you have nothing to go on as a Christian. Thus, Harris says: "Ancient miracles are less compelling than modern miracles (and modern miracles don't compel you): Christianity is predicated on the reliability of the gospel account of the miracles of Jesus. And yet, there are modern books cataloguing the miracles of Hindu adepts, written by educated Westerners. Why not grant these testimonials even more credence than the gospel? I would bet that you are not even inclined to read this literature, much

---

11. Harris and Sullivan, "Is Religion 'Built upon Lies'?" Online: http://www.beliefnet.com/Faiths/Secular-Philosophies/Is-Religion-Built-Upon-Lies.aspx/.
12. Harris, *The End of Faith*, 52.
13. Harris and Sullivan, "Is Religion 'Built Upon Lies'?"

less organize your life around it. Then why not view the gospel with the same skepticism?"[14]

The problem, for Harris, is that Christianity in particular relies on what it asserts are "historical" rather than simply metaphysical or interiorized experiential evidences. The bestselling New Testament scholar N. T. Wright's works are based on an examination of these evidences.[15] Yet all this does is to make Christianity a "contingent" faith that refuses to grant other contingent faiths any analogous personal authority. By all means, examine everybody's purported histories. But do believers actually do this? Of course not, Harris argues. Indeed, it is all "personal" and necessarily ends up being "my faith" against "your faith," which is not only small minded but dangerous. Why not simply accept the fact that religion tends to follow social location, period. If you are raised a Buddhist in a Buddhist land, the chances are much greater that you will be a Buddhist as an adult. Period. (This was Montaigne's famous claim, back in the sixteenth century.)[16] Belief is a product, at best, of chance circumstance, not rational truth.

Hence, claims to "special" authorities historically bound to your religion—like the Bible—are silly, Harris insists. At best they represent a "magical" mindset, at worst a deluded and therefore also dangerous (again) orientation. If you are willing to treat other religious books as "just books," you are bound by consistent logical practice to do the same with the Bible.[17] His argument continues:

> What is the intellectual justification for considering the Bible to be the inspired word of God, given how much bad stuff (like slavery) is in there, and how much good stuff (like all of science) isn't? Do you really think that no mere mortals could have written Mark, Matthew, John and Luke? Not even the combined talent of a first-century Virgil, Dante, Shakespeare, and Tolstoy? It seems to me that this textual claim really lies at the core of the matter: either the Bible is a book like any other great work of literature, or it's a magic book. Once one accepts it to be a magic

14. Ibid.

15. Cf. Wright's "historian's" attempt to explicate the "empty tomb" in *The Resurrection of the Son of God*.

16. See his claim that one's own country's religion is "always the perfect" one in his 1580 essay, "Of Cannibals."

17. So Spinoza, and later, in the nineteenth century, Benjamin Jowett notoriously insisted.

book, I agree that a wide range of religious implications follow; but if one doesn't accept this claim, it seems to me that the basis for being a Christian (as a opposed to anything else) evaporates. Would it really surprise you if God told you that the Bible was a product of fallible, human minds? And if this wouldn't truly astound you (in the way that finding out that George Washington never existed presumably would), how can you claim to be so certain of the doctrine of Christianity?[18]

The dangerous aspects of religion now emerge more fully for Harris. While he agrees that his interlocutor, Andrew Sullivan, is probably a fairly "moderate" person in his expression of religious belief—you are a nice guy, even if you are a complete idiot—he thinks that the lines between "moderation" and "fundamentalism" and fanaticism are nonexistent in any clear way. Once you accept the fundamentally irrational claims of any religion, you are, by definition, a fundamentalist, because you have put your reason in escrow for other illogical motivations. You have crossed the reason barrier.

> There appears to be no principled separation between religious moderation and religious fundamentalism other than a facility for (and an inclination to) doubt. But how much doubt is too much? Why not doubt the whole shebang, as I do? The pope seems to believe many things which you doubt. Do you have reason to believe that the pope is mistaken about the true doctrine of Christianity, or do you just not like the social consequences of some of his beliefs? Can you justify the intermediate position you've taken with respect to Catholicism in terms of truth and falsity (rather than consolation and its lack)? And if you disagree that the truth of an idea can be neatly separated from its consolations, what does the phrase "wishful thinking" mean to you?[19]

Indeed, the real problem is that there is no "logical" difference between the claims of "good" and of "evil" religions: they are all based on irrational assertions, whose lack of foundation makes the assertion itself a lie, and the acceptance of that lie constitutes a servitude to an illogic that is shared by *all* religions. "Don't you think Mormons and Muslims have similar stories to tell about feeling consoled in the presence of death, hearing voices, etc.?"[20] The fact that Christianity has produced

18. Harris and Sullivan, "Is Religion 'Built Upon Lies'?"
19. Ibid.
20. Ibid.

some good or helpful or kind people, or that many folk have embraced it means nothing, "is not an argument for its truth."[21] People in large numbers, as we know from history, can be and act like fools together. And in so doing, they do horrible, horrible things.

A DEFENSE OF CHRISTIAN RATIONALITY

What are we to make of these kinds of arguments? The first thing to be said is that the arguments in themselves are not new but rather derive from a tradition that, as I have suggested, finds its origins in a particular context of Western Christian conflict. Indeed, this context, in the sixteenth and seventeenth centuries, despite some of the reactive negativity involved towards religion, was also one that was more deeply informed by a positive desire to *defend* religious belief and put it to work. The notions of a "rational" system of argument that could be empirically tested—whether in the form of arguments by Bacon or Locke or Leibniz—derive from a peculiarly *Christian* impulse to find ways of reasoning that could bridge sectarian divides *among* Christians. Furthermore, the search for "universal" laws, that came from this Christian motive, was also a means of founding a missionary enterprise that could also embrace the sophisticated cultures—for example, the Chinese and the Indians—whose "natural reason" ought itself to respond to a message bound up with the Creator of such reason, God himself.[22] There is nothing straightforward or inevitable about how the empirical scientific method developed, first out of Christian impulses—actually, starting in at least the Christian Middle Ages—and then gradually apart from them. Virtually all the great scientists of the scientific revolution of the sixteenth to eighteenth centuries were devout Christians; and some, like Newton—and much to the chagrin of today's atheistic rationalists—were rather fanatical Christians to boot.[23] Rather, the *particular* form of this antitheistic scientism that we see today is, as Madeleine Bunting has said, more specifically *political*. It is not primarily disinterested at all. As Bunting writes:

21. Ibid.
22. On this topic, see Mungello, *Curious Land*.
23. Cf. Force and Popkin, *Essays on the Context, Nature, and Influence of Isaac Newton's Theology.*

What [the New Atheists] have in common is a loathing of an increasing religiosity in US politics, which has contributed to a disastrous presidency and undermined scientific understanding. Dennett excoriates the madness of a faith that looks forward to the end of the world and the return of the messiah. What Dawkins hates is that most Americans still haven't accepted evolution and support the teaching of intelligent design; according to one poll, 50% of the US electorate believe the story of Noah. He argues that "there is nothing to choose between the Afghan Taliban and the American Christian equivalent . . . The genie of religious fanaticism is rampant in present-day America." Harris similarly draws an analogy between Muslims and the American Christian right: "Non-believers like myself stand beside you dumbstruck by the Muslim hordes who chant death to whole nations of the living. But we stand dumbstruck by you as well—by your denial of tangible reality, by the suffering you create in service of your religious myths and by your attachment to an imaginary God."[24]

It needs to be said that the "political" argument, even from a purely empirical viewpoint, is not as clear cut as the New Atheists would like us to believe, as if citing the numbers of deaths associated with religious violence or egregious forms of past religious intolerance is itself an argument in the face of an otherwise unexplicated expanse of human history. A common response to these kinds of charges by the atheists is often, what about atheistically grounded violence, like Stalin and Mao? What indeed? As the novelist and essayist Marilynne Robinson has argued in numerous places, the moral vision of Darwinian natural selectionists has always been and remains deeply troubling, however much one wishes to dress it up.[25] Natural selectionists have almost *never* proven the leaders of movements for social justice. Even a militant atheist like Steven Weinberg admits that the "worldview of science is rather chilling" offering "no point in life."[26] Why think such a worldview could offer practical utopias? The anti-evolutionist movement among Christians in the nineteenth and early twentieth century was, Robinson argues, mainly a *moral* response of their own, to the dehumanizing vista the new atheistic scientists had opened up. Who proved right and wrong

---

24. Bunting, "The New Atheists Loathe Religion."
25. Robinson, *The Death of Adam.*
26. Weinberg, *Lake Views*, 241.

in this struggle is by no means obvious to the observers of the battle between "science and religion."

The evolutionary biologist David Sloan Wilson's book *Darwin's Cathedral* proved a tonic in the reemerging atheism wars.[27] Wilson is as much an empirical rationalist materialist as anyone. As far as I know, he is not a religious believer. But he had long taken aim at the claim by Dawkins that religion represented a kind of cultural "virus" that has early infected, for the worse, the cultural genetics of the human race. Instead, Wilson argued, religion has had a critical role in group *survival* and selection from a generally positive perspective: by ordering human life so that individual sacrifice makes "sense," the larger group is granted greater chance of survival, and this is assured through processes of cultural, and perhaps genetic, adaptation. Wilson underscores the exclusive character of religious belief systems—the inside/outside confrontation—but considers it, not a sign of religion's political failure, but a necessary and adaptive group dynamic. Using Calvinism as his first example of "an adaptive belief system," he concludes that such a belief system works best (1) when a moral system of rewards and punishments is established, and hence the consequences of prescribed behaviors are well known; (2) when this system is understood as fairly applied and thus its prescriptions do not benefit some at the expense of others in the group; (3) when the beliefs that justify its demands are easily learned and applied—hence dogmatically defined and catechized; (4) when individuals within the group are able to hold these controlling elements as a matter of internal limits, i.e. "believe" them through faith—rather than have them externally imposed; and finally, (5) should it resort to fiction to inspire action, when the fictions are judged by the actions they inspire rather than by their correspondence to reality.[28] In other words, according to Wilson, religion—and a highly developed, dogmatic, and institutionalized religion—can be "justified" as good for the species.

It is worth taking account of arguments such as Wilson's, if only to realize that the claims of a hard-nosed scientific scrutiny of the evidence, even upon purely Darwinian lines, does not grant obvious conclusions regarding the moral utility of religious belief. Indeed, the very nature of evidence here, and of what counts for evidence and how to assess it in such a political and moral perspective, is by no means self-evident. Most

27. Wilson, *Darwin's Cathedral*.
28. Ibid., 98–100.

religious people themselves are easily prepared to wonder if ridding the world of religion, let alone of Christianity in particular, would somehow lead to the freeing of reason or to its further enslavement.

But let me raise a second concern about the New Atheists' fundamental presuppositions regarding "rationality" and its relation to the "truth"—one they construe only in terms of materialist empiricism. Remember, the notion of a universally "accessible" reason and logic, with therefore universally affirmable conclusions, is central to the New Atheists' vision. If everybody cannot agree to something, through common observation, evidence, and logic, that something cannot be true. But it is not just that such a universal reason and its conclusions seem unattainable in practice, because of our own limitations (as hinted at above). Rather, "universality" seems an arbitrary criterion for rationality. Why should reason be constricted to what *everybody* believes? After all, there are many areas of our life where, as rational human beings, we do not presume such universality: our judgments regarding food or music or literature; or of personality and friendship; or even of value and meaning. We are capable of providing rational standards about these things, and of reasoning according to them, but they are rarely universal standards. I keep telling my son that it is rationally demonstrable that Bach is a better composer than John Lennon or Queen. But my reason is inexplicably incapable of penetrating his reason.[29]

Of course we do not really want to found universal claims about salvation on the platitude of *de gustibus non est disputandum*—that is, "there is no disputing taste"—do we? Still, if there is such a thing as "musical reasoning," and not just arbitrary taste, what is "religious reasoning"? The main argument that the New Atheists put up is not only that Christian claims are not accessible to universal reason, but that they are therefore immune to the criticism of normal experience like immorality, suffering, and evil. That is why they are dangerous. A prominent editorial in the *New York Times*, shortly after the Port-au-Prince earthquake, proclaimed "if God exists, he really has it in for Haiti," and then wondered why in the world Haitians would gather to pray, sing hymns, and be strengthened by their faith in the face of the horror they have expe-

---

29. Oliver Sacks has written a range of stimulating essays that touch on the question of music and neurology as they impinge on issues like "appreciation" and perceived beauty. Cf. Sacks, *Musicophilia*.

rienced.[30] Of course, as a subsequent article detailed, the outpouring of prayer, worship, and song in the rubble was one of the most astonishing religious demonstrations anybody had seen in a long time.

THE NECESSITY AND CHALLENGE OF ATHEISM

So let us ask the question, how can Christians claim that their God, the God presented in the whole of the scriptures and preached upon throughout the history of the church, can be just or good or merciful or powerful or all knowing and so on? Especially if one cannot establish clearly the existence of such a God in the first place? Is it all avoidance? My response would go like this: it is just these elements of value—justice, goodness, mercy, power, even rationality—that are impervious to universal agreement. They are topics not amenable to purely ideal arguments, built upon universally agreed presuppositions. They are about *experience*—that is, they are about what hurts, what causes us to weep, what makes our minds "click" with recognition, what "works" pragmatically in the carrying on of our daily lives. The proper realm of adjudication of these matters—suffering, goodness, mercy, reason—is in the realm of experience, the realm of historical phenomena and their apprehension.

The main answer to modern rationalistic arguments against the Christian God, I would insist, is that of Christian *experience:* the phenomena of the Christian life that includes an array of psychological, spiritual, ethical, and historical artifacts, the main one being the "experience" of God itself. The Psalmist (e.g. in Psalm 73) cannot understand the prosperity of the wicked; his anger and complaints, however, lead to "bitterness," not to clarity about the world (in belief or in unbelief). Only the presence of God itself resolves the rational dilemma. After his complaints, he realizes that "I am continually with you; you hold my right hand . . . Whom have I in heaven but you? And there is nothing on earth that I desire other than you" (Ps 73:23, 25). This is much the same resolution that is given to Job's anguished perplexity: the presence of God, in all of its astonishing and ungraspable power and glory relativizes my suffering and confusion. "I lay my hand on my mouth," Job finally admits, when he hears God speak to him "out of the whirlwind," whatever exactly he means by that (Job 40:4, 6).

30. Bhatia, "Haiti's Angry God."

The New Atheist argument against the Christian God, then, lays out the existence of phenomena that seem to contradict Christian claims: suffering, genocide, religious hypocrisy, natural disaster, plural religions, contested miracles, the elaboration of materialistic "laws," the advances of the sciences, and so on. These are, as they rightly claim, data that must be respected by the Christian. Are none of these data, though, rationally coherent with Christian claims? My answer is simply that this is not how Christians reason or have ever really reasoned; it is not religious reasoning at all. The primary rational task for Christians is not to provide an inferential system of ideational relations—against which, of course, any particular datum of experience is likely to bring a question, given the infinite variety of experiential realities (assuming an infinite universe). The primary rational task for the Christian is to order data according to the priority of his or her experience.

The data Christians work with is almost the same as what atheists do, but not quite. It includes death, suffering, also life and joy, freedom (yes, even our secular legal systems assume human freedom, and so do Christians, however incoherent that might seem with other claims we make), beauty, evil, ugliness, goodness, regret, incapacity, and so on. We are all human beings, and Christians are no less open to the realities of human existence—its brutalities as well as its glories—as anyone else. I, for one, have experienced enormous evil and suffering in my life; and I am like most other persons in this respect. I do not deny it or avoid it. Although, it must be said, that the character of these phenomena are not accessible to anyone but me: only *I* can tell what it is like to have *my* mother die as a young person, and then a sister, and so on. Still, it is a real datum, not something without roots in a common world.

But Christians also bring to the table of their rational focus another datum, a "phenomenon," and a "reality." And that is the datum of God himself. Granted, this is not the same in kind as the datum of earth, sky, and rain; it is open to contestation, but then again so is anybody's (including yours) assertion of the existence of suffering and evil (look at Buddhists who say that suffering is in fact nonexistent). What counts as "suffering"? Is it universally understood? Harris thinks he will be able to prove the neurological basis of all human feelings, including "faith."[31] But because such feelings, in fact, vary infinitely in the face of various other

---

31. This kind of general approach has been popularized by Dean H. Hamer in *The God Gene*.

realities, it is hard to see logically how neurological identifiers can do anything other than locate the *operation* of still inexplicable experiences. The Christian "experience" of God may well be explainable in terms of individual or social psychology, but, again, so are many things to which we grant real importance in different realms (and psychology, including neurological psychology in its implications, is the least scientific of the sciences, in my estimation). Reductive explanations are never, by definition, exhaustive inductively for they do not contain a demonstration of their own sufficiency, since we simply do not know what we do not know! Indeed, analogical reasoning would encourage us to *assume* elements that still await our discovery; and hence that "explanations" are always partial. With respect to the datum of "God" as an "experience," any reductive explanation for it must be able to deal with the unique character of its shape, which includes the kinds of mysteriously self-authenticating aspects that Anselm and others have grappled with under the heading of "the ontological argument." That is to say, the experience of God is a peculiar experience that is *sui generis*, and Christians rightly take this fact into account.

As theologians have insisted, in any case, the experience of God is "self-authenticating" in a unique way. It is not other authenticating; i.e., I cannot argue you into its acceptance on your part. But you cannot argue me out; not because of my stubbornness, but because those who have "tasted of the Lord" (Ps 34:8), as the psalmist puts it, apprehend something that is undeniable and inescapable as the totalizing orderer of a person and even a person's world in its own terms.

The unique character of the knowledge of God (something philosophers have puzzled over, with mixed results, and which Harris, as I noted, simply cannot comprehend) establishes this datum as an organizing frame of reference for all other data. That is its logical status. The existence of God—which, in Christian terms, is given partly through the experience of God within the context of Christian life—does not evacuate the world of other problematic data, e.g. evil, incapacity, suffering, and so on. Not at all. You can believe in God and none of these things goes away. Haitians pray and sing, but they have done so now among the rubble and dead bodies. But if you are a believer it *does* mean that all this other data must subsist in a *subordinate* relationship to the primary datum of God. That is what it "means" to "believe in God."

This is perfectly logical, if we accept that there is a logic that is religious at root.[32] No experience of suffering will shake my confidence in the existence, the goodness, etc., of God. (In fact, of course, it might, and we all know persons whom it has, but this is not a logical issue; for such experience often *does not* affect their confidence in God; and as atheists gleefully and painfully point out, Christians seem capable of adhering to their convictions in the face of incredible "counterevidence," understood in terms of ideational inference. Hence the perplexity of the *New York Times* editorialist.)

How then do Christians make sense of the world, a mixed-up and often horrible world, governed by a good and all-powerful and provident God? Briefly, in a mixed-up and highly ad hoc and often cumulative fashion, frequently rearranging and altering their connections between meanings, as necessary, in order to maintain the primacy of the datum of God (in Christian terms, of the "God in Christ Jesus.") They do this "in order" to maintain this primacy, in the sense of continuing to take seriously the character of the datum of God, as human experience is constantly shaped by new configurations of other, more contingent data. Christian rationality is highly unsystematic. But why should it be otherwise? ". . . though the earth should change, though the mountains shake into the heart of the sea; though its waters roar and foam . . . the Lord of Hosts is with us" (Ps 46:2–3, 7). To know God as God, to know God as the God of and in Jesus, is simply to recognize that the realities of earthly turmoil and natural order and/or disorder do not subvert the reality of this God. The "rationality" of faith, a rationality that is shared by many and attested to by many, though not by all people, works in this way.

CONCLUSION

Let me now try to extract some more mundane outworkings of this general view of things. First, there is the matter of acting "rationally" in a day-to-day way. Because divine "rationality" is about the compelling character of phenomena—the experience of God, which is not like any other

---

32. A good, if limited, approach to these kinds of issues, from a perspective influenced by Wittgenstein, is given by the British philosopher D. Z. Phillips. Among his many books, see *Religion without Explanation*. Another influential way of getting at this is given in the essays edited by Alvin Plantinga and Nicholas Wolterstorff in *Faith and Rationality*.

experience (and this must be emphasized) —all "evidence" for Christian claims is purely circumstantial—you try to fit together data, given the datum of God, in as coherent a way possible; but there is no central principle that can govern what or when evidence is finally noncontestable.

Great thinkers like Pascal—a very logical mathematician and empirical scientist—saw this. It is, by the way, the manner in which most of our life is organized with respect to relational being—how we make judgments about the rightness or appropriateness of this or that job, this or that encounter, this or that trust and self-giving. I do not throw away my spouse because of experiential inconsistencies, since there is a primary reality to which my marriage is bound. Instead, I work around inconsistencies of behavior and motive and outcome, confident that that primary reality ("one flesh," "until death do us part," or whatever) will survive and ultimately order the rest. "How can I be married to this person who has just wounded me?" I might ask. But rather than say, "Therefore it seems I cannot be married to her any longer," I say, "but I *am* married to her; therefore what I consider now a 'wound' is not the end of the matter, and must be refigured in my life." That "refiguring" is called forgiveness and it is governed by a prior—a primary datum—called love, however reapprehended with difficulty in such circumstances. The fact that so many people *do not* behave this way in their marriages does not make them more rational! A religiously "rational" person is one who is capable of forgiveness and change.

Second, what about this "magical" book we call the authoritative scriptures? How rational is that? Well, the Bible is misread if it is taken as a catalogue of historical ciphers or signs, like a newspaper. Again, in the Christian perspective that orders all phenomena according to the primary datum of God, the Bible as "Christian scripture" (the canon, that is), is an "icon" orchestrated by God, with Jesus Christ as its center and ultimate focus. I make no claims here as to the mechanism by which the Bible came together in this way; only that this is what it is understood to be by Christians who in fact believe in God.[33] Therefore, every event, story, teaching, etc. in the Bible has as its ultimate purpose the unveiling of Jesus Christ. How we perceive this happening—just as how we see the order of the world to be subject to God's love in Christ—is really an *ad hoc* affair. There is no single method by which Christians

---

33. A rich exploration of this tradition is given by Henri de Lubac in his multivolume work, *Medieval Exegesis: The Four Senses of Scripture*.

have ever done this. We will all have different ways of doing this. But, the story of Abraham and the divinely ordered sacrifice of his son Isaac, to take one famous example, cannot, in this perspective, be read as an example of God's cruelty. It is rather read as something that points to Jesus Christ—a "type" of the passion of Jesus for instance. This is the traditional reading of the text, from the New Testament on. Atheists may find this somehow too "neat" a way of denying the Genesis story; but the story of God giving up his own "beloved son" in love for the world, is hardly neat. Only humbling and transforming. A rational person need have no trouble reading the Bible as a witness to a merciful God, if that person believes that God is the orderer of all things and all meaning, which is what it *means* to experience God through belief: the signs of the Bible's narratives are providentially organized to display the mercy of God to the believer, though perhaps not to one who reads it as a purely historically referential document.

Third, the fact that we cannot be completely clear in our articulations about God is not a sign of irrationality at all, but represents the actual relationship of human knowing to the datum of God as experienced. To speak of God as "incomprehensible" is not to affirm that nothing can be known about God. It means simply that our apprehensions of this primary and ultimate datum are partial, but true as far as they go, and not without extraordinary fruit for the one who so apprehends. "Anthropomorphism" as a theological, let alone rational error, is misunderstood if we think it refers to any attribution to God of some aspect of creation. It is only in error if such attribution is seen as exhaustive of its referent. Not only is there nothing wrong with attributing to God a "voice," or an "arm," or even (within strict limits) "anger" (and "love" too!), it is absolutely essential that such attributions be made. God is *at least* a person, at least tangible in terms of human and created experience. This is what divine love is all about: communicating the self in a way that is trustworthy. The primary datum of God confirms this. We err only when we assume that the shape of such tangibility exhausts the meaning of reality, and when we make exclusive judgments on their basis.

I doubt very much if these kinds of remarks will persuade new or old atheists of much, except perhaps of my own inability to "face the facts." But the new atheists' own remarks do not include the possibility that one of the facts to be faced is God's own life, even in its seemingly inequitably distributed experience; and if so, that it will stand at the summit of factuality's hierarchy. I do not deny the blasphemy of evil, or the conundrum this creates for our explication of the world's immediate order. But atheists cannot properly make room for the reality that, for those who "know" God in some basic way, there is a perfectly rational—indeed, a necessarily rational—way of living in the broken and conflicted world we are undeniably in, even while praising God and rejoicing in God's presence and sovereign love.

Of course, there is no reason an atheist should grant such a possibility, since he or she does not share in the knowledge that I claim is fundamental to its granting. Perhaps they even think it supremely unfair that they do not. Good: I hope they do, since that at least demonstrates, if only negatively as it were, that "fairness" grasps after faith. That, in the end, is one of the best nonreligious arguments for religion. Fairness grasps after faith. For I do not doubt, in the end, that the very questions that atheists raise may be a part of such a process of knowing, or coming to knowledge in its deepest, most faithful, form. "Stop worrying and enjoy yourself"? Hardly. God bless the atheists. Not only do *they* need such blessing, as all of us do; but they are doing the rest of us a favor, by driving us back to the bedrock of all truth: the fact that God gives himself to us, not we to him, in the first instance. "In this is love, not that we loved God but that he loved us and sent his Son" (1 John 4:10).

6

Does God Condemn Non-Christians?

George Sumner

DRIVING TO A CHURCH conference in Richmond Hill, a suburb of the city of Toronto, recently, I was surprised to see, a block from the Pentecostals and the Catholics, across the street from the shopping mall with its stores and fast food, a vast construction site for a Hindu temple dedicated to the elephant-headed god, Ganesha. Though still scaffolded, the edifice already rises in golden splendor. I should not have been surprised, since Toronto is one of the most multiethnic, multifaith cities in the world; still I pondered what it meant for my ministry day at an Anglican church, that, but a few blocks away, prayer and sacrifice will soon rise up to the son of Shiva, lord of creation and destruction. What does it mean that my church, English by way of Rome and Jerusalem, sits virtually next door to this faith born by the banks of the Ganges? Even if we live in a town much smaller than Toronto, in some way the new reality of followers of once isolated religions now thrown up against one another is familiar to us all.

This essay is simply an effort to "unpack" this experience, which assumed dramatic proportions in the great Ganesha temple. With it a question forces its way into our mind, a question often merely implied and left unuttered: what difference does it make to my faith that Christianity in fact stands as one religion among many? This one basic question then flows into many tributary questions: if I, as a Christian, believe the claims of my own faith to be true, what can and must I say about the claims of others? Finally, can all these worshippers of Ganesha, next to whom I ride the morning subway, really be damned?

It is easy to imagine two very clear-cut but different responses to questions such as these. On the one hand, we might utterly reject what we see at the Ganesha temple: its claims are false, its effect pernicious, its adherents damned. On the other hand, we might accept Ganesha worship on an equal footing with our own Christian faith: the different religions are but different roads up the same mountain. But if we think more about the matter, we realize that we are not really satisfied with either answer. We sense, on the one hand, that something right and true can be found in the temple; we may have met someone whose apparent sanctity makes a blanket assumption of damnation hard. On the other hand, the religions are, quite plainly and simply, radically different. To say that all things their followers actually proclaim or practice do not matter (since they all amount to the same thing) is to do them the disservice of not taking their actual religious lives seriously. These observations leave us in search of a middle ground, not in the service of a lukewarm commitment to the truth of the Christian faith, but rather as a place to balance a full commitment to truth and uniqueness of the gospel and a charitable and generous attitude to other beliefs. Such a goal will certainly have an appealing ring for Anglicans! But is it possible consistently to inhabit this middle space?

RELIGIOUS PLURALITY

We cannot help but acknowledge that we do not pursue this perspective somehow suspended in midair, but seek it as we find ourselves in a very particular place and time culturally. After all, we have become conditioned to think about plurality, including that of religions, in terms of our consumer culture. But one problem (among others) with consumerism is that it only seems to offer a plurality of choices. For each alternative has become a commodity, an option at the seeming disposal of the choosing will, though all subserve the will of those presenting the menu. This is hardly how the traditional Muslim (whose religion after all means "submission") sees the nature of the choice before human beings between obedience and rejection of Allah. Consumerism only seems to offer options, but actually reduces all to the status of commodity.

In fact, Christianity ought to be happy to compete where there is a real array of different options. That is, after all, how the faith began in the first three centuries of her history, when the church was successful in converting much of the empire. In the crowded streets of second-century Alexandria, sectioned off as it was into ethnic regions, real debate existed between Jews, philosophers, mystery religionists, and Christians. In such a world the first great Christian theologian, Origen, sharpened his skills of argument and interpretation. The early "apologetic" (the word has to do in Greek with offering a defense) writers sought only to ward off imperial persecution so that Christians could live in peace and make their case in the marketplace. There have been other moments, unfortunately few, in the history of the Christian mission, when windows of choice and debate opened. For example, the fourteenth-century Mongol emperor Akbar listened intently (if indecisively) as Muslim clerics and Jesuit priests showed their debating wares. Christians have no reason to fear or resist these moments of religions side by side in the bazaar; they underline the distinctiveness of the gospel's offer of and the accompanying need for conversion, a decisive turning of heart and mind.

There is a second aspect of our contemporary context we need to bear in mind as we commence the work of finding the middle ground in a Christian understanding of other traditions. I have in mind the confusion in Christian minds about our own faith. Understanding Christianity is enough of a challenge, much less Sikhism! For it turns out that the question about other religions has become acute at the very moments when faith in Christ itself has weakened. In the age of the Enlightenment, with the rise of modern science in the nineteenth century, pluralism emerged for the same reasons and for the same people, who were also questioning the claims of the creed. One need only read a play like *Nathan the Wise* by the German philosopher Gotthold Ephraim Lessing, in which the religions are all indistinguishable golden rings. It turns out that pluralism is as contemporary as carriages and periwigs! Christians, now as then, can only hope to find the right approach to the beliefs of other traditions if they are clear about their own.

But which Christian belief can be the starting point for the appropriate approach to other religions? For we as Christians do not believe only one thing, but rather hold a series of beliefs outlined most concisely in the Nicene Creed. This may be the initial clue we are looking for. What if there is not one thing Christians need to say in response to the challenge of other religions, but rather a series of things? What if the trouble with competing Christian views of our neighbors is that we have tried to sum up our attitude by making use of only one claim, when a fuller picture may be given if we say several things, based on several beliefs, simultaneously?

CHRISTIAN BASICS

The place to begin is, "in the beginning," with the Bible. By listening there we learn what we as Christians believe about God's creation. In Genesis 1, God's creation is variegated, a rich profusion, and at the same time it is ordered, each creature having its place. Over it all, God pronounces his blessing: "it is good." At the culmination of the creation story God forms the human, to be in God's own "image and likeness." There has, of course, been a great debate about the meaning of that phrase "image of God," but it surely includes the idea that God entrusts to humans some role of ordering, caring for, and appreciating his creatures and the created order as a whole.

Just as God made the world and gave it order, so has God also entrusted to humans a role in preserving that ordered creation. Here an example may be helpful. A Papuan tribe may have its own laws governing courtship and marriage, hunting and eating, warfare and reconciliation. These laws may seem in many ways cruel and contrary to what God intends. At the same time, they may serve to preserve and order the lives of the people of that tribe. We would not want to equate those tribal customs with God's will, but they may also, to some extent, serve a function related to God's creation. Just as that creation is manifold, so too are the customs and systems of law for the many peoples of the earth. In such a way we might say that the sharia of Islamic peoples subserves order, teaching virtues like kindness, humility, and discipline. Insofar as it does this, it may be understood as an "order of creation." According to this understanding, there is something valuable and God-given in the religions themselves. They are, from this perspective, creaturely artifacts that support the ordered nature of creation itself. At the same time, it is easy to see how this view might come to be abused, for features that are oppressive and contrary to God's will might come to be "blessed" as

God-given when they are, in fact, opposed to the divine will. But that leads us to our next topic.

In those same opening chapters of Genesis we also learn that human beings have rebelled against God and so have caused the corruption of their own nature. Such sinfulness affects not only their "baser" nature, but their whole person. (This is what the tradition actually means by "total depravity": not that there is nothing good in us, but rather that there is no portion or corner of us unscathed). This is supported by the story in Genesis 3 itself, in which the serpent tempts Adam with a religious desire, the aspiration to be like God (Gen 3:5). Our religious dimension is sinful, as is every other dimension, but here in our religiosity our rebellion against God is particularly vivid. This is confirmed by Saint Paul's account of the rebellion of humans against their creator in Romans 1, where he gives the following account of the connection between sin and religious worship: "Claiming to be wise, they became fools; and they exchanged the glory of the immortal God for images resembling a mortal human being or birds or four-footed animals or reptiles" (Rom 1:22–23).

SIN AND REDEMPTION

Now at the heart of the Christian understanding of the human person is our two-sidedness, like the face of Janus in ancient Roman lore. We are at once creatures in the image of God and sinners; there is no way to separate or sequester one from the other. Precisely in the religions we see how inextricably interwoven the two are. In Hinduism, for instance, the belief in castes is part of a whole system of beliefs that give order to the world, at the same time that it subserves the interests of the powerful and suppresses the hopes of the weak. The Navajo belief in hozho, often translated "beauty," is at once a sense of the connectedness of all things, and an invitation to manipulation of the spirits for (sometimes malevolent) human ends.[1] There is no way to separate out the good and evil aspects of the religions, any more than we could surgically remove the sinful parts of our minds.

The distress of our sin leads to the question of redemption, God's response to that distress. This is the next chapter of the biblical plot we

---

1. See the works of Clyde Kluckhohn on Navajo culture.

are retelling: "For while we were still weak, at the right time Christ died for the ungodly" (Rom 5:6). The important point here is that no account of something general called "redemption" will do, for Christians know of no other kind of redemption apart from the person and work of Jesus Christ. That is quite simply what the Nicene Creed affirms when it describes Christ as one who is "very God of very God" and lived and died "for us and our salvation." Under the rubrics of creation and sin we could include the Christian faith alongside Islam or Juju or Buddhism. Likewise, Christianity is a created thing, as well as a source of social order: any potluck supper will tell you that. Additionally, the Crusades, the Inquisition, and acquiescence to the Holocaust on the part of many Christians should suffice for the sinfulness issue. But when we come to the point of redemption, here alone Christianity is in a unique position, precisely because redemption entails and requires the specific Redeemer, Jesus Christ.

If redemption is something that various religions do in various ways, then by virtue of this commonality it must be something we humans have a hand in. But at the heart of the Christian message is the radical message of grace: somebody else, Jesus, did this for us, while we were yet helpless. For this reason alone and not for any virtue in us, Christianity is incomparable and, by being so, it is unique. What we mean by "redemption" is the new relation to God and the new kind of life that follows from what Jesus has done for us, realized as we accept that work in faith. In other words, what Christians mean when they say "redemption" already implies the person of Jesus; he is packed into the definition itself. Redemption can be defined in this way: it is that relationship we have with Jesus, who is God's Son, which brings us into relationship with God Himself by means of Jesus's life, death, and resurrection. "Redemption," then, is a "gospel-specific" word on the lips of Christians. For followers of Jesus Christ redemption in general would for Christians be, by definition, no redemption at all.

THE UNIQUENESS OF JESUS

If this is true, then Christianity's third relation to other religions must be one of utter difference and uniqueness located in this Jesus, combined with the other relations we have spoken of, like a third overlay of an overhead projector. In this third relationship it is more difficult to draw a line of comparison from Christianity to other religions. By definition, this third relationship, tied to the person of Jesus, resists immediate comparison. We can only proceed by analogy, by an act of imagination, although we bear in mind that the key thing for Christians, the factor that rules the very content of redemption, is who brings it, Jesus Christ, the one factor Christianity shares with no other religion.

Such uniqueness is clearest if we return to the example of a Muslim at prayer. As he kneels in reverence, his notion of the nature of the divine (Allah) whom he addresses has its own specific content. For example, as a Muslim he is told by the Koran that God may never become incarnate. For him this would imply a second god and is thus blasphemy, the very antithesis of redemptive belief. Islamic tradition calls this heretical belief shirk, by which is meant an explicit denial of the Christian claim regarding Jesus. Denial of Christ is embedded in Islam's sacred text itself. Utter difference and disagreement cannot be avoided.

But at this point, we must face head-on a challenge from our culture. Yes, Muslims and Buddhists, across the globe or across the street, may be after something quite different. But why cannot their goal work for them and our goal work for us? Although ours may even be the best and truest, why cannot theirs be true enough to redeem a life? Steak is best, but one can just as easily live on hamburger. This question is most salutary, for it drives us back to our own scripture to see more clearly what our own faith claims. Consider, for example, the following verses from the opening of the epistle to the Hebrews: "Long ago God spoke to our ancestors in many and various ways by the prophets, but in these last days he has spoken to us by a Son, whom he appointed heir of all things, through whom he also created the worlds" (Heb 1:1–2). We have been talking about the relationships between Christianity and other religious traditions with a view to the biblical story of salvation. But all chapters of this story are not equal: the story has, Hebrews reminds us, a climax: namely the advent, death, and resurrection of Jesus Christ. This is the full and final revelation of God, the very coming of God himself into his lost humankind to save them: "the Word became flesh" (John 1:14) and "in him all the fullness of God was pleased to dwell" (Col 1:19) are, for example, making the same point using different terms. Other ways may have values that can be built up into virtues, but human lives have, claim Christians, only one ultimate goal.

Of course history did not end with the resurrection, although at the heart of the faith is the claim that Jesus's coming again is to confirm and make clear what he has already brought about through his death and resurrection. The "something more" of the second coming is not separate from the great events of the cross and the open tomb, but rather both together make up the "fullness of time" to which Hebrews refers. In other words, if we take seriously the kind of claim the New Testament makes—that Christ is the center or focal point of all history, both before and after—then there is no history to which his advent does not pertain. There is no human life that can happily remain with another, separate goal, oblivious to the goal set out by Jesus at the "fullness of time," all human time.

If, then, we look back at our verses from Hebrews, we can see that Jesus's inheritance of all things at the "fullness of time" has the very same universal reach as does the creation in which he, as second person of the Trinity, also shared. The technical term for this in theology is "eschatology," which means the idea of the "last things," or the end time. One of the great discoveries of modern critical study of the New Testament has been that eschatology—the thought that these events in Jesus' life usher in the end of all things—lies not at the periphery, but at the very heart of the New Testament message. If this is so, then it follows that the claim made by Jesus must have the same universal reach for all persons, in all cultures, and in all places and times. To believe that Jesus is who he claims to be is to believe that he by right makes that same claim on all the people of the earth.

THE CHURCH

The publication of this claim throughout the world is the business of the church, and so we come naturally to the fourth "moment" within the story of God's dealing with his creation and his people, the time of the church. In the New Testament, we learn that the mandate of the church is given on the occasion of Jesus' ascension, which in turn "unleashes" the gift of the Holy Spirit on the Day of Pentecost (Matt 28:16–20; John 20:19–23; and Acts 1–2, all of which testify, in various ways, to this connection between Jesus's resurrection and ascension, the giving of the spirit, and the church's mission to the nations of the world).

We would do well to review at this point what we have already discovered. We have identified three relationships between Christianity and the religions. With an eye to creation, we can see that systems of belief provide structure and support order in the created order and may, at times, even open adherents to the Creator. We can see that all such communities represent, at the very same time, human pretension, and the urge to "build ourselves a city, and a tower with its top in the heavens" (Gen 11:4). As divine response, Christianity claims uniquely to bear the name of the one in whom God acted, decisively, on behalf of all of humankind. Fellow-orderer, fellow-rebel, and witness to the divine response—these are three different, simultaneous relationships, so that already we have seen that the question of the relationship between Christianity and the religions deserves not one but three answers.

So we cannot say that there is a single relationship between the Christian faith and other traditions, but rather a weave of several connecting threads. In this same vein we can conclude that accounts of the relationship that try to give a monochromatic account are mistaken. For example, an account of other religions which saw them as essentially human longing for God which is fulfilled in the gospel would capture a part of the truth based on creation.

At the same time, we must grant that the Christ-centered relation, in which uniqueness is emphasized, has pride of place, since it addresses the goal or climax of human history: this is, to reiterate, what New Testament talk about "eschatology" is telling us. In other words, Christians believe that Jesus Christ faithfully shows what we can know of God's coming reign and will sit at his Father's right hand in that reign. So, while there are several things we may want to say of the religions at once, the crowning word must belong to Christ. It is not the only thing to be said and therein lies the validity of criticism leveled at Christian "exclusivism," but without any downplaying of Christ's unique place in the plan of salvation.

CONVERSION

To live is to meet followers of other traditions who come into constant contact with Christians. When that takes place, people have a blessed collision with Jesus Christ. Thus a Tamil Christian talking with her Hindu cousin, whereby the cousin comes into contact with the good news about Christ, but through the medium of the church with all its flaws, for "we have this treasure in clay jars" (2 Cor 4:7), or in "earthen vessels," as the King James Bible has it. In Acts 17:30, Paul tells us that "God has overlooked the times of human ignorance" and now is the time to convert, turning to Jesus Christ. In the conversation between believer and cousin, the time "before" is over and the time of decision, of the kingdom, dawns. After the encounter and, by God's grace, conversion, the new Christian becomes part of a church in the midst of the other religion.

There then commences (and continues) the task of understanding one's old beliefs and practices in light of the new. So which beliefs and practices are to be rejected, which retained, and which transformed? Here the various strands come into play, for a debate will surely ensue about which elements are creaturely blessings of creation, which signs of our fallenness, and which capable of use in explaining who Jesus the Christ is. Can an African Christian speak of Christ as the ultimate chief of the new clan? Can he or she attend a traditional initiation rite? Which portions must be omitted? The judgments are piecemeal and contestable. But the lead must be taken by the local Christians, those who know best the culture in which they live and the religion from which they have come. Throughout they must remember that they remain the neighbor of the non-Christian for they have no particular claim on truth or sanctity. But the Christian is the one "in the right place at the right time," the place where God has given his gospel. By grace they are "ambassadors for Christ, since God is making his appeal through us" (2 Cor 5:20).

CONCLUSION

Do Christians then have a view of other religious traditions? Can that view be said to inhabit the middle ground we have sought? No. Christians have many views, a series of perspectives, because the religions themselves are diverse, because the beliefs we ourselves bring to the question are many, and because Christians will differ over how to add the aforementioned pieces together. The unity of our response is simply the unity that is the person of Jesus Christ, through whom all things were made, who forgives sins, who is himself the fullness of God incarnate. It is with

Christ that all humans, including adherents of other religions will, now by proclamation, or else on the last day, have to do.

This in turn means that the right relationship of the church to other bodies of religious believers requires that the church be about the business of proclaiming the one who "makes the difference." The church has to devote itself to the practice of witnessing or proclaiming the unique and decisive work of Jesus Christ. Here a bit of everyday wisdom helps. Questions we ask when some real issue of life bears down on us are different from questions asked out of mere curiosity. If you are a school teacher "in the trenches," questions about how to teach first-graders to read have a deeper weight and urgency. Something similar is true for the church: congregations actually proclaiming the good news to members of other traditions who try to make sense of their unbelieving grandparents are asking different questions than those sitting in their armchairs, although the words appear to be the same.

Where one loses sight of this context, then the more secondary questions come to claim center stage. "Could an ancestor who had never heard the good news be saved?" That question implies a time "before" the proclamation and so assumes that the proclaiming has taken place. Where this question is asked by a church that does not proclaim, or perhaps a church looking for an easy out so as not to proclaim, the question assumes center stage, and its answer becomes the general rule, rather than the special (and problematic) case. So, in sum, the relation of Christianity to other traditions rightly depends upon the church's dedication to the practice of witnessing, the act of claiming the truth for all even as we strain to make ourselves understood by others with assumptions very different from our own.

7

Why Evangelism?

Being Caught Up in the Swoop of Grace

John P. Bowen

When I was growing up in Wales in the 1960s, we always knew when out driving that a very straight road in an unlikely place was usually of Roman origin. The Romans knew well that the shortest distance between two points is a straight line, and, in the interests of getting their army from A to B as efficiently as possible, they (literally) cut corners. What they did not care about, of course, was the view. They were not tourists; neither were their armies known for their appreciation of beautiful landscapes. For the rest of us, we know that roundabout routes are slower and less efficient but generally more interesting. So in approaching this subject of "Why evangelism?" I should warn you that I plan to take the scenic route. Do not worry that it seems indirect: I promise we will get there in the end and enjoy the scenery along the way. After all, we are not a Roman army.

First, then, a story. I have a friend in Western Kenya, John Njuguna, who is a church planter. I asked him once how he did his church planting. He said, "Well, I move into a neighborhood. If necessary, I learn the language. And, as I get to know my neighbors, we discuss what God is like. I tell them I am starting a church in the village, and we will be meeting under a certain tree on Sunday mornings if they would like to learn more." They come, they believe and are baptized, he calls the bishop to send a pastor, and then he goes off somewhere else to do it all again. He has done this more than a dozen times.

WHAT IS GOD LIKE?

John has an amazing gift. Among other things, I am intrigued by the fact that the first thing he talks with people about it is not whether they believe in God, or who they think Jesus is, or whether they are interested in church, or any of the things we might expect, but this deceptively simple-sounding question of what they think God is like. It is indeed the most important question we can ever ask or hope to answer. A. W. Tozer once said, "What comes into our minds when we think about God is the most important thing about us."[1]

Classical Christianity has always taught that God is Trinity, Father, Son and Spirit. To many, this sounds like an unnecessary complication to the simple idea of an omnipotent Creator whom we call God. Thomas Jefferson for one looked forward to the day "when we shall have done away with the incomprehensible jargon of the Trinitarian arithmetic . . . and got back to the pure and simple doctrines [Jesus] inculcated."[2] There are still Christians who feel that way.

Yet one reason the idea of the Trinity has always commended itself to Christians—apart from the "hints and pointers" in scripture that this is in fact an accurate way to speak of God—is that it sheds light on aspects of human life that are not explained adequately by the simple idea of "God."[3] In particular, the doctrine of the Trinity says that at the heart of the universe is not the image we are sometimes given of a lonely God who creates because he is pining for something to love, but rather loving, joyful, dynamic triune relationships. The relationship between the persons of the Trinity has sometimes been referred to as *perichoresis*, which some translate as "dance."

For many people, even lifelong Christians, the idea of the Trinity engaged in a dance comes as something of a shock: is it not rather irreverent, even blasphemous, to think of God in such a, well, human way? But it is not meant to be a literal picture, of course. Like all of our

1. Tozer, *The Knowledge of the Holy*, 1.
2. McGrath, *Understanding the Trinity*, 110.
3. Gunton, *The One, the Three, and the Many*, 215.

language about God, we are stretching our minds to understand what is really beyond us, and using the figures of speech which seem to us to come closest to describing the indescribable. So *perichoresis* is not meant to make us think of strobe lights, a heavy beat and sweaty bodies, but of joy and exuberance, of fluid movement, and rich harmony. There is no loneliness in the Trinity but a dynamic fullness of love and joy.

But love and joy always overflow. So one way to think of the creation of the world is as the overflow of the love of the Trinity, the eternal God making everything in order that all things—from angels to atoms—might take part in that great cosmic dance. The Baptist theologian Paul Fiddes imagines it like this: "If we use the image of a dance, then there is a kind of 'progressive' dance in which participants move outside the inner circle of dancers to make contact with others, and then come back in again, bringing other dancers with them. So the dance goes out from the Father and back in again to the Father. The Father sends out the Son through whom the Spirit proceeds as the life-giver in creation, and in the Spirit created persons return in worship through the Son to the Father."[4]

If we play with this image a little more, we may think of the archangel leaving his place in one of the inner circles of the dance and appearing to the Virgin Mary in order to invite her to take her own central place in the dance by bearing God's incarnate Son, and she accepts his invitation. When her son grows up ("sent" from the inner to the outer circle of the dance by the Father), we may think of him inviting others to join the dance too.

There was a popular Christian song in the 1960s called "Lord of the Dance" (words written by Sydney Carter), which adopted this same imagery of the dance. The words are put into the mouth of Jesus, and they show the connection between the dance of creation and the incarnation and work of Jesus: "I danced in the morning when the world was begun /. . . I came down from heaven and I danced on the earth; / at Bethlehem I had my birth." The song goes on:

> I danced for the scribe and the Pharisee,
> But they would not dance and they would not follow me.
> I danced for the fishermen, for James and John:
> They came with me and the dance went on.

---

4. Fiddes, *Participating in God*, 75.

> Dance, then, wherever you may be;
> I am the Lord of the Dance, said he,
> And I'll lead you all, wherever you may be,
> And I'll lead you all in the dance, said he.[5]

Of course, there is a reason that human beings need to be invited to the dance. Quite simply, although we were created with the capacity to be wonderful dancers, we have decided, individually and as a race, that we do not want to be part of the cosmic dance. We want to do our own thing, to dance to our own beat, or indeed not to dance at all. We would not dance and we would not follow God. The old-fashioned word for this is sin: not just "doing something wrong" (as we so often think) but disrupting the dance of the universe by opting out and refusing joy.

But for those who follow and join the dance, taught the movements by the Holy Spirit, what they discover is that they have a place in the dance: they begin to live the life for which they were designed, they begin to turn into the person their creator designed them to be, and they find joy. In the end, all who join the dance find that the steps and figures they are learning are actually part of the dance not only of this world but of eternity. C.S. Lewis captures some of the awesomeness of this vision at the end of his second space fiction novel, *Perelandra,* where the characters have a mystical vision of eternity, where the whole universe is dancing with God and "each movement [of the dance] becomes in its season the breaking into flower of the whole design."[6]

We have come a long way since I suggested we were going to come at our topic via the "scenic approach." Now, however, we are finally approaching our destination, and you will see why this is a better way to arrive than along a Roman road.

WHAT IS EVANGELISM?

In spite of many efforts in the past twenty years, not least the so-called Decade of Evangelism in the 1990s, evangelism still has a bad press.[7] But

---

5. © 1963 Stainer & Bell, Ltd. (Admin. Hope Publishing Company, Carol Stream, IL 60188). All rights reserved. Used by permission.

6. Lewis, *The Cosmic Trilogy,* 343.

7. Throughout the worldwide Anglican Communion, the "Decade of Evangelism" was an initiative to emphasize spreading the gospel during the 1990s.

it need not be that way. There are fresh ways to think of evangelism, and here is one of my favorites: evangelism is God's invitation for people to join the eternal dance of joy. It is as simple as that. Evangelism is not the invention of evangelists or of evangelicals, though their names might suggest that. It is not the property of street evangelists or televangelists or door-to-door evangelists.

At the heart of the word *evangelism* is the word *evangel*, a Greek word meaning "good news." What is that good news? The amazingly good news is that the love and joy of the triune God, which long ago overflowed to bring the cosmos into being, and which continues to reach out into every corner of that cosmos, has not given up on this world, in spite of the fact that we repeatedly turn away from God and from joy. Indeed, the love which always overflows has reached out supremely in the coming of Jesus Christ into our world, to live and die and rise again for us ("I am the life that will never, never die"), and to invite us back into the dance of joy. Evangelism is basically the communication of a message, an amazing message from God and about God, a message of joy, or an invitation to rejoin the dance. Because of this, evangelism is primarily God's idea, not that of any human agency; and God, not any human being, is the supreme evangelist, the bringer of the invitation to the dance.

WHY EVANGELISM?

In a sense, the question "Why evangelism?" has already been answered. The world needs evangelism because the world needs the evangel. The world needs evangelism because the world needs God and the world needs joy. The world needs evangelism because the world has forgotten the music of the dance, has forgotten that its feet were made for dancing to the music of God and with God, and without evangelism the world will not know that it is invited.

Of course, when people ask, "Why evangelism?" this is not generally the sort of answer they are hoping for, although for a Christian it is the most central. In my experience, however, people also want to know the answers to questions such as "Does evangelism imply that Christianity is right and every other religion wrong?" or "Can evangelism ever be anything other than disrespectful?" and "Is it ever appropriate to speak to someone else about something so personal as religion?" Supposing there were satisfactory answers to those questions, there still remains the very basic question: "What should I say?" Even if these are secondary questions, they are still important to consider. Let us look at them in that order.

Does Evangelism Imply That Christianity Is Right and Every Other Religion Wrong?

This question is treated at greater length elsewhere in this book, so I will deal with it only briefly here. C. S. Lewis, as so often, is pithy and helpful in his comments on this topic, in *Mere Christianity* and elsewhere. He says basically that Christians rejoice to acknowledge truth in any and every religion, since all truth is God's truth. At the same time, however, he argues that there is something unique about Jesus Christ which marks him out from every other religious founder in history.

His first point that there is truth in every religion is a reflection of the fact that God is creator, and not surprisingly there is evidence of the creator everywhere in the creation, rather as the distinctive style of a painter can be recognized in her paintings. His second point also has a parallel in art: you learn something about an artist from her self-portrait that you do not learn from her landscapes. Jesus Christ is God's self-portrait in a way that God's other works of art are not. The best that other religious founders can do is to help their followers deduce the character of the artist from the landscapes. Neither the Buddha nor Muhammad, neither Lao-Tse nor Confucius, neither Zoroaster nor Joseph Smith ever hinted at a divine identity for themselves and nor did their followers claim such a thing: indeed, they would have been horrified at such a suggestion. Yet Jesus gave clues to his true identity that his followers made explicit after his resurrection: Jesus Christ was God come to earth. Christianity is different from other religions primarily because Jesus Christ is different from their founders.

To revert to the dance image, we can say that there are echoes of the music and even the distant sounds of dancing feet, to be found everywhere in God's world, and whoever wishes to may attempt to join in, however falteringly. But in Jesus, God comes in person to take us by the hand and show us the steps. As the traditional carol, *Tomorrow shall be my Dancing Day*, puts it, Jesus comes "to call my true love to my dance."

So how does a Christian respond to a person of another religion? Firstly, with deep respect: here is a person in the image of God and a person for whom Christ died. Lewis points out that (apart from the sacrament) nothing should be treated with greater reverence than our neighbor and, we might add, that is true whatever their religion may be.[8]

Second, we will want to listen to what our friend has to say about their religion. Apart from anything else, it will deepen our understanding of them and what is valuable to them. But we will also want to listen for what we may learn of God from them and their insights.

But, thirdly, as we grow in our friendship with them, we will talk respectfully about our own faith, and particularly what we believe to be unique about Jesus Christ. Whenever friends share what is important to them, each is enriched and changed. I believe that when I talk about my faith in Jesus, he himself is able to bring home the truth of who he is to my friends without any pressure from me.

I remember one Muslim friend who said to me, "I want to know how it is different to live as a Christian from how it is to live as a Muslim." After we talked about it, he commented, "It seems to me that for a Muslim, I can find the answer as to how I should act in any situation in the Koran, whereas for you, the Bible gives you general principles, such as 'Love your neighbor as yourself,' and then it is for you to work out how that applies in any given situation." I thought that was a valid insight into what it means to be a follower of Jesus, but it was much more meaningful as a conclusion he drew from our conversation than if I had announced it dogmatically myself. I tried to bear witness to the truth as I understood it in Jesus, and the Holy Spirit helped my friend understand it.

Can There Be Such a Thing as Respectful Evangelism?

The way Christians practice evangelism must reflect the nature of the evangel. The poetry of the gospel has to be set to the music of the dance. It is deeply incongruous if a Christian tries to bully someone into believing that God loves them! Bullying and love are incompatible. Anger and violence and manipulation are not consistent with the good news of God.

A message about love will be communicated with love. A message about joy will be communicated joyfully. A message about a dance . . .

---

8. Lewis, "The Weight of Glory," 109–10.

well, Brian McLaren teases out what that means about evangelistic communication: "I think of [evangelism] like a dance. You know, in a dance, nobody wins and nobody loses. Both parties listen to the music and try to move with it. In this case, I hear the music of the gospel, and my friend doesn't, so I try to help him hear it and move with it. And like a dance, I have to ask if the other person wants to participate. There's a term for pulling someone who doesn't want to dance into a dance: assault. But if you pull someone in who wants to learn, and if you're good with the music yourself, it can be a lot of fun."[9]

Can such evangelism happen? Does it happen? Frankly, it happens all the time. Wherever I go, I meet people who have become Christians in recent months or years. Often I will ask them how it happened. Not once have I had someone say with a grimace, "Well, I was kind of bullied into it. I never meant for it to happen, but now I'm scared to back out." Inevitably they will tell me, often with a smile, about friends who cared for them, answered their questions, gently asked them to Christian events, loaned them books, and (as often as not) drank endless coffee with them. In other words, a message about following Jesus was communicated in a loving manner which made the message believable.

I met Emily and Catherine when they started coming to our church, but I did not hear their story till much later. In her first year at university, Catherine had found herself in a residence room with an over-enthusiastic and not-very-sensitive Christian. Fortunately, she had a friend in residence, Emily, also a Christian, though of a different stripe, to whom Catherine could complain about her roommate, and who patiently gave Catherine a different kind of answer to her questions. Not surprisingly, it was Emily who helped Catherine come to a lively faith in Christ and encouraged her to come to church.

Not that the other kind of evangelism does not happen, as Catherine and many others have experienced. That is not my point: my point is that it does not work, in the sense that it does not create lifelong passionate Christians. If anybody does respond to that kind of evangelism—and I fear they do, often in the pressure of the moment, because I have seen the damage it can cause—it does not last. They wake up the next day, or the next month, and realise that the choice they have made was a coerced choice, not really a choice at all, and not what they really intended. Those people are very hard to convince that maybe there is truth (and

---

9. McLaren, *A New Kind of Christian*, 62.

life) in Christianity after all, simply because they have been so badly burned. Or, to change the image, they have experienced a travesty of the dance, more than a bruising rugby game than anything else, and the result was broken bones, and a resolve never to repeat the experience, however often they are told that was not the real thing.

But anyone who cares about whether evangelism can be respectful is not in imminent danger of being a disrespectful evangelist. That kind of care for persons is deeply compatible with the gospel. Anyone who cares that much for people—if they care equally for the gospel—will make a highly influential and much-loved evangelist.[10] That, however, begs the answer to the third question.

Is It Ever Appropriate to Speak to Someone Else about Something as Personal as Religion?

What people are "allowed" to talk about varies from culture to culture. In North America, it is easy to talk about sex but difficult to talk about religion. In Africa, it is the easiest thing in the world to talk about religion, but highly inappropriate to talk about sex. On the one hand, I would say that in both places, "openness" does not equal "depth." On the other hand, both would benefit from a little more openness on the taboo topics, since both are so deeply significant for human life.

So is it ever appropriate? That depends, not only on the culture but also on the relationship. With those I really trust, I can actually talk about most things like my personal failings and insecurities, my relationship with God (or lack of it), my fears about sickness and death, and so on. But the relationship has to be a strong enough bridge to bear that kind of traffic. How does a relationship come to be that strong? Think about your own most meaningful relationships. They took time to grow. Little by little trust grew. Your friend showed himself trustworthy in a little thing, so you decided to trust him with a slightly larger thing, and then a larger thing again. It is like a plant that wants to grow: it puts out small, tender shoots, and if they find the right environment of sun and rain, it will put out bigger shoots and bigger shoots until it becomes a tree that can withstand most storms. That is one way that an environment can grow in which one can talk about religion.

---

10. Thiessen, *The Ethics of Evangelism*, 145–46.

But relationships can develop more quickly than that. I remember once inviting my next-door neighbor to a carol service at our church around Christmas time. He said he could not come, but the next day he e-mailed me a poem he had written called "Fundamentalism." At first I was worried: perhaps he thought I must be a fundamentalist because I had invited him to church. But no; it turned out that he was eager to discuss religion and faith and church, and our e-mail correspondence about such topics went on for six months. (You may think this seems strange between next-door neighbors, but if you are both introverts, it is perfectly natural.) We were simply two people who had an interest in the same topic (though from very different points-of-view) and we were delighted to have found each other. My experience suggests that there are many in our society who actually have a pent-up hunger for discussion about spirituality, but our cultural reticence holds them back. A casual comment that we may make about church or spirituality actually makes it easy for that conversation to begin, almost as if we were in Africa.

This suggests another answer to the question. I suspect that the reluctance of many of us to talk about our faith is actually because our faith is so internal and so deep and inarticulate that we feel we would not know what to say, even if someone asked us a direct question. So we project our reluctance onto the other person: "I couldn't possibly talk about it and I'm sure they feel the same."

One response to this is to say that anybody can learn to talk about their faith. Not everyone will be brilliant apologists like C.S. Lewis, not everybody will have answers to the difficult questions often raised against Christian faith, but not everybody has to. For one thing, the New Testament lays great store by the power of "witness," a simple word which, as in a court of law, is simply a matter of saying, "This is what I know." It is not uncommon for that unpolished word of "witness" to be more effective than many brilliant arguments.[11] Which leads us to the final question.

What Should I Say?

The story is told of a preacher who spotted a famous agnostic professor in his city-center congregation week after week and began to prepare his sermons with the goal of convincing the professor to become a

---

11. Percy, *Good News People*, 103–7.

Christian. After several months, the professor made an appointment to see the pastor and said that he wanted to follow Jesus and to be baptized. The pastor naturally was curious as to what had led him to this conviction, hoping to learn which of his sermons had done the work. "Well," said the professor, "as I was leaving church one Sunday, I gave my arm to an elderly lady who was struggling with the steps. Having thanked me, she looked me in the face and said, 'Young man, are you a follower of Jesus yet?' And immediately I knew that I wasn't but that I wanted to be. So here I am." It may be an apocryphal story, but it makes an important point, as the simple question of a woman with no theological training and no ability to preach had more effect than any number of carefully crafted, intellectually challenging sermons. This kind of thing happens all the time, which is of course humbling to those of us who *are* theologically trained and often find ourselves preaching. But it is encouraging to the vast majority of Christians who are not. Sometimes the amateurs are better dancers than the professionals.

The simplest place to begin about this matter of "witness" is to think to ourselves:

- What is it that keeps me going to church?
- How would my life be the poorer if I stopped going? What exactly would I feel I had lost?
- Have there been times in my life when I have sensed God's presence, or received a wonderful and unmistakable answer to prayer?
- What is my favorite hymn, and why am I attracted to it? What are the words of that hymn which specially touch my heart?
- Are there Bible passages, or places in the liturgy, that always give me comfort or strength, or that bring tears to my eyes whenever I hear them?

When we have answers to these kinds of questions, we are close to the heart of our personal "witness," like what it is that we could say about our faith in a court of law if asked to testify under oath.

You may protest: "But what I have to say is such a personal thing and so undramatic. How could it possibly impress someone else, or be helpful to them?" You would be surprised. For you to say in an appropriate moment, or in answer to a question such as "Why do you still bother with church?"—"Well, I find God gives me strength when I am frightened," or "I don't really understand what it means to say Jesus died for me, but I find it immensely moving"—can be very helpful.

Why evangelism? Because for some other person, that simple thing that you have to say about the importance of your faith may be precisely the good news they have been longing to hear. Or, to put it another way, your experience of the dance, however hesitant or stumbling, may encourage them to try a few steps for themselves.

There then is one response to the Christian who hesitates about evangelism because they do not know what to say: every Christian has *something* to say if they stop and think about it. It will not be something we will blurt out on just any occasion—after all, it is deeply personal and intimate—but we can take courage in both hands and say it when the time seems right. The result, though it may surprise us, will be joy for us, quite apart from the effect it may have on anyone else.

A CASE STUDY

So far, I have talked as though evangelism is a solo effort. Speaking for myself, however, I am always encouraged and reassured by remembering that evangelism is always a team effort.[12] To illustrate this, let me tell you a story of something that happened to me a few years ago. James was a seeker. When he arrived in Toronto as a graduate student that fall, he was looking for something or someone to help him understand Christianity. Then, through a succession of links, he got in touch with me with a view to meeting which we did.

Over the weeks that followed, we talked about many of his questions like the historical basis for Christianity, the reputation of the church in the world, and not least what it might mean for James to live as a follower of Jesus. Then, some time before Christmas, he emailed me in the middle of the week to say, "I've opened my heart to God in the way that we've talked about. I didn't expect to feel different, but actually I do—I feel more alive than I've ever felt before."

From that point on, our weekly conversation took a new turn. In particular, we began to read the gospels with a new intensity, like two disciples of Jesus trying to learn from our teacher. The first time we did this, to my surprise, James brought a bible with him. I did not even know

12. Bowen, *Evangelism for "Normal" People*, 81–86.

he owned a bible. Out of idle curiosity, I pulled it across the table towards me, and opened the front cover. There I read, "To James, from Dave." It was dated a few years earlier. "Who's Dave?" I asked. "Oh, Dave was my best friend in high school," he replied. "He was a Christian, and we had lots of discussions about faith over the years. But he never managed to persuade me. Then, when we graduated, he gave me this."

Our bible studies continued through the school year. They were lively, intriguing, edgy, and often humorous. As the spring drew on, he said one day, "By the way, I have a friend coming to see me at the end of term. I'd like you to meet her." "Who's that?" I asked. "Meredith and I dated through university," he replied. "She was a Christian. Towards the end of our undergraduate years, I asked her if she would marry me. She told me she couldn't marry someone who wasn't a Christian. At the time, I thought, what is this fascist religion where you can't marry whoever you want?" James smiled ruefully. "Now I understand perfectly." So one fine May morning, I was introduced to Meredith. As I shook her hand, I smiled and said, "Nice to be on the same team as you." Because I was.

So who was the evangelist in James's life? Me? Well, in a way I suppose so. Certainly I was the person who just happened to be around when he decided he wanted to be a follower of Jesus. Maybe our discussions were the final nudge he needed. I do not really know. But I do know that Jesus several times spoke of the work of the kingdom (of which evangelism is a part) like farming, a process with several stages, from sowing to reaping, all of them overseen by God. Paul understands this principle when he writes, "I planted, Apollos watered, but God gave the growth" (1 Cor 3:6).

So in James's case I was the reaper. But, of course, I could not have done what I did unless Dave had sowed the seed and Meredith had watered that seed. It was almost as though Jesus had me in mind when he said (also in the context of evangelism), "Others have labored, and you have entered into their labor" (John 4:38).

I sometimes wonder how Dave felt when he and James parted ways after high school. He had certainly "labored" to be a good witness, but I think in his place I would have felt discouraged: "I had so hoped that James would become a Christian, but he didn't. If only I had been smarter, prayed more, been a better friend. Maybe that bible will help him, if he reads it." I wonder if Meredith felt the same. Each of them knew him for three years. Over that time, they bore consistent daily witness, by their lives and (as opportunity offered) by their words. I, by contrast, knew James for three months. Frankly, I had the easy job, the fun job, for me, anyway, pure joy.

But God, who oversees the whole process of evangelism, used all of us in different ways to help James move to become a follower of Jesus. The work of evangelism is the work of a team of people in the Body of Christ. When people finally become Christians, then, as Jesus knew, "sower and reaper . . . rejoice together" (John 4:36).

So evangelism means teamwork. You may not be an "evangelist," but you can contribute something unique to the work of evangelism as Dave, Meredith, and I did. It may be your personal "witness" to your faith, as we discussed above. It may equally be your ability to be a trustworthy friend to someone. It may be that you could invite someone to church, perhaps for a special occasion like a carol service at Christmas or a back-to-church Sunday. On such occasions, the warmth of the community itself, and of course lively worship and an engaging sermon, can communicate more clearly than the words of any single individual. Perhaps you could host a dinner party in your home where a well-known local figure (a politician, perhaps, or an athlete) who happens to go to your church could talk about their faith and answer questions. The possibilities are endless. What can you contribute to the team?

THE EXAMPLE OF JESUS

There is one further answer to the question, "Why evangelism?" Christians are basically followers of Jesus, learning to live with the blend of "grace and truth" he demonstrated. Thus Jesus taught us to love God and neighbor, so we try to do likewise. Jesus taught us to forgive and modeled how to do it, so we too try to forgive. But Jesus also modeled evangelism—how to invite others into the cosmic dance of the Trinity—and so another part of our discipleship is to learn what he has to teach us about evangelism, and it put it into practice. So we need to ask: How did Jesus evangelize? Here are four key aspects.

He Was Clear about the Evangel

The evangel is a message which needs to be made known. But no messenger can be effective who does not know the message. The message of Christianity is not (as Douglas Adams suggested) that "nearly two thousand years ago . . . one man [was] nailed to a tree for saying how great it would be to be nice to people for a change."[13] The message is a little more than "be nice to one another." Mark's gospel shows Jesus announcing his message from day one: "Jesus came to Galilee, proclaiming the good news [the evangel] of God, and saying, 'The time is fulfilled, and the kingdom of God has come near; repent, and believe in the good news'" (Mark 1:14–15).

In other words, the time has come when God is establishing his reign on the earth, and human beings are called to "repent and believe," that is, to give up their self-directed ways and give their lives to following God's agenda as followers of Jesus.

It seems to me that every Christian should have some sense of the message. Not that you have to make a long speech about it at the drop of a hat, of course, but each of us needs to have a sense of "what it's all about." Imagine someone going door-to-door collecting for cancer research. The basic thing they need to say is: "Would you like to contribute to cancer research?" They may add a word about why they are collecting as with "I'm a cancer survivor myself" or "My mother died of cancer," in effect a word of personal "witness," as we discussed above, but they also need some sense of what cancer is, and what the treatments are, and what the money will go to even if no one ever asks them. They do not need to be experts, but they do need to know broadly "what it's all about." Apart from anything else, that knowledge would fuel their enthusiasm for the (often tedious) task. They need to see the overall picture into which their Saturday afternoon door-knocking fits. This is why the apostle Peter (in a Christian context) says, "Always be ready to make your defense to anyone who demands from you an accounting for the hope that is in you" (1 Pet 3:15).

If someone asked me what Christianity is all about (and they do from time to time), I would usually say something like this by trying to be faithful to Jesus' message but to put it in everyday language: "God designed the world to be full of joy. But human beings regularly fail to cooperate with God. We prefer to run our own lives and resent it when God tries to "interfere." God might have chosen to give up on this world, but he decided instead to renew everything, to eradicate sin and evil and suffering, and to restore the world to joy. He sent Jesus to live and die

---

13. Adams, *The Ultimate Hitchhiker's Guide*, 5.

and rise again as the centerpiece of his plan to restore everything. And now God invites men and women everywhere to follow Jesus and to cooperate with this cosmic restoration plan."

You don't have to use my summary, of course, but I believe we each need some kind of summary of what "the Christian message" is, just as Jesus did.

Jesus Also Talked about the Love of God and Showed the Love of God

I passed a church sign the other day that advertized the coming Sunday's sermon title: "Walking the Talk." My guess is that the pastor's message was going to be, "Let's not just talk about our faith: let's make sure we live it out as well." Of course, both are important, and it may be that there are some churches where people talk a lot about God without living "a Christian life," but my hunch is that for many Christians, the problem is the opposite: they try to follow Jesus in terms of how they live their lives, but they are tongue-tied when it comes to saying anything about it. Jesus, however, did both. I am not sure if it is helpful to say, "His actions spoke louder than his words," but it is probably better to say that his actions demonstrated the truth of what he taught (he said the kingdom had arrived and he proved it by doing the works of the kingdom) and his teaching explained what he was doing (my works tell you something about who I am). Words and works in balance, beautifully integrated.[14]

I wonder which side of the equation you come down on. If you are that rare animal, a Christian who talks a lot about her faith but does not actually try to live following the example of Jesus—well, you know what to do. As Jesus says, "If you know these things, you are blessed if you do them" (John 13:17)! Enough said.

But if you have the more common problem, of doing your best to follow Jesus's teaching but saying nothing about Jesus, here too is a challenge. The story is told of a Christian man who felt that it was better to share his faith through actions rather than by words. Six months after he had made this resolution, a colleague accosted him at the water cooler. "You know, Pete, there's something different about your life, and I reckon it must be something to do with your religion." Pete beamed. It had

---

14. Bowen, *Evangelism for "Normal" People*, chapter 4.

worked. "Let me guess," Jeff continued. "You're a vegetarian, right?"[15] So yes, the actions lend authenticity to the words, but the words are needed to explain actions that are otherwise inexplicable. Let us learn to do both.

Jesus Went to Parties with "Nonreligious" Friends

Jesus was known for consorting with undesirables to such an extent that a common criticism of him was: "Look, a glutton and a drunkard, a friend of tax collectors and sinners!" (Luke 7:34). Why would a religious leader do such a thing and apparently not worry about his reputation? I suspect one simple answer is that he liked people, liked to hang out with them, and enjoyed parties. He probably took pleasure in the fact that the phrase "friend of sinners," though meant as a criticism, was actually an affirmation that he was doing his job! The effect of those gatherings was to create an environment in which people felt comfortable and were open to hearing Jesus's message.

I asked some of my students recently whether they had grown up in churchgoing homes. Several had not, so I asked them how they had come to faith. One after another, they talked about friends who had invited them to a church or to a youth group, often a social event, where they had experienced love and had decided that they wanted Christian faith for themselves. That pattern is repeated time and time again around the world and in every century: people become Christians because they have a friend who is a Christian who then invites them to an event. This to me is the pattern of much of Jesus's ministry too. People are open to learn new things in an environment with a friend they trust.

Hence the saying one sometimes hears that "people belong before they believe." It is too easy to assume that, once people figure out that they want to be followers of Jesus, they will find their way to a Christian community: believing followed by belonging. I cannot deny that that happens, but it is more frequent for people to begin hanging out with a Christian community, and in that context to become Christians.

Many Christians who think they cannot be evangelists can invite friends to a Christian event. There are two problems with this idea, however. One is that Christians do not have time to make or sustain friendships outside the church; the other is that churches do not generally plan social events to which non-church friends can be invited. Churches

---

15. Ibid., 96.

which want to be accessible to non-church people, however, will figure out ways to change this.

Jesus Invited People Not Just to Hear about Discipleship but to Experience It

Jesus did not spend a lot of time arguing about the existence of God, or the reliability of the Bible, or why God allows suffering. But he presented the message of the kingdom and then invited people to get involved. His message to the crowds ("repent and believe") was immediately followed by the summons to the first disciples: "Follow me!" These were not two different messages: when the disciples left their nets and followed, they were actually showing what "repent and believe" means. They repented (left their old lives) and believed (started following Jesus). There was only a certain amount they could have learned by continued listening to Jesus: the most important part of what they learned, they learned on the road with him, watching him, asking him questions, taking responsibilities here and there for his work. It was as they shared life with him that they came to understand who he was and began to believe.

This should be encouraging for those of us who find it difficult to speak about our faith. Helping someone move towards Christian faith may not begin with a conversation about faith at all, nor even an invitation to an event at church (good though those things are). It may begin with an invitation to join in whatever ministry you are yourself involved in.

Suppose you are involved in a soup kitchen. Why not invite your friend who is not involved in church to help you out one lunchtime? I have never come across a church with a rule that says, "Only church members may serve lunch here." All are grateful for the help. But a funny thing often happens as you work side by side. The activity of working in a Christian ministry alongside Christian people actually helps others grow into Christian faith, almost without noticing.

I heard just such a story recently, of the friend of a church member who began helping out at the church's food bank. After a couple of years, it was obvious to everyone, including himself, that his attitude to God, Jesus, and church had completely changed: he had become a believer, even though he was not quite sure when or how it had happened. If it is true that some people "belong before they believe," it is equally true that for others they actually "behave (like a Christian) before they believe."

THE SWOOP OF GRACE

I began by suggesting that evangelism begins in the overflow of the life and love of the triune God, as human beings are invited to give up their self-directed lives and learn the steps of the Great Dance. So there is a process that begins in the heart of God and ends with us, that begins with the past (if we can speak of "the past" with God) and leads to our experience in the present.

But evangelism can be understood in the opposite direction too, not this time from the top down (as it were) but from the bottom up. Take James, whose story I told above, for example. On one level, it is the story of several ordinary Christians seeking to be faithful to Christ, "bearing witness" to James in whatever way seemed appropriate. Yet clearly there was no human agency coordinating their efforts: "Okay, thank you, Dave. You have done your part. Now we will hand it over to Meredith." Of course not. Yet there is a sense that there was a supernatural agency at work in James's experience: as Dave, Meredith, and I tried to be open to the prompting of the same Holy Spirit day by day, we were available for the Holy Spirit to work in and through us to achieve the result of James coming to faith. Thus behind the work of these human agents was the work of God the Spirit, the one who calls out the movements of the dance.

Yet this was not the beginning of God's work on behalf of James. We can go back further yet. The gospel of John says that "as yet there was no Spirit [given], because Jesus was not yet glorified" (John 7:39). For John, the time when Jesus is glorified is when he is crucified. Thus, after the cross and resurrection, the Holy Spirit is given to the disciples in the upper room. On the day of Pentecost, Peter also links Jesus's glory and the gift of the Spirit, though his emphasis is not so much on the cross but on Jesus's glory in the resurrection and ascension: "This Jesus God raised up, and of that all of us are witnesses. Being therefore exalted at the right hand of God, and having received from the Father the promise of the Holy Spirit, he has poured out this that you both see and hear" (Acts 2:32–33).

What does this mean? I described the sequence of events which brought James to faith in Christ, and suggested that it was a sequence overseen by the Holy Spirit. Now I want to add another piece to the jigsaw and suggest that the process actually began, not with Dave and James becoming friends in high school, but in the death and resurrection of Jesus Christ two thousand years ago! From those amazing events, the Holy Spirit has flooded out in all directions, seeking to draw all people everywhere into the dance of God's kingdom. Dave, and indeed every follower of Jesus, has been the recipient of the work of the Holy Spirit in this respect. If we understand that we are all spiritually in need of God's grace, that is, the work of the Holy Spirit. If we acknowledge that Jesus is the saviour of the world, that is the work of the Holy Spirit. If we try, however falteringly, to follow the dance steps of Jesus in our lives, that is because of the Holy Spirit.

Another way to say this is that God is passionately concerned for a world in need, sin, and brokenness, and from the moment human beings went wrong, God has been at work to put things to rights. This is what theologians call the *missio dei*, the mission of God. Thus there is a step further back in time, even before the coming of Jesus to live and die for us: Jesus's coming is simply the climax of God's redeeming work in the world. God has always been at work in the world for good, dealing with evil, promoting the good, working through willing people, but in Jesus the creator enters his own story, the king comes in person to put his kingdom on a new and solid footing.

Do you see how this sequence is leading us back and back, from James's experience, first to the events of Jesus's passion, and then to the heart of God in concern for the world? It is an amazing picture. But there is one more step, and this will bring us back to where we started. Why is God involved in a mission to the world? Why does Jesus come? Why does God send the Spirit? It is because of what God is like—the question of John Njuguna—and the answer of Christianity that God is overflowing love. The Trinity is a loving, dancing, overflowing, irrepressible, dynamic three-person God. Once we see that, the rest flows inevitably: of course this kind of God will care for a needy world; of course this God will humble himself to become a man and die for that world; of course this God will work across all nations to create his kingdom; and of course this God will call James and you, and me, to be his children and his apprentices.

Some call this movement, from the heart of God to a fallen world and back to the heart of God again, taking us with him, the swoop of grace. The closest the Bible gives us to a summary of this is Paul's hymn in Philippians 2: "Christ Jesus . . . though he was in the form of God, did not regard equality with God as something to be exploited, but emptied himself, taking the form of a slave, being born in human likeness. And being found in human form, he humbled himself and became obedient to the point of death—even death on a cross. Therefore, God also highly exalted him and gave him the name that is above every name, so that at the name of Jesus every knee should bend, in heaven and on earth and under the earth, and every tongue should confess that Jesus Christ is Lord, to the glory of God the Father (vv. 5–11).

Can you envision this swoop? It looks like this:

Jesus was in the form of God

He emptied himself

He took the form of a slave

He was born in human likeness

He became obedient to the point of death … on a cross

God highly exalted him

God gave him the name that is above every name

Jesus Christ is Lord!

Why evangelism? Because evangelism is part of the *missio dei*; evangelism is part of the work of God to put a broken world back together; and evangelism is the announcement that God is at work in and through Jesus Christ to restore the cosmos.

Why evangelism? Because the Lord of the Dance, in smiling love, has held out his hand to us to invite us to join the eternal cosmic dance and begun to teach us the steps. Now he asks us to learn a new and unfamiliar step, where we turn from the dance and reach out our hand to someone else and invite them to join, so that they too may experience new life and joy as they begin to experience the dance for which they were made. How can we refuse?

8

Who Is My Neighbor?

The Perplexities of International Development for Communities of Faith

David D. Kupp

> I am so angry at what has been done, and continues to be done, in our world. It is hard to believe that the nightmare is real. We seem trapped in grotesquely unjust systems, more and more dominated by power, greed, delusion, denial, ignorance and stupidity, fuelled by the symmetries of terrorism and fundamentalism. For some Christians . . . this takes the form of a perversion in which the Sermon on the Mount and the Parable of the Good Samaritan have no place.[1]

TAKE A DEEP BREATH: the smells tell you many stories. The odors and aromas of international development range from the savory to the stinky. They waft upwards everywhere you go—from the spicy soup pot in the Thai village to the open sewers in the slums of Addis Ababa. From the welcome, warming smoke of a First Nations hearth in the depths of Canadian winter, to the pungent sweat of the coffee pickers on the Guatemalan highlands, and to the heated, spittled anguish of a displaced people marching the streets demanding justice from their oppressors.

Understanding and engaging international development is a study in nineteenth- and twentieth-century triumph and befuddlement, suc-

---

1. Chambers, *Ideas for Development*, ix.

cess and failure, compassion and greed. So, our task here is challenging—to sort through one or two of the perplexities presented by recent decades of international development, bringing in several places filters of Christian faith and practice, and finally understanding how to engage our neighbors in today's global village.

There are a number of fundamental, but interrelated questions about the perplexing nature of international development:

- What is it?
- Why is it so hard to nail down?
- Where is international development going?
- What is the biblical-theological baseline for development?
- What is the best way for a person of faith to engage?

INTERNATIONAL DEVELOPMENT: WHAT IS IT?

Definitions of international development have ranged widely according to the different actors involved, their values, contexts and era. As you can imagine, the range of definitions is wide. In essence, what development is depends on one's experience of it—as the subject or object of development, which is driven by one's relationship to wealth, poverty and power, and the place, time, ethnicity and sex into which one has been born.

From the practitioner's perspective, whether volunteer or professional, academic or technical, international development work encompasses almost every imaginable vocation and skill set, with a broad palette of roles in its broader universe. Development players appear in many guises:

- the Gucci-clad economist striding through the doors at IMF headquarters in Washington DC
- the African anthropologist sitting under the tree with the Maasai herders on the Tanzanian plains
- the Asian NGO bureaucrat behind a desk in the capital city, wading through a stack of partners' project reports
- the church volunteer leading an after-school neighborhood tutoring program

- the relief veteran stockpiling supplies for emergency preparedness.

From the economists' perspectives, international development begins with the "bottom billion" of our earth's inhabitants who live on less than a dollar per day. Joining them are the additional three billion people that will be added to the world's population by 2050, almost all of them in countries of the global south. If we follow James Wolfensohn and others, four different levels of national prosperity, prospects and challenges are emerging:

1. Rich countries with high and steadily rising living standards, but with a pressing need to face new global realities, including their shifting importance in the world.
2. Middle-income countries, mostly in Latin America and the Middle East, need to break out of their low or highly volatile growth path.
3. Rapidly growing developing countries, such as China and India. They are fast reducing poverty at home, contribute greatly to basic global economic indicators, and are emerging as significant aid donors. But they need to address the soaring inequality and environmental damage that threaten their long-term prospects.
4. Poor countries, many of them in sub-Saharan Africa. Their economies are stagnant or regressing. They cannot achieve sustained poverty reduction unless they drastically improve their development policies, governance and basic institutions.

Further complicating these basics are the realities *within* each nation-state—every country and region in the world exhibits its own dynamic between the rich and the poor, against its own backdrop of historical, political, social and economic inequities. Development ceased decades ago to be simply about economics and prosperity, and slum dwellers would describe a very personal and local set of experiences to illustrate their perceptions of good and bad development. For Korten these slum dwellers fit into the "excluded" class; their perspective on development is through the eyes and everyday experiences of grassroots poverty. Viewed through the lenses of more localized human experience, Korten tabled these three classes of citizens in the 1990s. (The data in this three-citizen table is now dated, but the categories remain illuminating.)

Earth's Three Socio-Ecological Classes[A]

OVERCONSUMERS	SUSTAINERS	EXCLUDED
The top 1+ billion	The middle 3–4 billion	The bottom 1+ billion
> US $7500 per capita	US $700–7500 per capita	< US $700 per capita
(Cars, meat, disposables)	(Living lightly)	(Absolute deprivation)
Travel by car and air	Travel by bicycle and public surface transport	Travel by foot, maybe donkey
Eat high-fat, high-calorie meat-based diets	Eat moderate diets of grains, vegetables and some meat	Eat nutritionally inadequate diets
Drink bottled water and soft drinks	Drink clean water plus some tea and coffee	Drink contaminated water
Use throw-away products and discard substantial wastes	Use non-packed goods and durables, and recycle wastes	Use local biomass and produce negligible wastes
Live in spacious, climate-controlled, single-family residences	Live in modest, naturally ventilated residences with extended/multiple families	Live in rudimentary shelters or in the open; usually lack secure tenure
Maintain image-conscious wardrobes	Wear functional clothes	Wear secondhand clothing or scraps

A. Adapted from Korten, "Civil Engagement in Creating Future Cities," based on Durning, "Asking How Much Is Enough."

For nongovernment organization (NGO) representatives, development should be primarily defined and driven by the visions and goals of the local champions, families, community groups, civil society organizations (including churches), service providers and local government players that are the primary combatants of poverty. It is these local stakeholders that shoulder the core tasks of creating hopeful, healthy, and inclusive communities for their future generations and stewarding the community and natural resources. Although NGOs strive to meet various donors' expectations, they also know that meeting development's challenges has no static, readily available definition, but requires fresh analysis with local partners every step of the way in every context, along with effective dialogue and listening, and new partnerships among community, government and market actors.

NGOs most commonly depend on multiskilled "development workers" to form the backbone of their local initiatives and partnerships. The common image of the development worker of the 1960s and 1970s was that of the *technician:* installing, distributing, inoculating, building, delivering services. The picture grew over time to capture the development worker as the *facilitator:* listening, negotiating, mobilizing, connecting, training, partnering. Contrary to a common Western misperception, the NGO development worker is not a role commonly filled by outsiders and expatriates. Community development work is almost inevitably carried out by locals and nationals, not outsiders.

Diversity of Missions, Values, and Practices

We can see then that there are various ways to do development, and to engage internationally, and every practitioner and development organization is convinced that some ways are better than others.

Development actors and organizations have widely varied mis-

International Development Spectrum

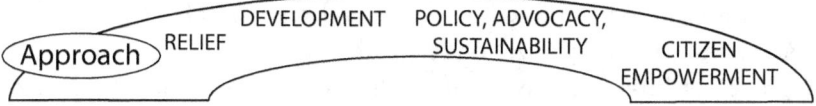

sions, strategies and behaviors, but it is possible to locate them along a spectrum. In their earliest years, many organizations acted as relief agencies, having been founded in the midst of a response to a disaster or emergency (e.g. the Red Cross in 1863 to aid battlefield casualties; Mennonite Central Committee in 1920 in response to famine in Russia and the Ukraine; CARE with its aid packages to survivors of World War II; the Anglican PWRDF as a result of the Springhill, Nova Scotia mine disaster of 1958). Over time most organizations decide to move along the spectrum or employ more than a single approach. Others build missions and strategies that engage all parts of the spectrum, for reasons of their organizational history, identity and reach, and they develop a range of activities according to the partners and the contexts in which they operate. The missions, values and activities of every organization also evolve over time in response to the ongoing debate and learning within the industry on what constitutes "good" or "sustainable" development.

This attempt to capture the full range of approaches and activities

of development players may satisfy no one entirely, but it begins to illustrate the diversity and complexity involved. It inevitably encourages various players to debate and explore the ethics, merits and appropriateness of various approaches and roles in different contexts. One function of this type of development spectrum is to help organizations align rhetoric with behaviors. Although the categories of a spectrum like this are certainly porous and fluid, the relationships between a particular approach and its range of actions, goals and resources have limitations. For example, if an organization's new mission and strategy calls for the approach of "citizen empowerment," then any historical activities of, for example, building infrastructure and delivering services no longer align with the mission, and new activities must be developed which, for example, strengthen local citizen groups to achieve their own local objectives.

There are numerous and continuous attempts to refine and evaluate the different parts of the development spectrum. One that has proved more durable than others is Korten's four-generation explanation. Korten built his framework primarily with NGOs in mind, but it can also be applied to other development players in the bilateral and multilateral aid world.

Strategies of Development-Oriented NGOs: Korten's Four Generations[A]

	1st-Generation Relief and Welfare	2nd-Generation Community Development	3rd-Generation Sustainable Systems Development	4th-Generation People's Movements
Problem Definition	Shortage	Local Inertia	Institutional and Policy Constraints	Inadequate Mobilizing Vision
Time Frame	Immediate	Project Life	Ten to Twenty Years	Indefinite Future
Scope	Individual or Family	Neighborhood or Village	Region or Nation	National or Global
Chief Actors	NGO	NGO plus Community	All Relevant Public and Private Institutions	Loosely Defined Networks of People & Organization
NGO Role	Doer	Mobilizer	Catalyst	Activist/ Educator
Management Orientation	Logistics Management	Project Management	Strategic Management	Coalescing and Energizing Self-Managing Networks
Development Education	Starving Children	Community Self-Help	Constraining Policies and Institutions	Spaceship Earth

A. Adapted from Korten, *Getting to the 21st Century*.

In reality, these four approaches (whether in the development spectrum above or Korten's) are not mutually exclusive or sharply delineated; they may coexist within organizations and often overlap in the field. Applied in practice, the four approaches and Korten's four generations have not proven to be fully comprehensive: there are other variants. The critical set of variables which saves these categories from overgeneralization is how they are each applied: unless mixture and balance is appropriate to within the specific context, time and human location of their application.

When does giving bread become a snake? Even a simple approach such as providing food aid can go wrong, and do more harm than good. Somalia is a well-studied case from the 1980s and 1990s where international food aid created a cascade of destructive effects. "Somalia is probably the most egregious example of Western patronage gone berserk. Huge amounts of economic relief aid were dumped into Somalia, transforming the country into the "Graveyard of Aid." But the massive inflow of food aid in the early 1990s did much to shred the fabric of Somali society."[2]

The food aid imported to Somalia depressed the food prices in the local markets and wiped out the economic rationale for local farmers to grow grain. It made more sense for them to travel to distribution centers for food rations. The large amounts of food aid created profitable looting opportunities for armed youth and greased the wheels of foreign contractors linked to politicians in Rome and Mogadishu. Ultimately the same resources fuelled arms purchases and war by the Somali president, Siad Barre, against his own people.

So complexity and context inevitably play key roles. If we apply the classic "give a fish" analogy to Korten's four generations, it might follow this sort of progression:

	1st-Generation Relief and Welfare	2nd-Generation Community Development	3rd-Generation Sustainable Systems Development	4th-Generation People's Movements
Fish Analogy: from the local perspective	"Give me a fish, and I can eat for today."	"Teach us to fish, so we can eat when you're gone."	"Let's agree on the best way to fish and who has rights to access the lake."	"Let's organize ourselves for a sustainable fishery, and our place in a secure food economy."

As Korten's table hints above, each development approach seeks to answer an underlying problem, which is built on a particular understanding of poverty. The problem of poverty has been variously defined, but the past few decades of development practice and learning leave little room today for simplistic, single-sector analyses. Poverty exists in

---

2. Ayittey, "How Western Charity Helped Destroy Somalia," Ch.8 in Ayittey, *Africa in Chaos*.

context and is multifaceted. It cannot be adequately comprehended or generalized by means of a single variable, such as income or economic purchasing power, nor tackled via a particular technical intervention focused on any single sector, such as health, microenterprise or infrastructure. Comprehensive attempts to understand poverty must now incorporate a range of variables.

Until two hundred years ago, we were all poor; at least, most of us, apart from a tiny elite of rich and powerful rulers, landowners and merchants. For millennia, it was clearly in their interests to tell stories and develop theologies and ideologies that portrayed such poverty as natural, even ordained. For thousands of years, economic and population growth was relatively static worldwide. Until two hundred years ago "life was as difficult in much of Europe as it was in India or China. With very few exceptions, your great-great-grandparents were poor and, most likely, living on the farm. One leading economic historian, Angus Maddison, puts the average income per person in Western Europe in 1820 at around 90 percent of the average income of sub-Saharan Africa today. Life expectancy in Western Europe and Japan as of 1800 was probably about forty years."[3]

Merely a handful of the world's generations have lived within today's bubble of soaring population and per capita incomes, from which springs the current wrestling of ideas and understandings around poverty and development. It is the recent, staggering, and often hidden disparities between rich and poor, both North and South, that now generate the deep ethical and moral dilemma to which poverty reduction experts attempt to provide answers: why does the so-called myth of progress continue to leave so many behind? "Even as large numbers of Indians and Chinese were joining the consumer society, many in the two countries were left behind . . . While a part of the rich world was discussing techniques that would prolong the human life span to over one hundred years, millions were dying from easily preventable diseases, lack of safe water, or infections . . . for those who found themselves born in wrong countries, in wrong social groups, and of a wrong race or sex, a large part of the promise went unfulfilled."[4]

---

3. Sachs, *The End of Poverty*, 26.

4. Milanovic, *Worlds Apart*, 2; Morrison, "Poverty and Exclusion," in Haslam, Paul, et al. *Introduction to International Development*, 232.

But whose understanding of poverty and development is best? The responses of the nonpoor to the poor range dramatically, from "Hands

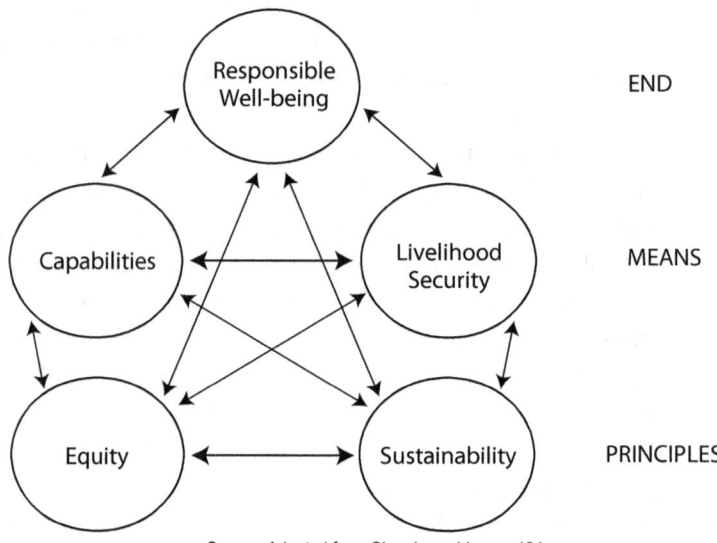

Source: Adapted from Chambers, *Ideas*, p.194.

off! It's their problem and their fault, not ours" to "We're in this together. Our histories and futures are all interwoven." For decades leading up to and following World War II, the experts were often external to the problems of poverty: rich countries armed with their modernization strategies told poor countries how to change, goaded by the various carrots and sticks of colonization and the Cold War.

For Chambers it is the local, poor household that captures the essence of poverty in its various forms of material, social, and structural "entanglement" across five dimensions of life. Chambers describes these dimensions of poverty as an interactive system that he calls the "poverty trap." The poor are entangled in this poverty trap. For Chambers it is therefore essential that development becomes a process of disentanglement from this multifaceted web of poverty. Chambers's decades of involvement and research in local situations of poverty and development around the world push him towards a development approach which builds on a set of underlying *principles* (the various dimensions of sus-

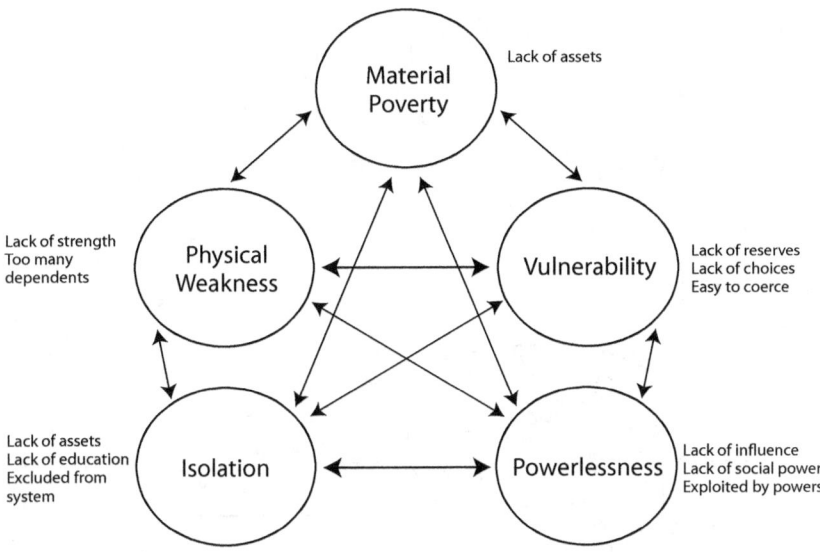

Source: Chambers' model of poverty as "entanglement."

tainability and equity), and employs a set of *means* (in the local realm of capabilities and livelihood security) in order to deliver development's *end*: responsible well-being.

Most critically, Chambers is the pioneer of participatory poverty assessments, where the poor themselves engage in decision making about what it means to be poor and what underlies their situation. Participatory poverty assessments are employed jointly in the hands of the poor and development facilitators, using the tools of physical and social mapping, participatory diagramming, measuring and modeling, and stakeholder meetings. Chambers praises and elevates "the analytical abilities of poor people. Whether literate or not, whether children, women or men, they showed that they could map, list, rank, score and diagram often better than professionals."[5] Here begins an important shift: participatory assessments do not just redefine the *what* of poverty; they redefine *who* gets to define poverty.

---

5. Chambers, *Whose Reality Counts?*, xvii.

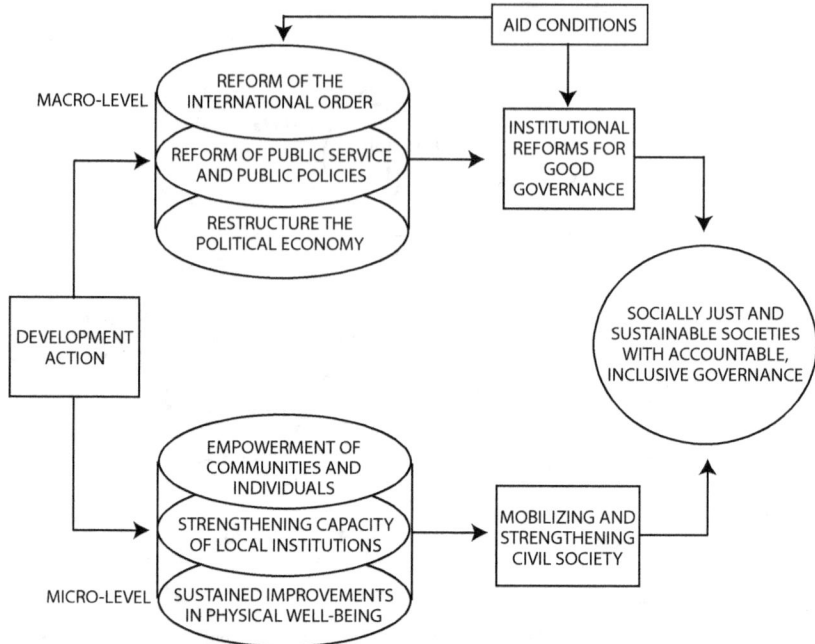

Source: Derived from Fowler, *Striking a Balance*.

Alan Fowler and Amartya Sen are also worth highlighting here, as two more voices among the important chorus of critics seeking to reestablish development's boundaries as "pro-poor" during the past couple of decades. Sen is a Nobel Prize–winning economist who with others rejects the narrow dominance of income and consumption measures as long championed by the World Bank, in favor of seeing poverty as the deprivation of a person's elementary capabilities. The resulting "Capabilities Approach" seeks to expand a person's freedom to achieve, choose, access and convert resources into well-being.

Fowler helpfully pushes forward the poverty-development map by situating the individuals, households and communities of the microcontext alongside the macroworld of the national and international economic, political and social order. Thus the critical local tasks of empowering individuals and communities, disentangling the poor, strengthening their local institutions, and building sustainable livelihoods and well-being can only take place within the larger environment of improving policies and governance, increasingly responsible public services and political sector, and a reformed international order. Only together can these micro and macro means deliver the overall goal of development action: "socially just and sustainable societies with accountable and inclusive governance."[6]

For Jayakumar Christian all of these contributors add value to the task; he too sees that poverty is generated out of a system of disempowerment. He describes a world where progress against poverty is being made, but never fast enough: "It appears the playing ground is tilted against the poor."[7] Building on Chambers, Friedman, and others, Christian uncovers the captivity of the poor to the god complexes of the nonpoor. However, a more holistic understanding of poverty must also incorporate a spiritual lens on powers, principalities, lies, and deceit. From his work within and outside of India Christian finds social systems everywhere reinforcing the powerlessness of the poor, trapping them in a multileveled and interactive biophysical, social, political, economic, religious, and cultural system of disempowerment—a "web of lies."

The nonpoor play a key role in the lives of the poor in their neighborhoods and across the world through a series of "god complexes," as they succumb to the temptation to play God in the lives of the poor and to generate and sustain the web of lies by which they themselves and the poor are held captive. Christian argues that poverty essentially has to do with power—the "power that keeps the poor powerless." He reviews and agrees with a wide range of historical assumptions about poverty, both secular and Christian. For example:

- The poor are poor often because access to available resources is blocked.
- The poor who fall below so-called poverty lines need essential social safety nets.
- The poor often need help improving basic social and economic practices.
- Structural inadequacies that skew wealth distribution need fixing.

And from a church perspective:

- Both the poor and the nonpoor equally need personal, social, economic, and political transformation.
- The poor lack modernization, and the church is often well placed to provide development projects.

6. Fowler, *Striking a Balance*, 11.
7. Christian, *God of the Empty-Handed*.

- The poor are the victims of flawed public policy, controlled and exercised by the nonpoor, which calls for prophetic challenge from the church.
- The love of Christ is the irreducible motivation that drives Christians to serve the poor and the nonpoor.

Ultimately, the sum of Christian's explanation adds up to "the tragic marring of the identity of the poor," in (1) their systematic exclusion as actors in their own situations, and (2) their deeply internalized belief in their own "poverty of being," a fatalism about being godforsaken, and their ultimate disempowerment in identity and value.[8]

This helpful and multivoiced chorus of definitions for poverty and development has not reached its end and climax here. The most recent challenges within relief and development demand continual adaptation by development theorists and practitioners.

WHERE IS INTERNATIONAL DEVELOPMENT GOING?

It is fair to say that over the past decade or two attitudes to development have shifted substantially. This is not the place to replay the entire history of development, with its roots in mercantilism, global trade, slavery, colonialism and missions. Suffice it to say that the most recent era of international development that arrived with the Marshall Plan at the end of World War II has surely ended. So too have the 1950s aid paradigm and practices that sprang from it, with their focus on short-term technical, commercial and economic gains.

Development has become concerned with long-term changes across a wide range of issues, from conflict prevention and resolution, to human rights and child well-being; from trade and social investment to environmental sustainability. On the side of "official" aid, three primary focuses now tend to dominate the agendas of the bilateral donors: growth, sustainability and justice.

The UN Millennium Development Goals (MDGs) arose in part from the attempts of UN and donor agencies to rebuild their reputations out of the shambles of the perceived development failures of the 1960s–1980s. The MDGs may already be a partial success in the sense

---

8. Myers, *Walking with the Poor*, 76.

that they have refocused the global aid agenda around poverty and have gathered a community of government and multilateral partners around a common set of goals. However, the eight MDGs and their eighteen associated targets are saddled with the challenges of inadequate funding and a looming set of 2015 deadlines.

The UN Millennium Development Goals (MDGs)[A]	
Goal 1	Eradicate extreme poverty and hunger
Goal 2	Achieve universal primary education
Goal 3	Promote gender equality and empower women
Goal 4	Reduce child mortality
Goal 5	Improve maternal health
Goal 6	Combat HIV/AIDS, malaria and other diseases
Goal 7	Ensure environmental sustainability
Goal 8	Develop a Global Partnership for Development

A. Online: http://www.un.org/millenniumgoals.

But even over the short lifespan of the MDGs several large forces have become redefining themes for how all development stakeholders respond, work and plan: urbanization, globalization, migration; sustainability, ecological footprints and climate change; amateurs vs. professionals; and local participation and ownership.

Urbanization, Globalization, and Migration

Stand on any street corner, at the heart of any major urban centre, and the city hits you straight in the face with its pulsating contradictions: dynamic, powerful, demanding, connecting, frustrating, excluding, protecting, conflicting. The modern city is the place and the experience we both love and hate, embrace and question. Our planet today is riding its second great modern wave of urbanization. The first wave rode the back of European industrialization into the nineteenth and twentieth centuries. The second wave, propelled by the forces of globalization, is now rapidly reshaping the villages, towns and cities of the global South.

Developing countries are being radically rebuilt by postmodern urban patterns of life, work, technology, and community. The feel and shape of these emerging urban settlements ranges broadly, from high-tech and formally planned to jarringly anarchic and chaotic. Thousands of municipal governments in developing countries flounder almost helplessly in the rising swell of slums and squatter settlements squeezed into their inner and peri-urban nooks and crannies, teeming with poverty and the informal dynamics of new urban dwellers and migrants.

The Developing World Is Moving to the City

Sometime in 2010–2011, the world's urban population will, for the first time in history, have surpassed the world's rural population. The global urban population has quadrupled since 1950, and in the next couple of decades virtually all population growth will be urban, at the urban-to-rural ratio of 27 to 1. A number of developing countries are already beginning to experience rural *depopulation*.

The developing world now accounts for 90% of global urban growth. Latin America is the most urbanized region of the developing world, with 77 percent of its population as urban. Asia has the largest number of urban dwellers, and will account for more than half of the world's urban population by 2030. However, urbanization is occurring most rapidly in sub-Saharan Africa, where urban growth rates average higher than 4 percent per year. Megacities (10+ million inhabitants) and metacities (20+ million inhabitants) are enormously important as "city region" centers of investment, communication, commerce and culture. Yet they are home to only 4% of the world's total population and are growing at the relatively slower rate of 1.5% per year. Most urban growth is (and will in future be) occurring in small to medium-sized urban centers, with striking impact on surrounding rural areas.

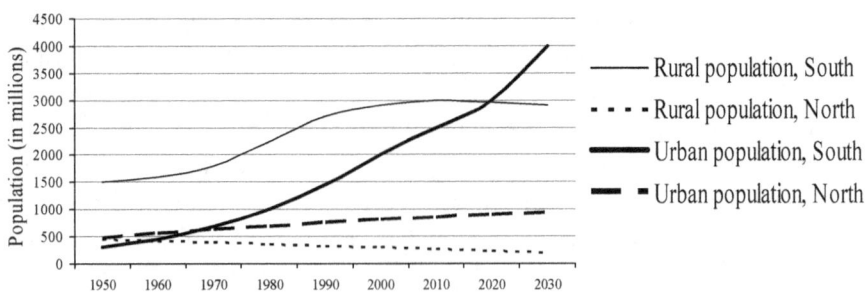

Source: UNDESA (United Nations Department of Economic and Social Affairs), 2005 (Available at www.un.org/esa/populations/publications/WUP2005/2005wup.htm).

Urban growth and migration is not a surprise, but it is a rational response to local and global changes in jobs and livelihoods. Urban populations are growing, moving and shifting today, like an ever fluid mass of jelly, squeezed in one direction by the forces of mobility and migration, pushed in another direction by rural–urban dynamics, and stretched and prodded by transient labor and market demands. These are forces that are both distant and immediate, generated by corporations and economic dynamics larger than nations and by local stresses as small and critical as the failing traditional farm.

In most cases high urbanization rates correlate with high economic growth. But urbanization is also driven by local forces, including postcolonial resettlement, civil unrest, shifts in pastoral and farming practices and prices, natural population increase and urban reclassification. Even attempts at rural development have proven to contribute to urbanization, through success in education and increased agricultural production requiring less labor.

The Rural–Urban Continuum

The classic rural village and the untouched wilderness tribe from memory and popular image no longer exist almost anywhere. Rural has now met urban, meeting mobile phones, buses, radio, TV, tourism, and jobs along the way. Movements of people, capital, goods, industry, information and diseases from cities to the countryside and back again mean that the linkages between urban, rural, and wilderness environments are pervasive and continuous almost everywhere on the planet. The policies and practices of development organizations must, therefore, now catch up to these linked rural–urban systems—traditional rural-only programming denies the new interpenetration of urbanism into rural settings. Urbanization is arriving everywhere, in the company of globalization, technology, information and decentralization, and is creating a series of new demands that apply all the way from the megacity to the village.

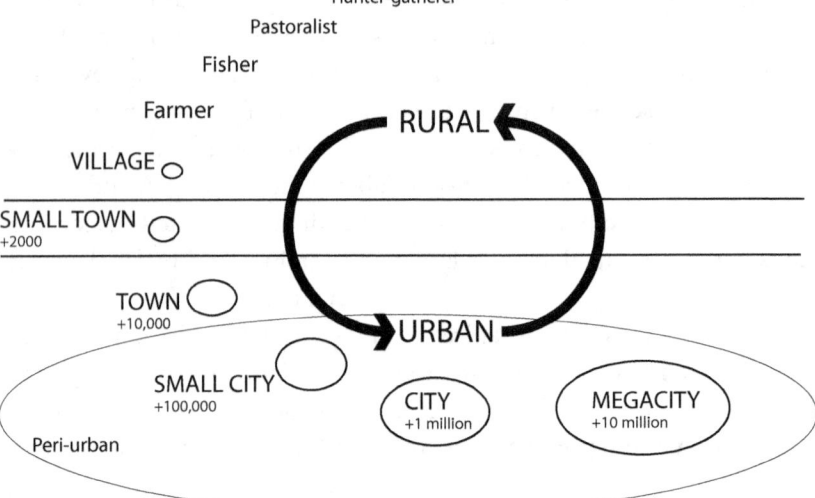

Previously rural households now have both rural and urban components to their livelihoods, including family members living, working and going to school in various locations along this continuum. Rural people depend on services and markets in their local urban centre. Every urban dweller and business has direct and indirect dependence on their immediate rural environment. Lives and economies are increasingly interconnected—across villages, hamlets, small towns, cities, and peri-urban areas. Nowhere is there a clear dividing line any longer between rural and urban; everywhere the tools of communication and the forces of globalization and migration are accelerating their interdependence.

Urban Poverty—Understanding, Finding, Measuring It

Urbanization has become virtually synonymous with slum growth in developing countries. One in every three of the planet's urban citizens—one billion people—lives in a slum, a ratio that is predicted to increase to two billion if current practices and policies continue. Slums are home to 72% of Africa's urban population, and are growing at 4.5% per year—outpacing Africa's overall urban growth rate. The UN defines a "slum household" as a group of individuals living under the same roof in an urban area who lack one or more of the following five conditions: durable housing, sufficient living space, access to improved water and sanitation, and secure tenure.

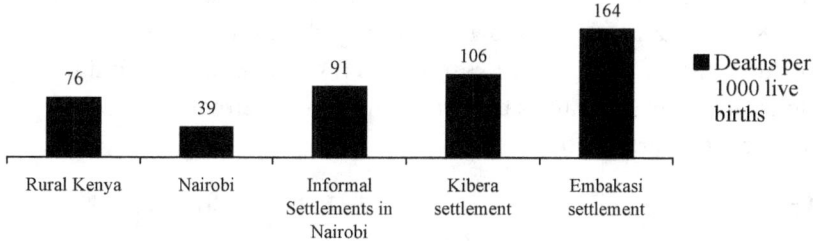

Infant Mortality Rates since 2002

UNDESA (United Nations Department of Economic and Social Affairs), Population Division. Urban and Rural Areas, 2007 (Available at www.unpopulation.org).

There is a geography to urban poverty that is distinct from rural poverty. Poverty manifests itself differently along the continuum from remote rural to megacity. Urban poverty is poorly understood, located and measured by many organizations and municipalities.

- Poverty in urban settings displays different symptoms than rural, regarding urban governance, land, shelter, basic services, livelihoods, coping strategies, justice, environment, and social dislocation.

- Aggregate urban data often hides poverty and local inequalities inside broad statistics. In the example from Kenya above, the infant mortality rates for the whole city of Nairobi (39/1000) look far better than the rate for rural Kenya (76/1000). But the rate for the whole city of Nairobi masks the actual rates within Nairobi's poor squatter settlements of Kibera and Embakasi: the high rates of mortality there only become evident if they can be measured separately, where they prove far higher than the rural rate.

- The scale of urban poverty is greatly underestimated by measuring it with rural income-based poverty lines that do not allow for the higher costs of urban housing, water, sanitation, health care, transportation, and schools.

- Many urban dwellers send significant cash remittances to their rural families.

Urban Poverty Now Matches Rural Poverty

In many cities urban poverty is becoming as severe as rural poverty. In countries such as Bangladesh, Ethiopia and India, four in every ten slum children are malnourished—a rate that is comparable to rural areas of those countries. In countries as diverse as Mozambique, Colombia, and Kazakhstan, rates of diarrhea among children are actually higher in slums than in rural areas. Similarly, HIV prevalence is significantly higher in many slum areas than in both nonslum urban areas and rural areas, particularly among women.

Are Some Development Organizations in Urbanization Denial?

Many Western and church-based NGOs have been slow to adapt to and engage with urban poverty. Their involvement in urban settings has been limited—few of the major NGOs are seen as major players in eradicating urban poverty. Many have no urban strategy or recognized best practices that distinguish between the various settings along the urban–rural continuum. On the other hand, local urban grassroots organizations, such as Slum Dwellers International, have been forging ahead, driven by their local leadership and the needs of their members.

The Challenges of Sustainable Development

The magnificent variety and wonder of life on earth is the joy of creation. Its diversity is the basis for our fullness of life. Yet the health of the planet itself provokes one of the most fundamental challenges for the next era of international development. As McKibben asserts, "we are engaged in the swift and systematic decreation of the planet we were born onto."[9] If everyone lived the lifestyle of the average Canadian or American we would need five planets to sustain the demand. Even as creation is now absorbing and reaping the results of two centuries of Western industrialization, that industrial and economic model for development now reveals its own underpinnings and assumptions as unsustainable environmentally. The resulting questions throw the development enterprise into sharp relief. It is becoming clearer that the global commons cannot survive the basic assumptions of traditional development (growth, access, consumption). The questions thus posed carry an additional edge for people of faith.

Through our growing demands for food, water, energy, materials, and space for our cities and infrastructure, human activities currently exert greatest pressure on creation in five ways: habitat loss, alteration

---

9. McKibben, "Climate Change and the Unraveling of Creation," 1196.

and fragmentation; overexploitation of wild species population; pollution; climate change; and invasive species.

For development practitioners, environmental sustainability has long been a priority at the local project level. But understanding the global implications of local ecological behaviors requires new tools: how do we determine positively or negatively whether our development models operate within the limitations of the planet? One example from the Global Footprint Network is the "ecological footprint"—a tangible tool that calculates how much natural resources we have, how much we use, and who uses what.[10] This ecological accounting can be applied to a nation, to a village or a city, to a corporation, to me as an individual, or to all of humanity. It then takes that measurement and determines how much productive land and water is required to provide the resources consumed, and to absorb the waste produced. The ecological footprint is being adopted by a growing number of government agencies, organizations and communities as a core indicator of sustainable resource use.

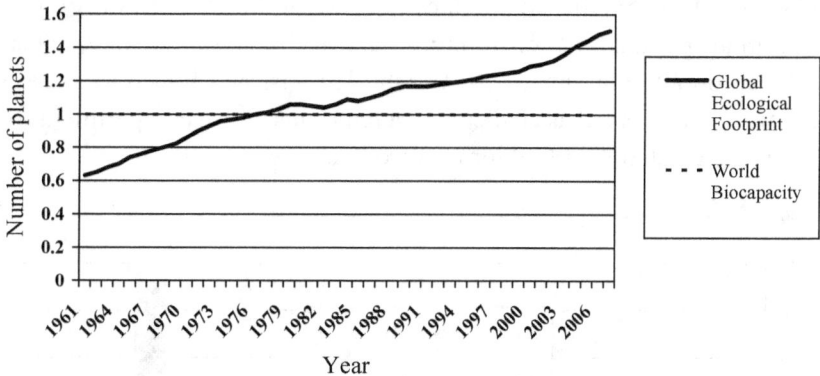

Source: Humanity's Ecological Footprint by Component, 1961-2006
(Global Footprint Network: www.twentyten.net/ecologicalfootprint).

At a global level, we were already in trouble several years ago. Humanity's ecological footprint is shown in the table above in number of planets. One planet equals the total biocapacity of the earth in any one year. Human demand on the biosphere more than doubled between 1961 and 2007. In 2007, the most recent year with available data, human activities used the equivalent of 1.5 planets of bioresources. With current UN projections for population growth, consumption and climate

---

10. Online: http://www.footprintnetwork.org.

change, by 2030 humanity will need the capacity of two Earths to absorb carbon dioxide waste and keep up with natural resource consumption.[11]

The average human's footprint is 2.2 global hectares (5.5 acres). In other words, to sustain the average person's resource demands for one year requires 2.2 hectares of biologically productive land and water. However, the earth has only about 1.8 hectares available per person. In some ways, it is not really very complicated—it is *all* about living within the bounds of creation. If we do not make choices to live sustainably, we cannot grow our food and we cannot eat. As many commentators have reminded us, great civilizations have risen and disappeared precisely on this issue, in such a way that they did not manage their biological commons, they stepped over the threshold of sustainability, and they waned and disappeared. In our case, globalization means that our biological commons now covers the entire planet, and once we step over the threshold of sustainability, there is no other pristine global commons waiting for us to move in. As Ronald Wright asserts in his *A Short History of Progress*, the twentieth century was a time of runaway growth in human population, consumption, and technology, placing a colossal load on all natural systems. Wright demonstrates how our modern predicament is as old as civilization, a ten thousand year experiment we have participated in but seldom controlled.

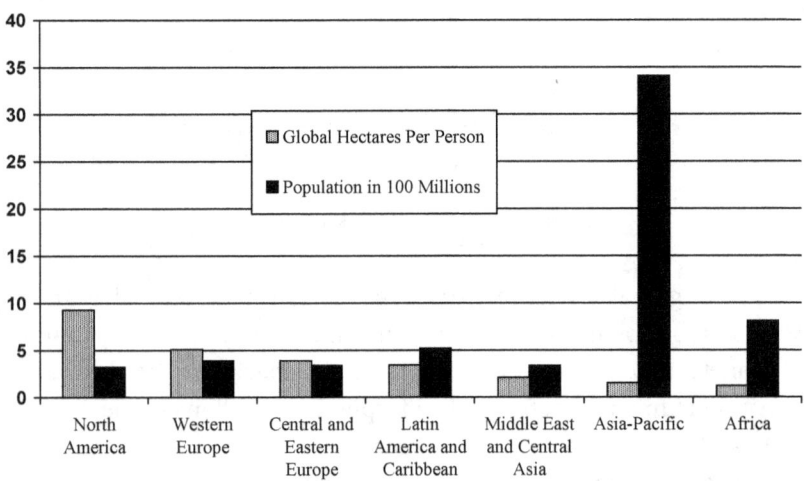

Source: R. Wright, *A Short History of Progress*.

11. Pollard, *Living Planet Report 2010*, 7.

The implications for development thinkers and practitioners have never been greater: only by understanding the historical patterns of human triumph and disaster can we recognize the inherent dangers of promoting and facilitating development. More than just the rhetoric of sustainability, we require a new and profound wisdom, as well as a transformation of our values and behaviors, as both the poor and nonpoor, to reshape where we seem to be headed. The planet's poverty and current ecological slide can only be answered by updated development models and practices that no longer assume economic growth based on increased consumption rates. Our current ecological imbalance is a direct result of classic development—the runaway success of industrialization gone global, amidst the dominance of today's market neo-orthodoxy. Even the optimistic, pro-poor models have missed or underplayed this crucial point, i.e. that our planet's stocks of natural biocapital display an increasing deficit and the powerful forces of the nonpoor are fighting for continued, unfettered access to reap the remaining biological stores.

As James Gustav Speth of the United Nations Development Programme asserts: "Sustainable development is, first of all, people centered. It puts poor people first. It meets their basic needs, including the need to attain self-reliance, and it enlarges their opportunities, including the opportunities to live a long and healthy life, to be educated, and to have the employment needed for a decent standard of living. Sustainable human development is also environmentally sound . . . and sustainable human development is participatory."[12]

While God's creation today displays the increasingly heavy impacts of human habitation across the entire planet, this conundrum carries a particular North/South dimension. We are increasingly familiar with the widespread deterioration of ecosystems in both the industrialized North and the developing South, evident in degradation of oceans, soil, water, air, and sacred sites, climatic change and the disappearance of plant and animal species. But societies in developing countries already bear an extra share of these burdens and more. In their struggles to meet their most basic human needs, the poor live with environmental stresses (mostly generated by the nonpoor) that can push them over the edge when drought, floods, erosion, food insecurity and failing human health strike and they are left with no safety nets or socio-economic cushion

---

12. Cobb, *The Earthist Challenge to Economism*, 118-19.

to break the fall. Environmentally sound planning and monitoring have now become indispensable practices for community developers.

Paradise Lost: Laying Blame

A number of critics have blamed Christianity as directly or indirectly responsible for the contemporary, global ecological crisis, both in the North and the South, seeing in the Judeo-Christian traditions the religious motivation for the raping of the Earth. Among the litany of accusers, Lynn White's now infamous 1967 essay provided an early shot across the bow of Christian environmental complacency, linking Christianity with the desacralization of nature and the consequent rapid nineteenth and twentieth century ascendancy of modern scientific, technological and human manipulation of nature.[13] Arnold Toynbee saw in Genesis 1:28 the divine directive to dominate and exploit creation.[14] Others similarly cite Christianity's appropriation of the dualisms of soul and body, spiritual and material, sacred and secular as fostering the devaluation and misuse of the Earth and the material world (e.g., Wendell Berry and ecofeminists such as Ruether and McFague).[15] Some blame Christian fundamentalist eschatology's negation of the present and its anticipation of a fabulous, newly created future world to be ushered in by Jesus.[16]

At minimum all these critics have motivated a healthy, vigorous rethinking by Christian development practitioners: how much was the Genesis mandate to "subdue the Earth" at the heart of Northern industrialist exploitation of the Earth? And then embodied in the post–World War II relief and development enterprise? On the other hand, how far should the egocentric, profit orientation of modern individualistic consumer economics take the blame for our rootless capitalization of other creatures and of the Earth's precious elements? The flurry of Christian theological response to the goads of White and others has produced much reflection and confession. It has also generated counter arguments, calling to the stand Irenaeus, Augustine, Francis of Assisi, even Luther and Calvin, the Benedictines and sundry modern Christian

---

13. White, "The Historical Roots of our Ecologic Crisis," 1203–7.

14. Toynbee, "The Religious Background of the Present Environmental Crisis," 146.

15. See Berry, "A Secular Pilgrimage"; Ruether, *Sexism and God-Talk*; McFague, *Models of God*.

16. See discussions in Bouma-Prediger, *The Greening of Theology*, 1–22.

thinkers and leaders, to demonstrate that "Christian belief and practice are not a necessary condition for the domination of nature."[17]

The ballooning theological discourse on ecology and development of the past three decades has also widened beyond formal religious systems such as Christianity and Islam to include the full span of indigenous religious groups, from the aboriginals of the Americas to the traditionalists of the African village. For some, this expansion of environmental action and reflection into a fully cross-cultural and interreligious arena has now created new possibilities for truly community-based engagement on sustainability. Meanwhile, the in-house dialogue on ecology, relief and development among Christians continues to need attention.

Local Participation: Who Owns and Governs the Development Process?

"Participation" joins "sustainability" in the pantheon of criteria ubiquitous in development programming these days. But what is identified as stakeholder participation in development programming may in fact point to many different behaviors. Participation may indicate stakeholder engagement that in reality is token, compulsory, or formal. In one locale participation may simply involve information sharing and consultation. In another locale it may describe spontaneous, locally driven and self-generated initiatives. Participation, then, has a range of types and degrees of power and engagement; these are often characterized as ladders. None of these ladders is finally definitive, however, for as Chambers insists: "Participation has no final meaning. It is not a rock. It is mobile and malleable, an amoeba, a sculptor's clay, a plasticine shaped as it passes from hand to hand…Ladders can thus be devised to fit particular contexts and needs."[18]

Ladders of Citizen Participation: Three Examples[A]

1. Citizen control	1. Collective action	1. Self-mobilization
2. Delegated power	2. Co-learning	2. Interactive participation
3. Partnership	3. Cooperation	3. Functional participation
4. Placation	4. Consultation	4. Participation for material incentives

17. Ibid., 7.
18. Chambers, *Ideas for Development*, 104–5.

5. Consultation	5. Compliance	5. Participation by consultation
6. Informing		6. Passive participation
7. Therapy		7. Token participation or manipulation
8. Manipulation		
Source: Arnstein	Source: Kanji and Greenwood	Source: VeneKlasen with Miller

4. Adapted from Chambers, *Ideas for Development*, 105.

The sort of development that transforms is development owned by local communities, to a degree represented by the upper portions of these ladders. Paulo Freire forty years ago taught us that change within communities best happens within relationships of discovery and trust, when it is driven inside out and bottom up, not outside in or top down:

> It is only when the oppressed find the oppressor out and become involved in the organized struggle for their liberation that they begin to believe in themselves. This discovery cannot be purely intellectual but must involve action; nor can it be limited to mere activism, but must include serious reflection: only then will it be a praxis.[19]

How important is the practice of putting people first, ensuring that the poor and their local community organizations become constructive partners and owners in the development process? There are plenty of evaluations that show the pragmatic benefits, including one from the World Bank's own files. It assessed water systems in the dry Himalayan foothills of Nepal, most of which were built by large aid agencies such as the World Bank, which imported professional engineers to identify the needs and do the work. The study showed that after just three years, 80 percent of the water systems built in Nepal were broken down. The same study assessed the water systems built by the community-based development organization World Neighbors, and found that 97 percent were still functional after fifteen years.[20]

The important difference in this case between the World Bank and World Neighbors is not size, but approach: the strategic choice for

19. Freire, *Pedagogy of the Oppressed*, 47.
20. Cobb, *The Earthist Challenge to Economism*, 129–30.

appropriate levels of community involvement and ownership from the very beginning, and every step of the way. National staff of NGOs like World Neighbors and others work relationally with local government and community-based partners typically before the concept and design of a project are explored. But where a developmental collaboration such as a water project should fit on a ladder of participation cannot be generalized. The best form of participation depends on context—what local capacities exist, where they fit on the ladder, and whether the chosen level of participation creates equity or winners and losers locally, e.g., because of gender practices.

The Future of International Development: Amateurs or Professionals?

Go to your favorite news source and you will often meet the latest champion of international development—the local social entrepreneur who has gone global. It has become fashionable to elevate the inspired man or woman with the right idea as heroes and heroines—energetic innovators able to tackle social problems and transform the lives of the poor. A recent example is Nicolas Kristof's article, "D.I.Y. Foreign-Aid Revolution," which ran as the cover story in *New York Times Magazine*. It outlines the journeys of three American women determined to improve the lives of the less fortunate. Seemingly ordinary women, without specific training in economics or development, these three have found innovative ways to provide affordable sanitary pads for women in Mozambique, support Congolese rape survivors, and education and shelter to orphans in Nepal. They each appear to share in large measure a streak of innovation, devotion to their cause, and superb determination to make a difference, "fuelled by some combustible mix of indignation and vision."[21]

These types of stories in the popular press encourage and warm the reader's heart. This is, after all, why development exists—to change things for the better. They also inspire debate. Some critics are emphatic that Kristof is wrong: amateurs are not the future of international development. "Unfortunately, such stories don't reflect reality. Spend a little time in any community in the world, and you'll see people from that community finding ways to improve it—not outsiders . . . Saundra Schimmelpfennig . . . has dubbed this the 'Whites in Shining Armor'

---

21. Kristof, "D.I.Y. Foreign-Aid Revolution."

storyline: Americans and other outsiders are uniquely positioned to bring change to a community, as if we are saviors come to deliver them from poverty."[22]

The critics list the challenges they see afflicting amateur innovators of aid projects:

- Their dangerously simplistic views of development
- Their implicit arrogance in thinking that outsiders bring solutions
- Their use of Western resources and power overwhelms indigenous resources
- Their impatience with NGOs and foreign aid agencies
- Local governments and civil society are bypassed, or barely acknowledged
- The first premise of aid—Do No Harm—is most easily breached by the outside group that comes without experience, with limited knowledge, and without long-term relationships or local accountability.

In favor of what the development amateurs bring, it must be said that:

- Many great movements and development organizations began with a single step taken by one inspired, angry, innovative individual.
- It is sometimes justified to criticize the established international development system and government aid programs.
- Sparks of innovation are the lifeblood of development and its need for constant, local adaptation through action-learning.
- Local patterns of oppression and nonpoor control of the poor can be "jolted" towards change by the shock of outsider intervention.

At minimum, these stories of amateurs provide cautionary tales. The aid world, including Christendom, is populated by relief and development organizations both professional and amateur, some with long, reflective traditions of learning and adaptation; others young and inexperienced. Aid efforts built on individuals with passion or on new group initiatives (e.g., a church congregation decides to launch its own project) may assume that their good intentions will translate into good work, yet

22. Algoso, "Don't Try This Abroad."

if they are accountable to nobody, and operate unaware of good practices or the normal codes of ethics or conduct for development agencies, the risks of failure and harm are high.

It may seem a truism, but in the end, every local development problem carries complexities within it hidden from the observer, especially the observer with outsider eyes. For example, experience teaches that building an orphanage—even as a last resort—may damage and destroy local cultures' practices of extended family social care. Externally donated materials and technicians always carry a potential distortion to local initiatives, entrepreneurs, and businesses. The arrival of an outsider may spell disempowerment when he or she lacks the finely tuned skills and behaviors of an experienced development facilitator.

WHAT IS THE BIBLICAL-THEOLOGICAL BASELINE? HOW SHOULD WE ENGAGE IN DEVELOPMENT?

Getting serious about development means diving into the deep end of life, in all of its perplexities. Here are six queries, or guidepost questions, to aid you, your organization, or church as you consider involvement in development.

Do We Have an Accurate View of Ourselves?

Tackling development calls for a close look at our self-interests and lenses on life. Am I aware of my privileges and how my assumptions and viewpoints on poverty, power, development, and justice are shaped by my access and opportunities? Ironically, the author and most of the readers of this essay are wealthy, which creates its own set of blinders for us. By global standards on income alone, Western-trained clergy, scholars, graduate students, professionals and the educated public (for whom this work is intended) are members of the richest elite in today's world. According to the Global Rich List, if your annual income is $60,000, you are in the top 0.95 percent of the richest people in the world.[23]

That creates the potential for all sorts of distortions in our discussion, awareness, and practice of development. At minimum we cannot pretend to represent the poor in our dialogue, but only the nonpoor. We need to be aware of how easy it is for us as elites to skew our interpreta-

---

23. See, http://www.globalrichlist.com.

tions of the world and of the biblical data in order to favor and create models that support our current economic and social status.

Can We Come to the Journey Truly Empty-Handed?

Can we rid ourselves of the pose that assumes that development is something "we" (the nonpoor) do to, for, or on behalf of "them" (the poor)? To combat our self-comforting theologies of poverty and development requires that we stop speaking, acting, and hauling our baggage long enough in order to listen. Genuine listening exercises with significantly different communities of poor and nonpoor means openness to absorb the full range of perspectives, ideologies, and theologies of poverty across the cultural spectrum. The call to "empty-handedness" is both the recognition of our own poverty and a Christian mindfulness that we are only human in the face of principalities and powers. Genuine recognition of our powerlessness opens us to the human and divine discovery of change theories built around dependence on God.

Are We Biblically and Theologically Diverse Enough to Engage Cross-Culturally, Whether Globally or within Our Own Neighborhoods?

There is no single or simplistic biblical approach to poverty within the Jewish and Christian scriptures. At a quick scan, the poor do emerge from the texts in roughly four categories:

1. the alien, or refugee, often displaced by war or drought;
2. the absolute poor, including orphans, disabled and vulnerable, often beggars;
3. the oppressed, who have lost their land, rights, and resources to the powerful;
4. the humble, living in subsistence, and often on the edge of too much debt.

But when we move beyond the biblical basics on poverty, the texts reveal a richer, more diverse palette of social, economic, and historical textures.

Similarly, there is no single and straightforward Christian theology of poverty and development. Relief and development is truly an ecumenical business. A quick review through past and present quickly builds appreciation for the diversity of traditions and theologies on poverty, justice, relief, and development. Consider the richness of a random sampling from recent decades, some diverse voices: the Lausanne movement awakening to the biblical holism; the increasing voice of Rome on ancient and contemporary issues of justice and peace; the Mennonite tradition of nonviolence and respect, delivering relational, grassroots community capacity building; the Anglican Primate's Fund's theology of action driving partnerships for sustainable development, relief, refugees, and global justice; Tear Fund's belief that Jesus's example takes them to the local church as the answer to poverty; indigenous church movements, that defy categorization but commonly reject "white" colonial and missionary Christianity in favor of accommodation between faith and local culture; and the community-based theologies within Latin American's theologies of liberation; and so on.

Each of these approaches arose out of relationships between specific vulnerable peoples and particular organizations and churches with passion and prophetic insights, melding with their joint struggles in a place that delivered their theology and vision for "fullness of life."

If the church has a common mission against poverty, it is to awake specifically and continuously to God's redemptive bias for the poor and the inequality of power relationships in every community setting and confront the principalities and powers among us and within our institutions that build and enforce those inequalities. That means challenging the nonpoor's systematic exclusion of the poor from access to education, wealth and the benefits of the system, seeking to play God in the lives of the poor. Each approach and its theological foundation have their strengths and weaknesses. As an example, liberation theology originated in the face of decades of completely inadequate attempts in Latin America to deal with poverty: effective theologies of poverty and transformation must be genuinely indigenous, not globally generalized pronouncements.

How Can We Ensure That We Are Giving Bread and Not a Stone or a Snake?

As Mary Crickmore suggests, we have a tendency to feel our own culture and its expectations are superior to others. But better advice comes from Proverbs and James, which call for a thoughtful humility that comes from wisdom. There are many local neighborhood and cross-cultural examples of organizations, missionaries, and churches bringing resources and projects that had unintended harmful consequences. These include: mission trips by volunteers that disempower local initiative and trades people; selective distributions (bicycles, supplies, food, seeds, tools, kits) that cause conflict; funds poorly targeted by well-intentioned donors that harm relationships and create discontent; resources and promises that promote false commitment to projects, partnerships and church ministries; and food aid that distorts local markets and farmers' livelihoods.

A better approach in a cross-cultural situation is to slow down and not drive "to just get it done" and fill space with activities, but to be very careful. This comes with time and relationships, and with appreciating the complexity of each context and situation, knowing that lasting change is hard work in any setting. According to Crickmore, "When we desire to "fix" a situation by giving money, let's first stop and examine what would be a genuine long-term solution. The modern world is complex. Unintended consequences happen every day to people who had the best of intentions. We shouldn't take the Golden Rule and apply it according to our first impulse. Rather, let's become learners. Let's take the time to be careful and wise."[24]

Do We Know Where We Fit Best, for Real Impact?

Identifying the niche for ourselves and our organizations within the broad field of relief and development takes time, experience, and expertise, but it is the place and role where we ultimately know we can make a difference and demonstrate a sustainable impact. Clarifying our mission, values, and skill sets helps, as well as developing understanding of the alignment that will make us most effective. Development practitioners often feel a tension over whether to work curatively or preventively and whether to tackle issues at the grassroots level or in public policy. For example, what is the most effective way to support cotton farmers in Mali? Is it through direct training and improved technology in the village, or through advocacy to stop U.S. government subsidies of their cotton agrobusinesses that depress the global cotton prices? Yoder, Redekop, and Jantzi capture and discuss the choices this way:[25]

---

24. Crickmore, "Bread, Stone, or Snake?"
25. Yoder et al., *Development to a Different Drummer*, 275–78.

Types and Levels of Action

	Levels of Action		
Types of Action	Local	National	Global
Curative	A	B	C
Preventive	D	E	F

They make five observations we can summarize here:

- Action at Area A (local and curative) is grassroots engagement, and is where many small organizations are most comfortable and active. Action here has minimal impact beyond the immediate partners; for example, a slum HIV & AIDS clinic, or a village tools and seeds project.

- If effective action is taken at Area F (preventive and global), then the need for action in all the other areas (A–E) over the long term is reduced. In the example above, successful advocacy that delivered a full reform of U.S. cotton subsidies would benefit vulnerable cotton farmers and their families around the world.

- Each type and level of action in this table is needed and appropriate in some context, and they are mutually reinforcing. This happens most powerfully when grassroots community organizations are strengthened to develop their own advocacy agendas and skills, and then join other organizations to network for both local transformation and policy changes on the issues that matter to them: child labor, primary health, education for all, and so on.

- Most faith-based NGOs spend most of their time, energy and resources on Area A, promoting curative action at the local level, with some preventive engagement in the same setting (Area D). The trend now is for NGOs to build on their base in Area A and expand to other areas.

- "Thus, more faith-inspired peace-and-justice people are needed at Area F, where the twin interests of being effective and faithful merge. Here there is less need for ambulance driving. The work is forward-moving, rooted in faith-motivated, life-giving values of peace, justice, and sustainability."[26]

26. Ibid., 277.

Can We Rethink Our Seminaries, Sunday Schools, and Sermons?

Development places a number of challenges in front of our church and religious institutions' assumptions and practices. In major part, relief and development—even the faith-based variety—is about economics, governance, and local and global citizenship. These are not the usual topics of Sunday homilies, and are not the usual fields of expertise studied by seminarians. But there is more compatibility than perhaps first meets the eye.

- Let us stop thinking that relief and charity by the church will fix the world—deep change requires deep engagement with civil society, policies and structures of government, business partners, and bishops.

- Let us allow our theologies of engagement and mission to evolve so that they can fully encounter today's versions of poverty, globalization, urbanization, climate change, and cross-cultural engagement.

- Let us encourage churches to go local first, and build their development credibility at home. Who in our neighborhoods is not experiencing the fullness of life for which Jesus came? Do we know who they are? Do we, and our churches and community organizations know how to find them, through the tools and approaches of local community assessment and mobilization? Are we engaged both in their lives, and in tackling the underlying causes of their vulnerability and poverty?

- Let us cease planting flags on little summits for our individual organizations and churches. The only way towards deep change and transformational development is through the challenging work of collaboration, with other NGOs, churches, government, service providers, and businesses.

- Let us encourage the church to take up its call for urban transformation. Some are fearful, defensive, hanging on to traditional pre-urban language and models. Some are resisting, calling the city evil and dark. But prophetic urban practitioners seek to respond incarnationally and holistically to their city and to the struggles of the urban poor, first listening and learning, then developing capacities for long-term ministries that transform.

"The future of the church in the city depends on taking up the gospel, the good news of Jesus and the kingdom, for the prisoner, the poor, and the outsider, not as the pretext for a mission strategy, proselytizing, or a programmatic enterprise, but as a living truth and movement that transforms."[27] In this way we will come to know who our neighbor is.

---

27. Gornik, *To Live in Peace*, 209.

9

Let's Talk about Sex

David A. Reed

MORAL JUDGMENTS ARE NEITHER naturally nor immediately self-evident. They are not of a mathematical sort, but as ethicist Philip Turner points out, they are cumulative and "serve to establish a burden of proof rather than certainty."[1] Practices are passed on to us extrinsically by home, church, and society, and are most potent when these circles of influence speak with one voice. But a society that celebrates freedom of individual choice is bound to break up the consensus of these moral forces.

Consequently, the swift pace of changing sexual mores in our culture has presented an increased challenge for Christians, and this is for three reasons. First, Christians can no longer depend upon society to enforce our particular sexual virtues. Second, this heretofore lack of need to actively contend for a Christian sexual ethic has perhaps allowed us to forget our own best reasons. Third, the progressive liberal stream of mainline Protestant ethical thinking in the past half century has created an alternative voice more adaptive to the prevailing culture within the Christian community itself. That is, Protestant Christians today do not speak with one voice on this matter.[2]

Culturally, sex is now a new frontier, especially in the wake of significant advances in human biotechnology. We are experimenting both

---

1. Turner, "Sex and the Single Life," 15–21.

2. The influential and now classic text that addresses sexuality from a liberal Christian viewpoint is Joseph Fletcher's *Situation Ethics*.

socially and technologically in ways that are certain to have far reaching effects for the future. The inevitable interplay between gospel and culture means that Christianity is not a mere morality play in which a story can be reduced to a few simple, absolute moral principles. Real life is not so tidy. Nor can scripture be reduced to a moral code of conduct, though such behavior codes are indispensable and practical guideposts for the journey. In writer Lauren Winner's words, the Bible is more like "a map of God's reality" that helps us ground our ethic in "the faithful living of the fullness of the gospel."[3]

Because our limited vision does not permit us to see immediately over the horizon to the future outcomes of our present actions, the task of thinking morally about our choices is to help us connect the dots, as it were, using as our template the kind of love and shape of human relationships made available to us in salvation history and particularly in the life, death and resurrection of Jesus. This essay will explore only one aspect of the sexual frontier before us: a theological reflection upon our changing social sexual praxis.

SEX AS A MIXED BLESSING: NEW FREEDOM WITHOUT A MAP

We begin by stating the obvious: we have been thinking and talking about sex for a long time, as long as humans could talk. We churn out erotic tales, sexual humor, and dirty jokes. We produce sublime treatises laden with virtues and vices. We exploit the power of sex to sell wrenches and automobiles to men, and we abuse the weakest, poorest, and most vulnerable members of our society.

But in our North American memory at least, sex is not what it used to be! Socially, sex used to be simple, and we had words to describe it. Everything fit neatly into our little categories. There were virgins, fornicators, adulterers, celibates, whores, and married folks. Though sexual mores have been anything but constant, the revolution of the 1960s produced in the Western world what can be best described as a new sexualized culture. In the process, we sanitized our sexual vocabulary of its moralisms and replaced it with the language of pleasure, fulfillment, choice, and the technically correct but sterile glossary of the sex-education classroom.

3. Winner, *Real Sex*, 30.

Sex is a complex social reality. Neither our culture nor respective Christian traditions agree on the list of sexual virtues and vices. Sex is never just an autonomous act. It is embedded in a social web of marriage, family, children, abortion, divorce, mental health, STDs, aging, laws, commercial advertisements, and cultural trends and norms. Surveys and studies track our sex lives. The information age has produced a generation that seems to know everything and nothing about sex.

The sexual revolution of the 1960s produced a monumental shift in our sexual attitudes and practices. Some of its effects have been positive. All the talk about sex, with the diversity and disagreements that have followed, has required both our Christian communities and society to engage in a deeper conversation. As Christians are being pushed out of the comfort of depending upon the prevailing social mores to enforce our beliefs, practices and prejudices, we are now being challenged to justify before a skeptical world our deepest and most distinctive convictions about ourselves as sexual creatures and the moral vision we wish to commend.

The sexual revolution has challenged us in four areas. First, it has provoked us to revisit the biblical view that *sex was created good*. A far too influential tradition of dualism within Christianity has relegated sex to an inferior but tolerated status. To be truly spiritual meant to be, in a way, sexless. The ideal was celibacy, or, if the effort was too daunting, castration. The rest of us joined the ranks of the second-class believers too weak to refrain from sex.

We are rediscovering that *sexuality is part of being human*, not just a series of acts defined as sexual. First, we are born male or female, and our being-in-the-world is sexual. Our sexuality is inherent in all human relationships, and should be celebrated as a gift of God. We are embodied creatures, whole and incapable of dividing ourselves into component parts.

Second, we can now *differentiate between sensuousness and sensuality*. All that is sensuous is not excessive dedication to pleasure, as *sensuality* suggests. We interact with our environment through the senses, which brings us much enjoyment in life; and our sexuality is woven into the fabric of our sensuous humanity. In a dualistic world, the pleasurable rewards of the human senses are shunned as dark tempters that lead us astray, particularly into the den of sexual sin. But a world that God made and blessed as good is one in which the whole person is caught up in delights stirred by the senses. In themselves, these delights are creational gifts for us to enjoy.

Third, we have begun to *respect and embrace the equality of women as sexual partners in our common humanity*. A closer examination of our traditional sexual mores reveals a dark sexist fault line that enforced the double standard of privileging men while repressing, scorning, and punishing women.

Fourth, we are *moving the reality of sexual orientation from closet whispers to public discourse*. Admittedly, this ongoing shift is generating much distress and division for all sides as our society continues to rewrite legislation, and our Christian communities struggle to articulate a faithful theology of sexuality and establish commensurate practices and policies. The positive contribution, though for many difficult to embrace enthusiastically, is that we are called to protect a vulnerable minority and compel the Christian community to address a new theological and missional challenge—not an unfamiliar discipline since the missionary days of the apostle Paul.

Finally, the church is being challenged to take responsibility for teaching and discipling in sexual matters; in other words, *to move from moralism to morality*. It is no longer sufficient to legislate a moral code, mindless of the reasons for adhering to it. It is not enough to lay before the faithful a way of living without accepting the responsibility for cultivating the kind of character that enables them to desire and strive for it. The church can no longer depend upon society, in either its laws or its inclinations, to do our work for us. Now is an opportune moment for a genuine retrieval of Christian memory.

Of course, informed Christians know that all is not well in post-1960s sexland. Freedom without boundaries is taking its toll, and human trafficking is reintroducing a new and insidious form of slavery that is spanning the globe. The church's response must surely be a single-focused condemnation of such dehumanizing empires, but must include compassion for their victims. In a sexualized culture, the offers of a meaningful and full life are myriad. The church will be wise to remember those who are burdened with guilt from a morality laden with rules and regulations, those trapped in malevolent systems of exploitation, those conflicted between desire and law, and those who have abandoned law for momentary happiness. For the church to talk about sex, it will need to listen in on a wider conversation.

SEX IN HISTORY: CLASH BETWEEN JEW AND GENTILE

How did we get here anyway? Current fashions in sexual matters are not entirely new. Our generation was not born in a vacuum, but we are the aggregate of previous ones, with the predictable reactions and visions of a "new future." History does not simply repeat itself, but the past does receive regular visits from a society that sometimes borrows wisely and occasionally plunders irresponsibly from its storehouse of ideas and practices. Today's sexual culture is a confused mélange of Judeo-Christian and pagan heritages, woven into our own distinctive cultural identity.

A sharp point of debate for Christians from the beginning has been the nature of persons, because both Jews and Christians held a radically different view from their pagan neighbors in the Greco-Roman world. Pagans lived by the ancient dualism between soul and body. The soul was superior to the body, and had the task of administering the desires and impulses of that body in an orderly manner. It was a hierarchical world in which the male was regarded as fully formed at birth and the woman was born a "failed male."[4] Male virility was a fragile commodity that men had to maintain by self-control in all matters, including by their disciplining of inferiors—women and slaves—which they customarily did with warm authority.

Unlike pagans, Jews and Christians, on the other hand, rejected this dualism in favor of a unified person—body and soul. The soul is not so pure and controlled that it can bear the responsibility of managing the flaming desires of the body. Both body and soul stand before the Creator God: "Body and soul faced him together: He had created both and would judge both."[5]

In Paul's writings, the battle is between the flesh and the spirit. Flesh is not one's bodily existence but that dimension of the person that wars against God. At the same time, the Christian believer is "a new creation," so that even the body shares in a mysterious way "a measure of the same spirit that had raised the inert body of Jesus from the grave."[6] On this basis, Paul makes the audacious claim that the body is the "temple of the Holy Spirit" (1 Cor 6:19).

---

4. Brown, *The Body and Society*, 10. I am indebted to Brown for the following discussion of ancient Roman and Christian views of persons.

5. Ibid., 35.

6. Ibid., 47.

Sexual acts are governed by this high dignity accorded the body, so much so that Paul describes sex with a prostitute as becoming "one flesh" with her. As historian Peter Brown comments, "It was a startling use of an image of physical joining usually applied only to husband and wife."[7] The implication is that what one does with the body in sexual acts bears directly upon one's view of the nature of persons, their sexual practices, and the relationship of the body to religious belief. For Christians, sexual acts are not extraneous to one's relationship with God. Sex, though it encompasses the internal qualities of intent and relationship with the other, does not dispose of the spiritual significance of the bodily act itself.

The attention Paul gives to sexual practices—their purpose and boundaries—suggests that the earliest church faced dilemmas that called for theological attention. Certainly, Christianity has had a checkered career in sex management.[8] It did not take long for the dualistic beliefs of the society to infiltrate the church, especially a new gnostic-type movement called Manichaeism that viewed all things material, including the body and its sexual passions, as evil and corrupt. Mandatory celibacy in the clerical and monastic orders of the medieval church institutionalized the superiority of the spiritual, consigning sex to a lower virtue and marriage to those with weaker resolve.[9]

The sixteenth-century Protestant Reformation restored sex and marriage to normative (though not exclusive) status within church and society. But it was the Puritans a century later that emphasized the unitive or relational more than the procreative aspect of marital sex. The Puritan marriage bed achieved a surprisingly high degree of sexual intimacy and mutuality.[10]

By the eighteenth century the influence of the Enlightenment was beginning to change attitudes regarding the importance of certain social institutions. Society was becoming more secular, and religion was being relocated from public life to the private sphere. Events of the past

---

7. Ibid., 51.

8. For a brief summary of changing attitudes to sex throughout Christian history, see Grenz, *Sexual Ethics*, 2–11.

9. In contrast, Paul advised believers to remain in their present state as a matter of expediency, since he anticipated the imminent return of Christ; see 1 Cor 7:25–31.

10. For a popular overview of the historical development of sexual intimacy within marriage, see Mace and Mace, *The Sacred Fire*.

century have extended that shift to sexuality. As theologian Stanley Grenz observes: "When sexuality came to be divorced from its theological context, sexual acts, like religious belief in general, were severed from the public domain and made exclusively private."[11]

The sexual revolution of the 1960s called for individual freedom and fulfillment. Its lasting impact resulted from the blending of the philosophy of individualism, the Romantic view that nature and human nature are inherently innocent and good, and the advent of the contraceptive pill. While this generation entertained the illusion of freedom with the pill, the reality is that sexual responsibility was simply transferred from the male to the female. It guaranteed pregnancy-free sex, but it also further objectified women as sexual playthings for men. Historian Lawrence Stone claims that this experiment in sexual freedom is unique in human history: "Before now, sexual libertinism has been confined to narrow elite circles, often around a court. Its dissemination among the population at large . . . is a phenomenon unique in the history of developed societies."[12]

SEX IN THE MODERN WORLD: COPING WITH SOLITUDES

Current sexual practices, however, no longer carry on within a traditional worldview, but rather one which rationalizes and sustains them. The one new fact in the long history of sex is the influence of what we call the modern world. While modernity is identified with the civilization that emerged in Western Europe following the intellectual and cultural upheavals of the Renaissance and Reformation, its effects are now being felt, perhaps differently, in regions of the world where advancement in science and technology is increasing rapidly. "Modernization" refers to the processes through which the modern world has been shaped by science and an industrialized economy. In order to shed light upon the particular challenges relating to our sexual lives, we will review briefly the distinctive character of modernization.

Educator-theologians Richard Osmer and Friedrich Schweitzer conclude that "differentiation" is a fundamental mark of modernization, particularly in differentiating the modern world from the past, and the

11. Grenz, *Sexual Ethics*, 9.
12. Quoted in Stafford, *The Sexual Christian*, 36.

various subcultures (workplace, family, religion, leisure, etc.) from one another.[13] These subsystems are called "spheres of life" or what Jürgen Habermas calls "lifeworlds." Each life sphere claims authority within its own orbit, but cannot impose that authority beyond its own boundary. This leaves the individuals who must pass, sometimes rather quickly, from one sphere to another with the complicated task of holding onto their identity as they go. Everyday life is a fragmented world in which these respective spheres are like pieces of a life puzzle that are essential but incomplete parts which the individual must put together in order for life to "make sense."

One alternative for coping with this differentiation is to remove oneself one step from all things material, such as cultural communities and even one's own body. The practical effect, however, is to reduce personal identity to a functional dualism in which the body becomes a mere conduit for fulfillment of the inner mind, emotions or soul; and the life spheres are only episodic and utilitarian occasions that hold no enduring moral power. The scientific and technological dominance of modernity only strengthens this tendency by providing various tools and techniques aimed at producing particular interior "enhancements," whether they are stimulation, tranquility, or pleasure. The moral sphere is corralled in the interior life of the person, while the naturally good body is allowed to roam unfettered.

A second practical effect of this differentiation is that no one institution or sphere can make a moral claim over the whole of one's life. In order to find a comprehensive moral worldview, one way is for individuals to take nothing of moral value from the various spheres and retreat into their own interiority where they hope to find the raw material to construct their personal and moral identity. But, as Osmer points out, this can only be carried out at the expense of invalidating the cultural realities within which they move and live.

As an alternative, he and Schweitzer propose that personal and moral formation occurs most fully only when the person is meaningfully involved in a particular moral community. This means that human formation requires an "ethos," that moral environment which is part of the real world, rather than as a set of moral abstractions. Only then can

13. Osmer and Schweitzer, *Religious Education between Modernization and Globalization*. I am indebted to Osmer and Schweitzer for the following summary of modernization, especially as set forth in chapter 2.

the individual gain an answer to the question, why be moral? or why be moral in this world? In other words, the most fertile soil for identity formation is when the self is embedded in "the substantive beliefs and practices of particular moral communities."[14]

The range and kinds of sexual practices that have rapidly moved from the margins to the mainstream of our culture suggest that many in our society are negotiating their way through the maze of life spheres with little moral guidance or communal attachment.

SEX IN THE CITY: LIVING ON THE FRONTIER

The sexual revolution, nearing a half century since its flowering, spawned a variety of attitudes and practices that have become part of mainstream culture. One is *hedonism*, sex as a form of recreation. The argument goes like this. Sex is primarily a biological drive, an appetite like the need for food and drink. Following the ideal of Romanticism, if it is natural, it must be good (nothing as natural as sex, eating, or sleeping should demand moral restraints). It may not be absolutely necessary for physical survival, but it is essential to psychological health. Therefore, sexual acts should not be regulated by society.

In addition, sex, like a good meal, is pleasurable. In our fascination with technology, sex is more like a toy attached to our bodies than an integrated dimension of our personhood. As in a game of tennis, one seeks a competent partner. The goal is not enrichment and growth of the other, but performance and the number of good hits! In some circles, sex à la carte has created the need for a new set of manners—such as how to behave on "the morning after" with your first-night bedmate and send the message that "one night does not a romance make."[15] The confusion of signals between partners in the new social order is what popular writer Wendy Shalit calls "guerilla etiquette."[16]

Some observers of the post–sexual revolution have concluded that, instead of a fulfilled life, sex without borders has produced a saturated generation with diminishing capacity for lasting relationships. A *Washington Times* article describes the fallout among young children

---

14. Ibid., 55.
15. Izzo and Marsh, "Modern Manners for the Morning After."
16. Shalit, *A Return to Modesty*, 236.

between ages ten and thirteen as "emotionally detached couplings of kiddies—oral sex as goodnight kiss between children who don't even pretend to be in love." One psychologist calls it "body-part sex . . . The kids don't even look at each other. It's mechanical, dehumanizing." As one thirteen-year-old boy bubbled, "[Oral sex] is something to do with someone . . . Sex is pleasurable. Why not now?"[17] Such early desensitizing robs a generation of its power to bond, especially for a life vow of fidelity. Though many have become tired of recreational sex, it still lures the most vulnerable, lonely, and immature, often with devastating consequences. Oral sex, for instance, is not always mutual, since young women are frequently pressured by boys with the unspoken message that his favor toward her will be conditional upon her performance. As the popular Christian writer Tim Stafford concludes, "A critical test of any ethical system, particularly for sexuality, is how it affects the young."[18]

Adult versions of casual sex are usually less blatant in their utilitarianism. They are more tasteful and discrete. But the dualism is still at work. In the film *Indecent Proposal*, we detect hesitancy as Diana (Demi Moore), in a bedroom scene with her husband, tries to rationalize her decision to have sex with another man for the offer of a million dollars: "After all, it wouldn't mean anything. It's just my body, it's not my mind, it's not my heart . . . We both slept with other people before we were married. So we just have to look at it like that . . . We'd just have to forget it ever happened . . . and never discuss it even happened, because nothing will have happened. Nothing that matters anyway."[19]

While the drive for pleasure seems insatiable, occasionally someone asks, "Are we having fun yet?" In the eighties this question produced a shift toward a greater emphasis on relationships, the time when one-night stands began to give way to coital delay for the sake of intimacy. This development is what Stafford describes as an *ethic of intimacy*. It sounds more traditional, and sexual activity is more contained. But in its cultural form alone, it is insufficient as an ethic for guiding one's conduct. The cultural ideal of intimacy, like the popular romantic view of love, is based on the values of individual freedom, sexual compatibility,

---

17. West, "Generation XXX."
18. Stafford, "Intimacy," 25.
19. Lyne, *An Indecent Proposal*.

the privatization of sex, sex without consequences, no double standard, and a situational standard that sex is for the emotionally mature.[20]

The ethic of sexual intimacy is occasionally reflected in the currently popular quest for spirituality. Here spirituality is not perceived as a journey into God, but a means whereby one achieves personal fulfillment and happiness.[21] One expression of sexual spirituality appears in the nature mysticism of the New Age and neopagan movements. In the words of one advocate, "sex is holy communion." Drawing upon various religious traditions and sexual practices, sex mystics turn recreation into sacred moments. One journalist concludes that this movement reveals "an undercurrent of sexual unhappiness beneath the surface of a culture that is outwardly carefree about sex."[22] In a culture that can now speak about spirituality without reference to God—that is, referring to a deeper interior self or human spirit—even secular sex therapists give attention to the "spiritual" aspect of sex. As writer Paula Rinehart comments, it hints at a longing in this generation for some deeper or transcendent meaning "as though it senses instinctively that sex is more than moving body parts."[23]

While the cultural appetite for sexual freedom remains strong, there are voices of dissatisfaction. One example is the New Marriage Movement, a coalition of scholars and practitioners, both secular and religious, that has produced a Statement of Principles in an effort to bring the "marriage crisis" into public discourse. The communication clearinghouse is an online newsletter called *Smart Marriages*, supplemented by a widely attended annual conference.[24] Among other things, it tracks various longitudinal studies that are now being conducted, including those that examine the long-term effects of sexual behaviors on the post-60s generation.

Another voice of dissent is what some call a "return to modesty," including the new but small celibacy or abstinence movement. Reporting what she sees as the sad end of an era of sexual freedom and loss of healthy social boundaries between the sexes, Shalit challenges outright the prevailing myth that sex is now so everyday that it really is "no big

20. Stafford, *The Sexual Christian*, 17–19.
21. See especially chapter 3, "The New Salvation," in Stafford, *The Sexual Christian*.
22. Butler, "Sex in a New Age Guise."
23. Rinehart, "Losing Our Promiscuity," 32.
24. See online: http://www.smartmarriages.com for news, archival material, and organizations associated with the new marriage movement.

deal." She recounts her disgust and that of many female students with college coed bathrooms, her shock at learning from the mixed college wrestling team that, "Oh don't worry . . . It's *nothing sexual*," her surprise that some good Jewish boys and girls were off on a camping trip and could sometimes even share sleeping bags because they were "just friends." Shalit's conclusion: "For all their experience, they were, in some fundamental way, prudes, because they were blind to the power of sex. They were "mature," which is to say, emotionally detached, but that meant they were essentially clinical about things that to me would seem extremely intriguing and occupy my imagination for hours."[25] As "K. C." from Atlanta concludes, "The phrase *casual sex* is the world's biggest oxymoron!"[26] The disturbing conclusion here is that a generation for whom sex is "no big deal" is one which has been numbed in areas which should be filled with heightened sensitivity.

The truth is, sex is a powerful force far beyond its capacity to sell automotive tools. This of course is not a modern discovery, as we read in Peter Brown's summary of the conclusions of the ancient pagan doctor Galen: "Here were little fiery universes, through whose heart, brain and veins there pulsed the same heat and vital spirit as glowed in the stars. To make love was to bring one's blood to boil . . . [The genitals were] the outlets of a human Espresso machine."[27] Given the exploitive power of such explosive sexuality, feminist Karen LeBacqz argues on the basis of the principle of vulnerability that "protective structures" need to be put in place, especially for singles.[28]

The new celibacy movement—both religious and secular—spans the youth generation from teens through the twenty- and thirty-somethings. While there has been continued pressure, mostly from conservative Roman Catholics and Protestant Christians, to provide abstinence-based sex-education courses, the results of experiments have not been entirely successful. A *New York Times* article concluded that those who took a pledge of abstinence delayed "much longer than those who do not make such a pledge of chastity."[29] But actually the delay was

25. Shalit, *A Return to Modesty*, 175–79.
26. Ibid., 235.
27. Brown, *The Body and Society*, 17.
28. Cited in Grenz, *Sexual Ethics*, 221.
29. Schemo, "Virginity Pledges by Teenagers Can Be Highly Effective, Federal Study Finds."

only eighteen months, and fewer Christian singles than nonpledgers used any form of birth control.[30]

These small but significant movements of resistance are indicators of discontent but so far have made no appreciable gains in changing the sexual landscape. It is all still there: casual and risky sex, delayed but meaningful relational sex, and a renewed emphasis on traditional marriage and chastity for singles. If the sexual revolution is dying, it is not evident in the statistics. But voices of dissent also persist. One movie critic, Suzanne Fields, makes the point in her review of *Magnolia,* in which a crude motivational speaker (Tom Cruise) spreads a peculiar message for men: "Seduce and Destroy." Fields's conclusion is that "the character is satirical, a dramatic symbol for the dead end of the sexual revolution."[31]

SEX IN CHURCH: BODY, SOUL, AND THE OTHER

There is no golden age of sexual morality in church history. We have tolerated practices from a sex-denying dualism to the double standard, and today for many, a reluctant acquiescence. So our claims must be modest at best.

At the same time, many thoughtful Christians are convinced that the current sexual experiment is an inadequate delivery system for the traditional Christian sex ethic. Our first task is to grapple with sexuality from our own distinctively scriptural authority and tradition. But as sex is a gift of God for all humanity, we believe there are good reasons for commending our vision to those outside the church.

One reason is that we believe *sex is grounded in personhood.* While sex is certainly a biological fact of nature, we must talk about it in terms of persons. The issue here is the popular claim that *sex is necessary* for a full and healthy life.[32] But sex in humans is a complex affair, an appetite unlike those that demand satisfaction to survive. To reduce sex to biological necessity is to rob persons of their human dignity and freedom. As feminist Camille Paglia states, the sexual freedom

---

30. Winner, *Real Sex,* 17.

31. Fields, "Chaste Chase." For a personal and up-close account of the difficulty of the American under-forty generation to enter into lifelong marriage commitments, see Straus, *Unhooked Generation.*

32. See Stafford, *The Sexual Christian,* 14–15.

delivered to us by popular psychology is more like "a new enslavement to ancient Necessity."[33]

If sex is more than biology, it must engage persons at the level of their humanity—psychologically, socially, morally, and spiritually. Philip Turner makes the point that for humans the biological drive is transformed into "sexual desire," a passion that is "peculiar to persons." It is a human achievement, a virtue, or, "a power of soul that we must come by in some way."[34]

This power of soul belongs to humanity in a manner that is not grounded in biology or even the human psyche, but in a source outside itself—a transcendent source called God—and in a mode called "the image of God."[35] Therefore, sex includes a spiritual dimension that both informs and shapes the human sexual life intended by God.

Another reason for commending the traditional Christian ethic is that we believe *sex is an intrinsic social reality*. Persons are social beings, not autonomous individuals. Humans do not merely *have* relationships; relationships constitute us as human beings. As Karl Barth states, "The humanity of every person consists in the determination of his or her being as being-together with the fellow human."[36] As persons we come to know ourselves only through interaction with others.

There is something about sexual desire that, in the end, is not fulfilled by mere physical gratification. We seek the relationship of others in an effort to overcome the loneliness of bodily isolation. In a word, we long for intimacy in its most profound sense. This is why the present pursuit of sexual satisfaction looks more like loneliness than love. The reason? It is the effect in society of a potent toxin brewed from the ingredients of individualism, sexual idealism, and social isolation.

Intimacy is not an independent commodity to be sought. The search for such affection strays into territory dangerous to itself and others when it is pursued outside an ordered social reality. Lutheran theologian Robert Jenson argues that for intimacy to thrive, it needs a moral and just community. As relational beings we need a public space for living out our humanity, including our sexual relationships, a place

---

33. Quoted in Clapp, *Families at the Crossroads*, 105.
34. Turner, *Sexual Ethics and the Attack on Traditional Morality*, 13–15.
35. See Anderson and Guernsey, *On Being Family*, 56.
36. Quoted in Jenson, *Systematic Theology*, 2:73.

"in which God calls us to be human in that we call each other to come together in justice."[37]

Jenson concludes that the older moral tradition made sexual ethics the "longest chapter," and for good reason. The human sexual encounter is more fundamental than all other forms of community. It is that place where persons are most physically present to one another as both subject and object. But to affirm this bodily presence with another person is to acknowledge an inescapable reality, that the body's "chief marvel is its sexuality."[38] Therefore, what one does in bed "is the area of my action in which the community has the most urgent interest."[39]

What does the institution called marriage in this public space look like?[40] Three characteristic marks that have achieved ecumenical consensus historically and across church traditions are: one-flesh unity, fidelity, and procreation.[41] We realize that not everyone is provided the opportunity or is called to the married state. We are only asserting here that marriage is the proper place for sexual union, which Christians have traditionally held to be God's purpose for humanity. The following three theological affirmations about the sexual act illuminate its relationship to marriage and divine purpose.

The first affirmation is that *sex in marriage is a kind of community described in Scripture as "one flesh"* (Gen 2:21–24; Matt 19:5; Eph 5:21–33). An individualistic culture may have difficulty in grasping the power of such a concept. Sexuality functions at three levels: the biological as innate drive, the affectional as sexual desire for another person, and the moral and spiritual as a bond of love between two persons. The first two are particularly subject to abuse and disregard for the other person. For instance, the first level is entirely self-centered, as its primary purpose is to satisfy a biological appetite. Relationally, it objectifies the other (it can be mutual objectification in the form of recreational, pleasure-based sex), and disregards the whole person (it becomes a form of dualism).

37. Ibid., 79.
38. Ibid., 88.
39. Ibid., 90.

40. It is only because of the limited scope and not lack of concern that this essay does not address directly the topic of sexuality and single persons. The focus here is specifically sexual practice as understood in culture and the church's teaching, with particular attention to its role in marriage.

41. These are the three traditional Christian virtues of marriage incorporated in most marriage liturgies and vows. See Stackhouse, *Covenant and Commitments*, 19.

While it may say, "I love you," it really means, "I love me and want you."[42] The affectional alone lacks stability, as it relates to the other through attraction but does not make provision for commitment, the unreliability of human emotions, or unpredictability of human circumstances. When the romance fades, the reasons for remaining together lose their power to persuade the will.

The moral and spiritual level recognizes that sex is a dimension of our whole being, body and soul, as well as our relationship with others. It is no surprise that sex management is a public and social concern for all societies. Because humans also seek transcendent meaning in life, sexual permissions and prohibitions frequently appeal to divine command.

For Christians, sex is a moral and spiritual matter. Scripture describes it in the most intimate terms as "one flesh," and as a sign of God's way in the world. It is a kind of love informed and enabled by the love of God revealed in Jesus Christ. This is why, in Ephesians 5, Paul employs the one flesh of marriage love as a metaphor of the sacrificial love between Christ and his church. For Stafford, it is this "loving monogamy" that sets the Christian view apart from other ancient forms of monogamy.[43]

One way we experience this loving union is by embracing in faith the marital sex act as a sign of Christ's unconditional love for the church to the point of sacrificial death. Practically, in marriage we are freed "from performance-pressure," and graced with the freedom to be transparent in the presence of the other.[44] Also, as Lewis Smedes describes it, "one flesh" signifies a "life-uniting act" (traditionally called the unitive purpose of marriage). It is an act of uniting body and soul. All other coital relationships are excluded since they do not combine the life-uniting act with a life-uniting intent.[45]

The second theological affirmation is that *the sexual act in marriage embodies a commitment of fidelity to the other.* Fidelity to another is a sign of God's unconditional covenant love. It also reflects a theologically realistic understanding of human nature, a point made abundantly clear by Ramsey: the human capacity for *fidelity* makes marriage *possible*, and the human capacity for *infidelity* makes marriage *necessary*.[46]

42. Ramsey, "A Christian Approach," 115.
43. Stafford, "Intimacy," 22.
44. Grenz, *Sexual Ethics*, 85.
45. Smedes, *Sex for Christians*, 128–30.
46. Ramsey, "A Christian Approach," 114.

For a frail human being to enter a lifelong, exclusive relationship with another fallible person requires an act of faith. The divine command is God's yes to us and the promise of divine assistance. This call is particularly acute in a time when prophets of hopelessness proclaim that because we live longer than previous generations, most of us do not have the personal and moral stamina to persevere in a long-term marriage.[47]

Jenson makes a more robust claim. The act of sex is a gesture, the sign of a pledge and not a technique, is one that "can be the embodiment of an ultimate promise: the promise of myself if it kills me, of shared life 'until death do us part.'"[48]

In addition, an exclusive and permanent relationship with another is the divine means by which we acquire the virtues necessary for developing "the ability to meld one's own interests with those of another."[49] Mutual submission is a virtue that requires years of practice.

Our capacity for infidelity makes boundary setting a moral imperative. Sex is inherently unstable. Smedes has it right when he states, "The inner self is at once a reservoir of moral power and a cauldron of moral turbulence."[50] Most of us have learned from life's struggles and temptations that—metaphorically at least—it is easy to get into heaven, but hard to stay out of hell! Self-deception and opportunism pervade our inner world of sexuality. Referring to the marital covenant, Turner urges us to acquire those virtues necessary "to contain desire within the bonds of love and direct it toward the fulfillment of love's purpose."[51]

The third affirmation is that *the sexual act in marriage embodies hope*. This hope is signified in the procreative purpose of marriage. Though today the unitive and relational purposes are separated from and sometimes cherished more than the procreational, the generative

---

47. The argument that former generations divorced less because their marriages were shorter is contradicted by the fact that it was largely the infant-mortality rate that lowered the average lifespan, and that the average age of marriage a century ago is comparable to today's age. See Popenoe, "The Top Ten Myths of Marriage."

48. Jenson, *Systematic Theology*, 2:92. The reality of divorce does not nullify this pledge. Both Scripture and history testify to the human struggle for sustaining lifelong vows. Marriages sometimes experience what the Orthodox Church calls a moral death, and may rightly be dissolved. But the vow of permanence remains, in both marriage and remarriage.

49. Turner, *Sexual Ethics*, 18.

50. Smedes, *Sex for Christians*, 213.

51. Turner, *Sexual Ethics*, 18.

dimensions are still present in any sexual act. The act that is life-uniting for a couple is precisely the *same act* that generates life. Even if the sex act is intended for making love, and even if appropriate means of birth control are employed, the act is still a procreative and life-giving one. Theological reflection will not see this connection as insignificant. But this may be the most difficult claim to be grasped by a generation that has no existential fear of pregnancy because the pill "unhooked" the physical connection prior to its own living memory. A traditional Christian ethic regards the family as the primary, though not exclusive or dutiful (that every couple *must* procreate), location for the birthing and nurturing of children. Among other reasons, adultery and fornication are viewed as inconsistent with Christian values precisely because they do not seek or intend to engage in sex *within a context* that welcomes children.[52]

SEX REDEEMED AND LOVE RESTORED

We do not deny that there are limited benefits in relationships outside the normative vision of the community called marriage. Good cohabitation is better than a bad marriage or risky sex. Christians may rightly support provision in civil law for the protection of persons in alternative or vulnerable relationships, even when these arrangements are the result of either choice or circumstance. Christians are bound by the gospel to exercise compassionate pastoral care toward all who struggle and fail.

But a Christian moral vision must also recognize that there are losses in these limited and temporary commitments. They are inherently unstable, women and children are at a higher risk, people can spend years trapped in a dead-end arrangement, and temporary benefits seldom outweigh the rich dividends of a faithful marriage.[53] The personal returns from a contractual society—one that makes short-term commitments based upon expediency and self-interest—are meager when compared with the benefits that come with a covenant of permanency.

The human sex act properly belongs within a particular form of community. In a way, we begin with the Christian community where

---

52. See Meilaender, "Sexuality," 71–78.

53. We do not imply that traditional marriages are always lifegiving. Many couples are trapped in marriages that are boring, hostile, or lonely. What is stated here applies to all relationships, including marriages.

we learn that marriage mirrors the intimate, faithful and sacrificial love of Christ for the church, and that its sign is one flesh, fidelity, and procreativity.

But this distinctive character of marital community seeks to be taken into the public sphere as an overflow of divine blessing. In this way the created order is being transformed. Though an unbelieving world does not know, it may still reap the benefits of a way of living that is the divine gift of common grace. After all, sex is also about the people we *don't* have sex with.

Why should the vision presented here be more compelling than culture's competing offers? Stafford is close to the mark in observing that "there are too many losers."[54] One has only to calculate the effect on the weakest members of society who have suffered at the hands of a self-indulgent generation. But, as Jenson points out, the God of judgment and mercy is never far off. While our culture sacrifices its weakest ones in indulgent worship to Moloch, that ancient Semitic deity who received the sacrifice of children, another voice may be heard: "As they call on 'Lord Moloch', they risk hearing, 'You called? I am the Lord. But my name is not Moloch and I do not savor the smoke of your children.'"[55]

The church is called to embody this word of judgment and mercy. Sometimes persons and even cultures drift so far from a Christian moral vision that they will only return by taking the long way home. It is a long way not because they stop to smell the roses, but because they make so many dead-end side trips into swamps and bogs. When they return, it is not our task to chastise. Those whose feet are bleeding and whose muscles are tired from the ordeal know well enough the wasted days and lonely nights. Only one who has tasted the joy of coming home can tell us what it was like to be lost. As Jesus's parable of a Wandering Son and a Waiting Father reminds us, do not post the Ten Commandments on the gate. Kill the fatted calf!

---

54. Stafford, "Intimacy," 24.
55. Ibid., 83.

10

Why Christian Spirituality?

Merv Mercer

IN A RECENT CLASS discussion concerning the characteristics of our culture at this particular moment of history, a student offered a particularly helpful image. Most of us have the picture of the sinking of the *Titanic* etched in our minds, particularly that frozen moment when our eyes take in the whole scene. The night is clear and dark with stars crisply bright; the water is silent, black and frigid; floating, freezing passengers are slowly being numbed out of existence; and lifeboats dot the sea's surface with huddling survivors. In the background the great ship *Titanic*, its stern lifting in the air and people leaping from its sides to their death, approaches the point at which it will split and slide effortlessly into the depths. The inhabitants of the lifeboats look back at the sinking ship realizing that their future, now orphaned from what had once felt secure, would never be the same. The stability and normalcy of the great ship had almost instantly been replaced by the relative insecurity of lifeboats afloat upon the dark North Atlantic. To the student, this picture was an image of our own society in the postmodern and post-Christendom moment in which we find ourselves. The *Titanics* of our world, the symbols of our self-pride and confidence, are sinking all around us leaving us confused about our survival. Those lifeboats represent the various options to which we and other members of our society are all committing ourselves. Many of us are anxiously stretching toward them although many of us have failed to reach any lifeboat at all, and are at risk of drowning. The lifeboats all have various names but certainly several are named for different forms of spirituality, from those of the eastern religions to assorted New Age varieties. One has to search hard to find the one named traditional Christianity.[1]

In a much broader sense the sinking of the *Titanic* is an apt image for the death of modernity as well. The state-of-the-art ship ("unsinkable," it was claimed) had failed to survive even its maiden voyage. Dismay at its loss was as much a horror at the failure of science and technology as it was grief for those who drowned. "How could such a thing happen?" was, and maybe still is, the question on everyone's mind. Many contemporary Christians, certainly Canadian Anglicans, have a similar response to the situation facing their church. How could the Christian church, the church of the establishment, find itself having to justify its own relevance to a culture whose very core values have Judeo-Christian roots? The short answer, I suppose, is that the church in many ways "hitched its wagon" to the culture in which it found itself; now it must suffer the culture's disillusionment and awareness that even the advances of technology fail to address the deepest human questions. It is hard to admit that there is a real sense in which the institutionalized Western church may have to go down with the *Titanic* in order to secure its survival.

The growing and often unspoken sense of despair felt by people in the pew has resulted in their being tempted by the notion that the goal of spirituality might become their comfort and salvation. People want to feel better in the light of what is the contemporary situation rather than to be challenged to move beyond the present crisis to what might be, "especially if such movement involves definite sacrifices or discomforts."[2] The risks that might lead us forward into true growth seem too much to bear, and any glimmer of being nurtured by the transcendent dims in the quest for solace and comfort in the immediate. The church has arrived at a crucial moment and it is essential that it reappropriate the truths of the Christian faith. To the extent that the question "Why Christian Spirituality?" focuses us on the faith's first principles, it will serve us well as we seek our way through this maze in this particular time in our history.

---

1. As we considered this image of the "sinking" of a culture, we wondered if the orchestra that went down with the ship, playing "Nearer, My God, to Thee," was perhaps a representation of the institutional church; there was no clear consensus on that.

2. Wuthnow, "Small Groups," 1239.

Contrary to what one might expect, this essay will not compare and evaluate Christian spirituality with the legion of other options available in our world. What actually distinguishes Christian spirituality is the biblical and theological truth from which it arises; it is to those realities that we must turn in order to answer our question. It is not time to be confused or depressed, either; rather it is time to reassert what the Christian saints have tested through their experience of God over thousands of years. What they have taught us is that the faith is not amorphous and unclear, but that its beliefs have order and structure. In other words, Christian spirituality depends for its vitality upon the personal appropriation of certain theological understandings; that is to say that such vitality arises from a "synthesis of faith and life,"[3] putting our faith to work in the texture of our lives. It is important, then, for us to engage intentionally with the central tenets and doctrines of our faith if we are to understand fully how this synthesis provides a baseline for our Christian spiritual life.

WHOSE WORLD IS IT, ANYWAY?

The meaning of our faith is undergirded by the appreciation that all we know of life has been created by God—the universe, our world, all creatures and humankind, including you and me. This assertion is critical to our having the right order of creation in mind; it recalls for us our creatureliness and locates us in the correct relationship to God who is at the center of it all as creator. Modern people seem to have lost their hold of this truth and reconceived the universe; in their realignment they have ironically placed themselves at its center. In pace with this reconception of meaning even the doing of theology has shifted: "At one time theologians argued that the chief purpose of humankind was to glorify God. Now it would seem that the logic has been reversed: the chief purpose of God is to glorify humankind. Spirituality no longer is true or good because it meets absolute standards of truth or goodness, but because it helps me to get along. I am the judge of its worth."[4]

---

3. McGrath, *Christian Spirituality*, 9.
4. Wuthnow, "Small Groups," 1239–40.

It has been observed that people "have a habit of turning everything toward themselves . . . to make even God into [their] own image."[5] This displacement of God, or if truth be known of ourselves, has cost us dearly. Our contemporary culture has sought its meaning in what humankind can discover through science and the other tools of modernity and, along the way, has lost any sense of transcendence and mystery.[6] There is still the abiding sense in our culture that we can "achieve self-knowledge without any reference to God"; the result is that our lives are often "empty, superficial and trivial."[7] In modernity's failure to resolve the reality of wars, famine, cruelty and evil, humankind finds itself without meaning and understanding, effectively lost and powerless. Jim Houston concludes that "not only is the modern world an idolatrous society, and an addictive society, but we are now also a loveless society."[8] At a cultural level, perhaps the most pervasive of human needs, to love and to be loved, has slipped through our collective fingers even as we loved ourselves too much.

Christianity teaches that "human fulfillment can only be fully achieved through a deepened relationship with God."[9] At the heart of this relationship is a creator God who loves what has been made and desires its harmony and peace. Referring to the Old Testament, the reformed theologian Karl Barth describes a God "who calls his own people to himself": "The revelation of the primacy of God and the station of man in the covenant is the work of God's word. This covenant (in which God is man's God and man is God's man) is the content of the Word of God; and God's covenant, history, and work with man are the contents of his Word which distinguish it from all other words."[10]

It is appropriate for us to be guided to God's continual reaching out to creation as the Old Testament records it. In the garden of Eden, God expressed a desire for intimacy with the humankind placed there,

---

5. Houston, *The Heart's Desire*, 49.

6. Even in biblical studies, scholarly use of historical-critical methodology has sometimes had this tendency. The Jesus Seminar is a good example of modernity gone awry, leading us down a dead-end street in terms of our faith and spiritual lives.

7. Eden and Wells, *The Gospel in the Modern World*, 188; Houston, *The Heart's Desire*, 16.

8. Houston, *The Heart's Desire*, 82.

9. McGrath, *Christian Spirituality*, 29.

10. Barth, *Evangelical Theology*, 20–21.

walking and communing with both man and woman. Even in their sinful rejection of God and their eventual dismissal from the garden God did not desert them, but continued to offer relationship to them and their descendants: "And the Lord God made garments of skins for the man and for his wife, and clothed them" (Gen 3:21). This offer was given more particular shape later in the covenant extended to Abraham and Sarah, and further to the ongoing reality of the people of Israel as Abraham's descendents (Gen 17:1–8).

In spite of its constant distancing of itself from God, humankind has been reminded time and time again that God's love absorbs all our shortcomings and failures and teaches us the true meaning of love. The call to a covenant love relationship with God, however, has most often been rejected by us. I am struck by the variety of ways in which love is configured by humankind as a product of human constructs. Unfortunately, when we put ourselves at the center of things we discover we are incapacitated, able only to manufacture hollow counterfeits. One has only to observe the empty and hazardous eroticism that has flooded our lives, from the sexual manipulation of the consumer to the more devastating fantasies of Internet pornography. Without the template provided through our encounter with God's love, from the center of all meaning, we are left to our own devices and fall abysmally short. Of course, the covenant named in the Old Testament is not the final word, but merely a signpost of God's desire pointing forward to the greatest gift, the Word made flesh: "Israel's history, therefore, points beyond itself; it points to a fulfillment which, although pressing forward to become reality has not yet become real."[11]

THE WORD . . . THEN, NOW, AND ALWAYS

It is to the Christ event and a new covenant that the Old Testament points. In that new moment in history, God made available to all of creation a new power to defeat all evil and corruption: "The Word of God is Gospel, that is, the good word, because it declares God's good work. In this Word, God's work itself becomes speech. Through his Word,

---

11. Ibid., 21.

God discloses his work in his covenant with man, in the history of its establishment, maintenance, accomplishment, and fulfillment."[12]

Jesus as the Word of God made flesh lived in the creation in order to become the means of its redemption. It is the decisive act of God in Christ that makes possible the return of the recalcitrant Israel to the eternal love of God. This same divine initiative is also the means by which all of humankind is offered reconciliation with God, receiving mercy, forgiveness, and love: "The Word became flesh in our place and for us, to overcome, take away, and eradicate the sin that separates us from God, the sin that is also the sting of death, the old element of our old nature and world."[13]

The touchstone of this act of salvation is focused in the person of Jesus Christ. No spirituality that is Christian can avoid having something to do with Jesus Christ, nor can it fail to recognize in Christ's redemptive act the model for all Christian spiritual life.[14] The "life–death–new-life" cycle will not only become the rhythm of redemption, but also the pattern in which we will live and grow. What Jesus's death and resurrection makes very clear to us is the cost of estrangement from God. If Jesus is required to die the "cross-death" in order to establish a new covenant between creation and God, if the cost is that great, then we are each faced with the real consequences of our own sinfulness in a whole new proportion. The consequences of our individual brokenness now take their part in a much larger cosmic story. It demands from us a more intentional recognition of and response to God's offer of forgiveness; it also calls us to a personal transaction in which we must inevitably face and accept our need in new ways and receive the gift God has given: "God's love is seen more clearly than before to be an atoning love; it brings sin back to God, overcoming the estrangement caused by our sin and rebellion. We are shown that to be self-sufficient and pretend we do not need God is to deny our humanity."[15]

To acknowledge our need for God is in many ways to die to our sense of self, just as Jesus did in his sacrifice. One can see the agony and extent of this struggle in Gethsemane, as Jesus, admittedly "deeply

---

12. Ibid., 19.
13. Ibid., 70.
14. Cunningham and Egan, *Christian Spirituality*, 7.
15. Houston, *The Heart's Desire*, 94.

grieved, even to death," prayed: "My Father, if it is possible, let this cup pass from me; yet not what I want but what you want" (Matt 26:38–39).

In the renewed community that encountered the risen one, we see that Jesus's resurrection lives on in the recovered relationship with God that results from the acceptance of the gift of new life, a life of peace, reconciliation, and righteousness. This cycle of death and resurrection marks both the birth of the Christian life and also prefigures a spiritual life in Christ that will echo a similar rhythm of death and new life as we mature in our understanding and experience of the faith. Each stage of a Christian's spiritual development incorporates some measure of self-emptying, a death, in order that he or she be more completely filled and sustained by the heartbeat of God. In the risen Jesus we see revealed both the face of God and our own future in the purposes of God.

We are now at the critical point upon which the balance of history hinges. Here too lies the point of deepest answer to our question about Christian spirituality. Our individual question—as well as the ultimate health of our culture and world—intersect in this "moment." Our own affirmative response to the Christ event also mirrors the best possibility for our culture's future. It is not an easy moment, though; its resolution also presents its largest challenge. Are we really ready to acknowledge our need for God? Are we unwilling to disown the self-driven goal of seeking to be "super-people" in control of it all? If human beings are open to their vulnerability as creatures made by God, then God has provided a means by which a redeemed relationship is possible. All are able to revel in the status of being the beloved—the means is provided, the banquet table is set.[16] On the other hand, if they are unable to appropriate this truth, then Christian spirituality is foolishness and a scandal to them. Make no mistake that this is the critical balance point in the quest for an answer to our question about Christian spirituality. The self-serving instinct, so thoroughly human, that we can generate our own redemption, collides with the immovable witness of the resurrection and God's direct intervention in the affairs of the world. We deny God's offer at our peril; all meaning in life is poured by God into the resurrection and all meaning flows out of it.

---

16. The parable of the Waiting Father (also known as the parable of the Prodigal Son) in Luke 15:11–32 is very helpful in helping us appreciate God's desires for us.

TRINITY AND COMMUNITY

The Christian experience of forgiveness and salvation, nurtured by a spirituality that makes such experience personal, literally saves us from ourselves. Having Jesus's work on the cross as our referential truth lifts us beyond our individualistic delusions and incorporates us into the cosmic story that is afoot. At the same time, it turns us to face our sisters and our brothers with new sight. We discover we are not alone, that God has formed us with a communal imperative. If we are to further our understanding of the uniqueness of Christian spirituality, we must look more closely at the nature of God's self-revelation as it is recorded in scripture. Consider the moment at which Jesus's earthly ministry was inaugurated, his baptism: "In those days Jesus came from Nazareth of Galilee and was baptized by John in the Jordan. And just as he was coming up out of the water, he saw the heavens torn apart and the Spirit descending like a dove on him. And a voice came from heaven, 'You are my Son, the Beloved; with you I am well pleased'" (Mark 1:9–11).

We see in this passage the apparently communal nature of the Godhead itself. God the Father speaks, the Spirit descends and the divine Sonship of Jesus is established. This confluence of all three persons of the Trinity at Jesus's baptism is an icon of the larger significance of Jesus of Nazareth: "Divine love is the revealed nature of the Holy Trinity: God who is the source of Love, Christ our Savior and Redeemer who is the communication of Love, and the Holy Spirit who is our reminder of that sacrifice of Love."[17]

Our spirituality connects us at one level to this divine community while at another level and at the same time bestowing upon us a place in God's earthly community, the church that scripture has identified as the body of Christ (cf. 1 Corinthians 12): "Life caught up in God is more like relating to a loving community than it is like relating to a loving individual. We turn to the Father, and he gives us the Son and the Spirit; we turn to the Son, and he shows us the Father and breathes the Spirit upon us; we turn to the Spirit, and he shows us the Father and the Son."[18]

The biblical texts of creation tell us that humankind is formed in the image of God, or *imago Dei*. The "basic correspondence between ourselves and God" might suggest that we are to reflect God's character

---

17. Houston, *The Heart's Desire*, 93.
18. Adam, "The Trinity and Human Community," 61.

and nature to some degree. Perhaps the community of the church is such a reflection.[19] As Christians, then, we are defined by and carriers of this Trinitarian life, imbued with "the relational life of the divine community of Father, Son and Holy Spirit."[20] Just as the ground of our faith is communal, so Christian spirituality "cannot be limited to an exclusively individualistic care of the soul."[21] Instead, the Holy Spirit forms us as community; reshaping us as the body of Christ; it is there that we are nurtured, trained and sent, and there that we experience and share God's love in relationships with others.

It seems clear to me that such a communal life may also provide a stumbling block to those in our culture. So many people today are engaging in some type of self-definition, struggling to discover themselves, often at the expense of others around them.[22] One only needs to peruse a bookstore's shelves to estimate the extent to which self-help guides are promoted or to observe the manner in which so many products are marketed toward the betterment of the individual. The call into Christian community stands in stark contrast to such a reality; in doing so it places before members of our culture a clear alternative that we must never diminish or undersell. The love of God is available to all; but it calls people out of their individualized and alienated lives into community and friendship as it is mediated within the Christian family. Far from emphasizing *the self*, the focus of the faith is very significantly on *the other*. One of the important tasks of Christian spirituality is to make that community an embodiment of Christ-given grace so that others will see clearly God's intent for all creation: "every Christian thinker, if he or she at all merits designation, begins from the experience of being reconciled, being accepted, being held (however precariously) in the grace of God. And this is mediated in the objective form of a shared life and language, a public and historical community of men and women, gathering to read certain texts and perform certain acts."[23]

---

19. Ibid., 53. There is obviously a much larger theological question at stake here. This is not the place to engage that question. I simply wish to hint at the possibility that the church reflects God's communal nature, and that to love God is also to love and participate in the church.

20. Eden and Wells, *The Gospel in the Modern World*, 194.

21. Cunningham and Egan, *Christian Spirituality*, 19.

22. The more global our awareness, the more penetrating this judgment becomes.

23. Williams, *Christian Spirituality*, 2.

Christian spirituality, then, is intricately tied to the shared acts of those who hold the same faith. It is the converting experience of their faith that brings cohesion to their community. Together Christians have "tasted and seen that the Lord is good"; it is inevitable that they would then desire to share the response that gives rise to their worship life.

Word and sacrament lie at the heart of that shared worship. The written text of scripture tells the story of God's love affair with creation; it is a reminder of what shapes the community of faith. As we hear it spoken, we are relocated into the memory of God's redeeming action and of our own reception of its grace. As Don Saliers has written: "The divine initiative calls forth a communal response that finds its own best being in praise of its creator and redeemer."[24]

By reliving this story over and over again, in the differing circumstances of our lives, we continuously discover the riches of God and learn to apply them in ever widening circles of influence. Insofar as the sacraments are the enacted Word in the life of the faith community, they too become agents of our ongoing and developing holiness. In a sense, both Word and sacrament disable time even though they are clearly placed within it. They recall the past, certainly, even as we gather around them in the present moment; but they also lay a claim on our future with God as well. They are enacted promise, not unlike Saliers's description: "The forms of being called to remembrance of what has taken place between God and our stories in the past give us a future as well. This suggests that authentic biblical worship is a peculiar kind of "future present," but always grounded in the mystery and suffering of real human history."[25]

Christian spirituality can never be divorced from worship because it is in these acts of remembrance that we freshly reappropriate God-with-us.[26] Because spirituality is holistic, that is to say tied to our whole person, it touches our emotional life and all that forms us. For that reason, our personal history and the course of all salvation history are both important. "Remembering is essential to our sense of identity. Our deepest emotions are intimately linked with how we remember and what we recall."[27]

---

24. Saliers, *Worship and Spirituality*, 28.
25. Ibid., 19.
26. Ibid., 36.
27. Ibid., 16.

I am deeply concerned by the manner in which history and tradition are discounted and ridiculed by our culture. This malaise of modernity, in which only the next discovery or new idea or spirituality option has meaning, is the systemic illness of our age. In order to live spiritually as Christians, we must value our faith memory and traditions. Among our traditions, let me name our most precious. Most importantly, I mean the historical moment in which Jesus the Christ entered our world to live and die in our midst; the Christian enterprise is ridiculous without that. I also absolutely wish to hold on to scripture as the corporate memory of the people of God; that is how we consciously hold onto the *story* of our faith.[28] I want to recall the God experiences recorded by Christian people throughout the ages and the history of the church—the mistakes that have been made and the joys known—over some two thousand years. The lives of the saints, for instance, offer untold riches. Not least, I want to treasure our personal histories, yours and mine, of encounter with God and the life of faith. Such firsthand witness lies at the heart of our mission as Christian people; we will share most ably what we ourselves know. I will always wholeheartedly resist the notion that such traditions are crutches that limit the future. Those who have disposed of memory in order to honor an idolatry of the "new" are, I believe, dangerous to the nurturing of true spiritual life: "Christians should be particularly wary of any dismissal of the past, because it is God's nature to reveal himself in historic acts[,] . . . we have tended to lose our memories of God's dealings in the past. Our insight has become so restricted to the secular world that we run into the danger of becoming culturally cut off from the flow of history."[29]

I am certainly not suggesting that history be uncritically accepted or blindly followed. We must recognize the shortcomings of many that have called themselves Christian and isolate such failures from our conviction about the truth of our beliefs. Our faith has historical axes that must be honored and traditions that must be treasured. Any summary dismissal of our past risks "throwing the baby out with the bath water."

---

28. Ibid., 36.
29. Houston, *The Heart's Desire*, 22–23.

NOW . . . AND NOT YET

If the pivotal moment in all of human history is the death and resurrection of Jesus Christ, then what significance is there to our church two thousand years later—and to what end do we talk about Christian spirituality? The answer lies in the connection God makes between then and now. The means by which humankind has been reconciled to God was accomplished through Jesus Christ's atoning death and resurrection. Although it is our defining truth, however, it is incompletely realized in our midst. Only at the end of time will we see it fully achieved in the new heaven and new earth God has promised. It is as if Christians carry dual citizenship enabling them to live in the promised kingdom of heaven even as they reside in the broken world of the here and now. They live in "the now" with a clear eye upon "the not yet" and their spiritual lives inhabit the intersection of those two realities. It is important to note that Christian spirituality does not serve itself; rather, it is the nutrient by which Christians are strengthened to live the gospel in the world between "the now" and "the not yet." In other words, it is inextricably linked to the unfolding purposes of God in creation. Christian spirituality is "a way of life," not a philosophical system of self-development; this distinguishes it from the vast array of alternatives that abound in our culture.[30] When we follow Jesus's instruction to love God and love our neighbor as ourselves (Luke 10:25–28), we are indeed living at the apex of Christian spirituality.[31] That is how we participate in ministry "between the times." What is required of us is that we actively apply our theological understanding of God's activity to the real world in which we live. That application involves our whole being, as "Authentic Christian spirituality must be holistic. Such a spirituality will recognize explicitly that we are human persons and not merely souls imprisoned in bodies."[32]

This type of engagement leaves no room for dualistic confusion or any suspicion that spirituality provides an escape from reality. Christian spirituality is fully engaged with life in all of its triumphs and failures. At the same time as it is rooted in the individual experiences of Christians, however, it is also connected to much larger consequences. For William Stringfellow it has a cosmic scale: "Whatever else may be affirmed about

---

30. Cunningham and Egan, *Christian Spirituality*, 9.

31. In this passage, Jesus is affirming the lawyer's own understanding of what must be done to achieve eternal life; it is an echo of Lev 19:18.

32. Cunningham and Egan, *Christian Spirituality*, 18.

a spirituality which has a biblical precedent and style, spiritual maturity or spiritual fulfillment necessarily involves the whole person—body, mind and soul, relationships—in connection with the whole of creation throughout the era of time. Biblical spirituality encompasses the whole person in the totality of existence in the world, not some fragment or scrap or incident of a person."[33] As Christians we take our place on God's universally large canvas and the brush strokes of our faithful lives become important elements in God's renewed picture of creation. We can only play our part, though, because we are equipped to do so.

Before Jesus undertook the work of the cross, he promised his disciples that they would be enabled in their coming discipleship by the sending of the Spirit: "If you love me, you will keep my commandments. And I will ask the Father, and he will give you another Advocate, to be with you forever. This is the Spirit of truth, whom the world cannot receive, because it neither sees him nor knows him. You know him, because he abides with you, and he will be in you . . . But the Advocate, the Holy Spirit, whom the Father will send in my name, will teach you everything, and remind you of all that I have said to you" (John 14:15–17, 26).

The role of the Holy Spirit is further elucidated a couple of chapters later:

> And when he comes, he will prove the world wrong about sin and righteousness and judgment: about sin, because they do not believe in me; about righteousness, because I am going to the Father and you will see me no longer; about judgment, because the ruler of this world has been condemned. I still have many things to say to you, but you cannot bear them now. When the Spirit of truth comes, he will guide you into all the truth; for he will not speak on his own, but will speak whatever he hears, and he will declare to you the things that are to come. He will glorify me, because he will take what is mine and declare it to you. (John 16:8–14)

The Holy Spirit witnesses to us about the truth of Christ and provides guidance for all those who choose Jesus as Lord. It is the Holy Spirit that bridges the gap between the cross and the present day; it is

---

33. Stringfellow, *The Politics of Spirituality*, 22. Michael Taylor emphasizes the same thing when he says, "In the Bible man is bound to God—'the image and likeness of God'—by virtue of his responsibility for the transformation of the cosmos in which he lives and has his being" (Taylor, *The Sacred and the Secular*, 191).

the Holy Spirit that keeps the promise of the kingdom of heaven clearly before us; it is the Holy Spirit that reminds us over and over again that we are God's beloved ones: "Positively, the freedom given us by the gift of God's love in the Holy Spirit empowers us, so that we can share that same gift with others. God became open to us and available to us in the gift of the Messiah Jesus. So are we to open ourselves to the world, make ourselves available to each other . . . freed from the need to be closed and self-protective because of the absolute affirmation given by God's gift of love, we can finally answer yes to the other as other, the neighbor whom we encounter every day."[34]

The apostle Paul tells us that this same Holy Spirit equips believers with spiritual gifts in order to build up the church, the body of Christ, to play its part in the world.[35] These gifts open us to the experience of God's power in our lives and relationships within the church. They exist primarily, however, as the means by which the church is equipped to be a powerful agent in the world. While the exercise of these gifts may fulfill us as ministering disciples we must be alert that they are always to be directed beyond the church toward the needs of the world. Vital spiritual experiences and encounters with God can sometimes make us possessive in an addictive way and tempt us into inaction in the world. Unless we are careful, we can enjoy the spiritual life in an indulgent kind of way. Take, for instance, the gospel record of Christ's transfiguration, as Peter suggested they set up three dwellings to keep Jesus, Moses, and Elijah there with them.[36]

I suspect that you and I are just as likely to try to contain and possess spiritual experience as the disciples who saw Jesus glorified. Peter, James, and John wanted to stay on the mountaintop and enshrine their experience, no doubt planning to bask themselves in the glow of their encounter with the holy. The point of the transfiguration for those disciples, of course, was that the privilege of seeing the transfigured Christ was meant to equip them for their return to the horrors of Jesus's Easter in Jerusalem, and to lay the foundation for the truth of the resurrection. Just like the disciples, we must subjugate our experience of the holy to the rigor of the mundane and the broken. We must always strive for a

---

34. Johnson, *Faith's Freedom*, 181.
35. Cf. 1 Cor 12–14.
36. Cf. Luke 9:28–36; Matt 17:1–13; and Mark 9:2–13.

balance between the transcendent and the immanent.[37] The new life that bubbles up within us as a result of vital spiritual experiences is not for us to own; rather it is given to us so that we will have a glimpse of the future God intends and offer it to others: "The new life is not a possession. It is, simply . . . a new world of possibilities, a new future, which is to be constructed day by day. Life, after all, implies movement and growth. And perhaps this rather banal and obvious point is an indicator of what must be central for any adequate understanding of Christian spirituality."[38]

To be participants in God's unfolding redemption of creation, inaugurated in Christ and to be completely realized at the end of the age, is to recognize that we live in a time "between the times," or "now . . . and not yet." We have seen Christ's resurrected glory, but we have not yet seen the completed renewal of the world. That tension is always with us, "But as long as we are here in time and space and human history, the tension between what is and what God intends will remain."[39]

This sense of incompleteness takes its toll on Christians and only spiritual vigilance will protect one from feeling overwhelmed by the strain of living between the ages. We carry the promise in our hearts and souls, but we know the burden of a world not yet the way God intends it to become. It is in this sense that our lives must be broken and we must be ready to be given for others.[40] It is for this reason that we must know the extent to which God has gone to reclaim us, to appreciate the measure of the gift. It is only out of our deep personal gratitude that we are able to offer gifts to others; and acts of righteousness are often costly and sacrificial. The rewards of being embedded within God's purposes for all of creation do make it all worthwhile.

IN SUMMARY

The spiritual life of a Christian is shaped by the Holy Spirit in some very significant ways. Let me describe them as shifts or movements because they are developmental directions in a disciple's experience, rather than instantaneous realities. They are the movements from

37. Cunningham and Egan, *Christian Spirituality*, 19.
38. Williams, *Christian Spirituality*, 8.
39. Saliers, *Worship and Spirituality*, 108.
40. Ibid., 84.

self-centeredness to God-centeredness, from Messiah to servant, and from isolation to involvement.

An immense perspective shift accompanies the movement from feeling that humankind is at the center of the universe to knowing that the universe belongs to God and that we are in relation to God at its center. This awareness generates an audible sigh of relief and reshapes our human task. Rather than feeling guilty for our failure to resolve human dilemmas, we can shift our focus to identifying and appropriating God's resolution of those dilemmas. At the heart of this discovery we find that we stand loved and forgiven, rather than judged and doomed. Take, once more, the parable of the Waiting Father in Luke 15, in which this reality is so richly presented. As the wayward son returns home, with confession and regret in his heart, he is instead overwhelmed by the welcome of his parent. There is no need to explain his previous misdemeanor and brokenness; it is only important to rest in the parent's arms as the beloved.

Related to our accepting the truth that God is at the center of everything is our transformation from messiahs to servants. In our recognition that the death and resurrection of Christ is the crucial moment of all of history and the source of our own and our world's reconciliation with God, we are relieved of any delusion that we are responsible for redemption. Our task is merely to receive God's gift in Christ and to be followers of Christ, "hearers and doers" of *his* word. Our effectiveness in the world is subsidiary to God's activity in Christ and the redemption of all things already accomplished. We are only to be faithful servants of God, obedient to his assignment of us to participate in the activities of God's household.

The final movement that transforms us is the movement from isolation to community. As Christians we enter into the community of faith, the company of those gathered who have also realized that God is the center and have received the truth of Christ into their lives. We need never feel alone in the face of the challenges of life or be overwhelmed by the assignment given us. The work of the Holy Spirit is to equip us for our calling and to shape out of us the family of God. We join a community that is transhistorical, composed of those who have borne witness to Christ for two millennia and of those who will do so after us. We are part of a large enterprise and that communal reality gives us comfort as well as purpose.

Thus the short answer to our question, why Christian spirituality? is quite straightforward. Only Christianity addresses the needs of the whole of creation. Only Christianity offers our world the reconciliation with its creator that the atonement has provided. Only Christianity encompasses a vision large enough to envision the fulfillment of a new heaven and a new earth. Like none other, Christian spirituality makes all of these truths personal to each believer and incorporates each believer as a participant in the redeeming work of God.

11

Celtic Christianity and the Postmodern Spiritual Quest

Thomas P. Power

THESE DAYS THERE IS a fascination with things Celtic, whether in music, art, literature, or film. Family outings over the years to an annual Celtic festival in Goderich, Ontario, have reinforced for me how pervasive the interest in matters Celtic is in North America and in how eclectic a manner that interest is manifested. For, as well as the staple and obligatory musical offerings (that seemed to gravitate between high-energy and deep melancholic strains!), there were booths selling crafts, food, and books, in addition to which there were instructional sessions in blacksmithing, flower-garland making, dancing skills, instrument construction, and language acquisition. In the course of a weekend thousands of patrons attended the festival. What accounts for this revival of interest at a popular and academic level in matters Celtic in our postmodern world and why for some might this have a spiritual dimension?

BASIC QUESTIONS

This essay attempts to answer these questions by addressing the following areas:

- First, it seeks to explore whether there is, in fact, a relationship between postmodernism and Celtic Christianity, and, if there is,

- Second, if such a relationship exists, how does it tally with the historical reality of the Celtic spiritual tradition? How legitimate are the projections and assumptions made of that tradition?
- Third, in what ways can Celtic spirituality be legitimately drawn upon in the service of the church today as a means of engaging the spiritual needs of contemporary society?

POSTMODERN CONNECTIONS

It is no accident that the revival of interest in matters Celtic has occurred within the larger context of postmodern culture. There are definite points of convergence, but I contend that this tells us more about the spiritual needs of our culture than it does about Celtic spirituality. At the same time, it is clear that there are distinct emphases within the Celtic Christian tradition that flowered between the fifth and the twelfth centuries and, because of the points of convergence between it and postmodern culture, can provide the church with a useful bridge or witness to that culture.

It is important to provide a context for this interest both within and outside the church by assessing the subject in a theological, biblical, and historical context that will do justice to the tradition itself and at the same time recognize the contemporary search for spirituality evident in our culture.

While there has been a large scale rejection of traditional religion in the wider culture, this is complemented by a search for the spiritual or sacred. This need is being filled by eclectic New Age philosophies and, of relevance to our topic, ancient (neopagan) religions, such as that of the pagan Celts. A neoromantic worldview permeates the exploration of ancient religions like that of the Celts with a focus on respect for nature, coupled with a quest for a golden era predating modernity, motivated by a belief in the existence of the noble or pure Celt. Such a nostalgic worldview is drawn to the Celtic past by what it perceives as wholeness and harmony. In anthropological terms such an engagement with historic native or indigenous cultures can be seen as a means of viewing the local or particular as possessing the potential to be universal. As expressed by one writer: "Going native amounts to travelling abroad or across ethnic boundaries to find some suppressed aspect of the self valued and on public display in another land or neighborhood, which one can then bring back as theoretical or cultural critique."[1]

In this context, there are distinctive ways in which the Celtic tradition appeals to contemporary culture. Our culture is characterized by a number of distinct features that together point to a spiritual crisis and search.[2] First, these include the fact that we live in a postrationalist world where the Enlightenment confidence in reason, progress, and science no longer prevails. In this context a spirituality deriving from the Celtic world has an appeal because that culture laid stress on the imagination, the intuitive, and the nearness of the spiritual realm or the incarnational. An apparent prerational, intuitive element in Celtic spirituality thus appeals: illustrated, for example, by the interlacing and spirals in the Book of Kells (a copy of the four gospels in Latin dating to circa 800 AD), and the carefree journeying of the monks which built on pre-Christian precedents.

Second, the postmodern generation is one that articulates a sense of betrayal because it feels it will not attain the prosperity, security, and fulfillment that previous generations did. Deriving from this some see in the Celtic world either a society of intimate communities embodying security, intimacy, and reliance; or a society that, in its monastic culture, included the practice of exile, journeying, and pilgrimage that involved a risky casting oneself adrift on the world and is thus appealing to postmodern insecurities in an empathetic way.

Third, postmodern culture supports religious pluralism in that it is a pick-and-mix culture that sees the selection of whatever seems appealing from different faiths and beliefs as legitimate in the process of obtaining a spiritual identity. Celtic spirituality becomes one option in this plurality of choices that combine to constitute one's faith; in this instance, its difference, earthiness and marginality being appealing and defining features. Boundaries between doctrine and distance in historical time are not seen as barriers in this assembling of one's spiritual makeup. Because the Celts were not heavily doctrinal or theological and

---

1. Shweder, "Santa Claus on the Cross," 78.
2. For identification of these features see Walsh, "The Church in a Postmodern Age," 1–5.

saw no division between the sacred and the secular, their spirituality has an appeal on this account also. Other boundaries are also eliminated in this spiritual quest. Thus because postmodernists efface the boundary between past and present, Celtic spirituality is appropriated and brought into the present as a living, immediate experience.

Fourth, the desire for a postindividualistic, communal context to life is prominent in postmodern culture because the social dimension to existence is seen as the solution to the alienation and isolation of the self seen as a characteristic consequence of modernity. In reaction to Enlightenment claims to the attainability of universal truth, postmodernists assert that truth becomes relative and specific to the community or locality in which it is generated. (In this regard the 1999 Irish film *The Waking of Ned Devine* contains identifiable postmodern themes). Community is crucial to the process of knowing and to identity formation.[3]

The Celtic countries, both historic and contemporary, appeal to the postmodern person because they are perceived as embodying tightly knit, intimate communities which establish their own norms of truth and practice. The emphasis on family, kin, clan, or tribe is regarded as furnishing the model whereby the identity of the individual is formed and protected, and in which knowledge and truth are generated in a communal context.

The communal dimension is important also because postmodernism is suspicious of all grand narratives or stories whether these be technological confidence, capitalism, or religion itself. Rather than being the vehicles to liberation, these have, in the estimation of postmodernists, proven to be the instruments of oppression and domination. All forms or expressions of metanarratives or worldviews, therefore, are suspect because the grand claims they make are seen as contributory to oppression. Christianity is one such metanarrative of which postmodernists are dismissive. But Celtic spirituality attracts because it is not a narrowly nationalist interest emanating from the Celtic countries themselves; there is also a wide, particularly North American, interest. Such interest is even cross-denominational. These attributes serve to defend Celtic Christianity against the charge of being a totalizing metanarrative.

A fifth point of convergence between postmodernism and the Celtic tradition is culture. Even in a cultural sense, the Celtic tradition generally has a certain appeal because, firstly, it laid no claim to a domi-

---

3. Grenz, *A Primer on Postmodernism*, 168.

nant worldview, such as that on Continental Europe and Britain south of Hadrian's Wall. The Celts were, rather, victims of a Roman imperial worldview and, hence, win the sympathy of postmodernists. Conversely, those areas untouched by Roman legions, i.e. Ireland and Scotland, are lauded for surviving with their own local narratives relatively intact. In contrast, with the decline of the Roman Empire, continental Christianity became increasingly materialistic and decadent by assuming the structure of the empire it served. Culturally, therefore, the Celtic world is viewed as a local narrative which in the early centuries avoided the appropriating nature of the Roman grand narrative. In succeeding centuries the Celtic local narrative itself struggled with the British colonial metanarrative. That the Celtic view has survived serves to validate the Celtic worldview in the eyes of the postmodernist.

A second cultural element is that the Celtic Christian world attracts because it is seen as a local expression of—or even a deviation from—the universalist norms of the Christian church in the early centuries. This found expression in its apparent ecological sensitivity, its high regard for the role of women in church life, its celebration of human creativity, its sensitivity to indigenous cultures, and its lack of hierarchical structures. Thus both secularists and Christians are attracted and sympathetic to the Celtic tradition (pagan and Christian) as a local expression or narrative that deviated from or challenged a dominant worldview (whether Roman, British, or Christian).

Sixth, postmodern culture is characterized by fragmentation, reflected in a plurality of views and perspectives, and it eschews integration of the different elements in life. Yet postmodernists seek a more holistic view of life and truth with an emphasis on the affective and intuitive as a means of counterbalancing the previous Enlightenment stress on reason.[4] The quest for such wholeness is seen as an attempt to recover the spiritual dimension of life. In this context, the Celtic tradition attracts because of its holistic character in that a dualistic division between body and soul, the physical and spiritual, the eternal and the present, and the sacred and the secular did not operate. Yet a holistic view of life did not imply a bland, uniform, or homogenous emphasis. For the Celtic Christian tradition at least allowed for a diversity of expression in different areas. Communally, there were the monasteries with their diverse but inclusive populations of ascetics, married monks, and crafts-

---

4. Ibid., 14.

people. Visually, there is the Book of Kells with its spiral patterns, interlacing, and profusion of detail on pages like the Chi-Rho page (fol. 34v), where the detail for the letters of Christ's name in Greek (XPI) cannot be contained within a rigid geometric pattern. The Celtic world appeals because it can seemingly embody ambiguity and diversity in unity.

The contemporary world is one that is increasingly media-saturated, virtual, simulated, and hyperreal. One of the overriding needs of our culture is the desire for personal experience as a counterpoint to this virtual world.[5] The Celtic tradition appeals because it is perceived to provide people with the real experience that they desire in a spiritual sense. It is seen as communal, relational, experiential, and earthy, providing a real experience of getting in touch with deep spiritual needs. Unspoiled landscapes and a vibrant natural world are attractive and appealing in an elemental way and are seen to fulfill and refresh people with meaningful experiences.

Seventh, postmodernity seeks to uphold and respect the "other" by a rejection of the colonial and racist experiences of history. Instead there is an acceptance and openness to those racially or ethnically different from us. In particular, such honoring of the other should express itself in hospitality.[6] The Celtic world, both historic and contemporary, is seen as welcoming to the outsider and stranger. Hospitality was not only a Christian practice but it was also a requirement of secular law.[7] The Christian faith as practiced in the Celtic world provides us with a model of how that faith adapted to the social structure of a rural society.

In seeking to honor the "other" postmodernists would advocate the removal of the patriarchal oppression perpetuated in the institutions of society, in association with the disavowal of colonial and racist tendencies. Ancient Celtic society is viewed as one in which women had a more favorable position than in other societies (there being instances of female druids, for example). From a church perspective the Celtic Christian church is seen as one that was inclusive of women's ministry and as one that had a positive attitude towards women generally. They would point to sayings like "There is a mother's heart in the heart of

---

5. Beaudoin, *Virtual Faith*, 73–95.

6. Dyrness, *The Earth Is God's*, 103–5.

7. Bitel, *Isle of the Saints*, 194–221. For the contemporary revival of interest in hospitality, see Pohl, *Making Room*.

God" and to the women leaders of the church like Bridget and others, as exemplary of the Celtic affirmation of the feminine.

A CHRISTIAN DIMENSION

Turning more specifically to Christian considerations and attributes, despite the reservations one might have about the wider culture appropriating elements of the Celtic past in an attempt to fulfill contemporary needs, Christians need not feel uncomfortable in doing so. The legacy from Celtic Christianity is impressive both in terms of its material remains (stone high crosses, metalworking, and illuminated gospel books), all of which are a reminder of an evangelical tradition that used the physical appearance of the gospels as a tool of conversion. Aurally there is an enduring hymn tradition represented in such well-known hymns as "Be Thou My Vision" and "St. Patrick's Breastplate."

The Celtic Christian heritage is a common one for the historic churches whose origins lay in the British Isles whether Roman Catholic, Anglican, or Presbyterian. While some in these different traditions see the revival of interest in Celtic spirituality as marginal to the life and concerns of the modern church; others see it as a bridge into the culture that can be used to effect by the church. Key elements exist in the Celtic Christian legacy which orthodox Christians can feel confident upholding, while these and other elements lend themselves to articulation as an entry point into the wider contemporary culture. There are a number of examples one can choose to illustrate this potential.

First, Celtic Christians (and, indeed, their pagan forebears) saw the divine as immanent in the world. They were ever mindful and aware of God's presence especially in creation. This aspect appeals to contemporary neopagans, who also seek to project the divine into all things even the self.[8] While belief in God's immanence has been overstressed as an aspect of Celtic Christianity (to the neglect of recognizing an equal emphasis on God's transcendence, reflected in the refrain "High king of heaven" found in the hymn "Be Thou My Vision"), Christians need to give greater acknowledgement to God's presence in nature and develop a vibrant theology of creation that will be engaging to our world. There is much in Celtic spirituality that would assist in this task.

---

8. Wilkinson, "The Bewitching Charms of Neo-paganism," 59.

A second instance is church structure. The ecclesiastical structure that came to dominate the church in Ireland up to the twelfth century was one based on the monastery rather than the typical diocesan model prevalent on the continent of Western Europe. This reflected social structures, as Ireland was a decentralized society and thus the monastery integrated well into localized power bases. Also, monasteries were complex in their community structure and in the range of buildings and functions they included.[9] Some would see the church in Ireland as a separate entity, outside the mainstream of Roman control. Certainly there were differences, notably over the dating of Easter and the style of the monastic tonsure, but these were not serious enough to justify the claim of a distinct church. The church in the Celtic areas was part of the mainstream of Roman Christianity, and in no way sought to promote itself as institutionally separate.

This aspect aside, there is an accompanying belief that in contrast to the bureaucratic and centralized nature of the modern church, the church in the Celtic diaspora functioned simply without stifling structures. This dimension connects with the postmodern suspicion of all institutions, especially organized religion, as totalizing and controlling.[10] The modern charismatic and house-church movements have appropriated selective elements from the Celtic tradition in support of their functions. An example of this is documented in R. Ellis and C. Seton, *New Celts: Following Jesus into Millennium 3*, which outlines the experience of the authors' Revelation Church movement in England.[11]

A third example is the position of Celtic Christians in relation to culture. Some regard Celtic Christianity as valid because it absorbed into itself elements of pagan culture. This syncretism is seen as positive and appeals to the stress on a plurality of choices espoused by postmodern culture. It also appeals because it provides a model of cultural engagement, something that is perceived to be absent in the modern church where we typically find either of two extremes: a distancing from or nonengagement with the world leading to isolation, or a total absorption by the world resulting in compromise. The Celtic Christian experience was neither of these. Rather it accepted elements of the pagan culture and transformed them for Christ. An example of this

---

9. Sheldrake, *Living between Worlds*, chapters 2–4.
10. Beaudoin, *Virtual Faith*, 51–72.
11. Ellis and Seton, *New Celts*.

is the traditional Samhain festival, the chief source of the present-day celebration of Halloween.

The Celtic new year began on November 1 and was preceded by a festival that honored Samhain, the lord of the dead, on the last day of the old year when he would unleash the souls of the dead. Since the festival marked the passing of the harvest and warm weather and the coming of winter, darkness and decay, it was associated with human death. On the evening of the festival, the druids (pagan shamans or priests) ordered the people to put out their hearth fires in order to ward off malevolent spirits, leaving the house completely dark. People then gathered at a central place where the druid built a huge new year's bonfire of sacred oak branches and sacrificed animals, crops and possibly even human beings (usually slaves or prisoners). During the ceremonies some wore costumes of animal heads, fortunes were told and other customs were observed to either honor the dead or protect oneself from evil spirits. At the end of the ceremony parts of the fire were taken back to one's home, and one's own fire in the hearth relit from the sacred fire as the new year dawned.

Celtic Christians did not treat paganism, the druids, or the world of the spirits as either imaginary or benign. They believed in taking back the darkness and the night. Thus they gathered to praise God in a service on Samhain eve. The churches would shine in the darkness as a beacon, showing they wished to take back every piece of territory from the evil one. They loved to take places of darkness over and make them hallowed ground. This illustrates the fact that because they lacked a dualistic view of the universe, Celtic Christians had a confidence in the victory of God and their approach to culture proceeded from that vantage point.

A fourth instance of cultural sensitivity or contextualization is the Trinity. The Celts in their pagan phase often expressed the divine in terms of triads or three-headed gods or goddesses. This practice predisposed them to be receptive to the Christian doctrine of the Trinity following the arrival of the faith. It became the Celtic model for Christian community. Building on the postmodern quest for community and on the recognition of Celtic Christianity's Trinitarian emphasis, the church can engage postmodern culture by exemplifying that God seeks the establishment of community in the highest sense. The Trinity is a social entity and thus provides a relevant model of the individual in relationship.

A fifth instance relates to the offering of sacrifice (sometimes human) by the pagan Celts to their fickle, unfriendly, terrifying gods. In contrast, the Christian God was loving, sought the deliverance of his people, and did not want them to feed him with sacrifice. Rather, he sacrificed his only son for our redemption, and wanted to feed us through his body and blood. No human sacrifice was needed again; rather we are to live for God and others.[12]

The idea that a God would lay down his life for them, was awesome news for the Celts and depicts Christianity working effectively within their cultural referents for transformative effect. Thus the example of Celtic Christianity's relationship with the pagan culture it was in contact with provides a model of how the church should be in creative and transformative tension with the culture around it.

A sixth area concerns environmentalism where there are some commonalities of concern between postmodernists and Christians. Postmodernists maintain that adherence to the collective metanarratives of economism, progress, and technicism has been destructive of the world's environment. This forms part of the betrayal that this generation feels: not only are they not going to have the standard of living that previous generations had, but the legacy of earlier prosperity is industrialism and environmental disaster, making it a problem of enormous proportions, the solution to which requires the allocation of resources which otherwise might have been used to ensure the continuity of earlier living standards.

Christians feel guilty about this too as they are seen to have contributed to the destruction of nature which proceeded either from an inadequate articulation of a theology of creation or, indeed, the entire absence of such. Life on earth is fragile and there is a need to cooperate with the earth. In contrast to this destructiveness the ancient Celts are seen as environmentally conscious, in touch with nature, respectful of the created order, and as recognizing God's presence in nature. However, though Celtic Christians demonstrated sensitivity to nature, perhaps more so than their European counterparts of the time, there was nothing distinctively Celtic about appreciating God's presence in the natural world.[13]

---

12. Hunter, *The Celtic Way of Evangelism*, 83.
13. Márkus, "Rooted in the Tradition," 19–21.

CONCLUSION

Interest in Celtic Christianity in its modern revived guise encompasses within itself a mixture of contemporary concerns (originating within and without the church), and a historical dimension that embodies an apparently selective rediscovery of elements from the Celtic past. The Celtic past of the early centuries is viewed and indulged in as a golden age of innocence, simplicity, and unspoiled beauty. With all these claims being made about the Celtic world by Christians and postmodernists alike, there is a clear danger of constructing a romanticized world that is more reflective of contemporary needs and concerns than what was actually present in that world itself.

Much of the interest in Celtic Christianity deriving from the needs of postmodern culture is in many ways a construct reflecting the superimposition of these needs and their projection onto the past. There is a danger that proponents project onto the Celtic past a tableaux of their own needs which in many cases has only a superficial relationship to the actual past.

While postmodernity may be criticized for the selectivity with which it chooses certain features from the Celtic past to appropriate and while there is some deviation in the application of such a selection, nevertheless such an interest represents a crucial bridge for Christians to utilize. Such an interest is to be commended as it opens people to receiving the message of the true God. This approach finds its biblical sanction in Acts 17:16–34 where Paul acknowledges the spiritual predisposition of the Athenians but transforms it for Christ. The Celts had the same approach in their evangelizing efforts in that they affirmed the culture in which they found themselves and won it for Christ.

Celtic Christianity provides us with a rich and orthodox legacy from which we can learn much about the nature of spirituality, relationships, trust in God, and devotional practices. One can recommend exploring this spiritual tradition for the rich spiritual insights it provides as long as these are consistent with scripture. Discernment is critical but at the same time we must be open to the joy that Celtic spirituality has to offer.

12

Is Worship a Waste of a Good Sunday Morning?

Annette Brownlee

IN A CHAPTER OF her spiritual autobiography *Traveling Mercies*, Anne Lamott tells us why she makes her son, Sam, go to church. She points to some obvious reasons that have to do with parenting: she is bigger than he is, she drives and he does not, and he lives in her house. In other words, she can make him do it. But the real reason is because of what she wants to pass onto him: "I want to give him what I found in the world, which is a path and a light to see by."[1]

Lamott found the light and path she wants to pass onto her son when she stumbled into St. Andrew Presbyterian Church in Marin City, California. She was about thirty at the time, living on a houseboat, a drunk, a drug addict, probably pregnant, searching for God, but appalled by Christians. In her autobiography, she writes that the music drew her into the church: first to the doorway and no farther, always leaving just before the sermon. At that time Jesus made as much sense to her as Scientology or dowsing.[2] But the singing began to melt something stiff and rotting inside of her; it wore down the boundaries that kept her isolated, tricking her into coming back to life. Yet she still had to leave before the sermon.

Lamott learned that she was indeed pregnant with a man she hardly knew, broke, drunk, and in no position to raise a child. It was at this

1. Lamott, *Traveling Mercies*, 100.
2. Ibid., 47.

point that she reached her lowest ebb. After an abortion she drank and took pills for six nights straight and when, on the seventh, she began to bleed heavily, she was so disgusted with herself that she could not ask for help. Her fear sobered her quickly and she went to bed. After the bleeding finally stopped, she felt a presence. It was so strong she turned on the light to make sure no one was there. But she knew beyond a doubt that it was Jesus. She writes: "I thought about my life and my brilliant progressive friends, I thought about what everyone would think of me if I became a Christian, and it seemed an utterly impossible thing that simply could not be allowed to happen. I turned to the wall and said out loud, 'I would rather die.'"[3]

The sense of Jesus's presence followed her around all week. The next week she went back to church and for the first time she stayed for the sermon. It might as well have been about extraterrestrials, but the last song did something to her. "It was as if the people were singing in between the notes, weeping and joyful at the same time, and I felt like their voices *or something* was rocking me in its bosom, holding me like a scared kid, and I opened up to that feeling—and it washed over me."[4] She ran home crying, opened the door of her houseboat, stood there a moment, took a long breath, and said out loud, "All right, you can come in."[5]

The light and path that Lamott discovered—and is determined to pass onto her son—is no small thing. It is not about good morals, Christian values, or becoming spiritually awake. Lamott reached out for a life preserver thrown to a dying woman, a preserver with the name of Jesus Christ, son of the living God. He not only saved her from her downward spiral, but began to gradually transform her each day, making her new. She turns to a line of a George Herbert poem to describe Christ's power in her life:

> And here in the dust and dirt, O here,
> The lilies of his love appear.[6]

Lamott discovered this light and path in a Presbyterian church *by hovering around its worship:* "A choir of five black women and one rather Amish-looking white man making all that glorious noise, and a congre-

---

3. Ibid., 49.
4. Ibid., 50.
5. Ibid.
6. Ibid., 51.

gation of thirty people or so, radiating kindness and warmth."[7] After her conversion, she began listening to sermons, reading the Bible, and—after a year of sobriety—she was eager to receive baptism, in which she was marked as Christ's own. She found a community.

What does her insistence that her son come to church teach us about worship? In her second book of reflections on faith, *Plan B: Further Thoughts on Faith,* she is still arguing with her son about going to church. Now fourteen years old, Sam knows a thing or two about God. After all, in the first twelve years of his life, Sam and his mother probably missed church about ten times. Sam argues that he can spend time with God just as easily elsewhere as in church. His argument is one almost every parent has heard from their teenagers and every pastor has heard from their adult parishioners. The variations of the argument reflect age, geography, and income. I can worship God at the beach, cottage, cabin, golf course, with my friends, hiking, or taking it easy after working the night shift. For Sam it is hanging out with friends. His mother compromises but does not relent. She writes:

> Why do I make him go? Because I want him to. We live in bewildering, drastic times, and a little spiritual guidance never killed anyone. I think it's a fair compromise that every other week he has to come to the place that has been a tap for me: I want him to see the people who have loved me when I felt most unlovable, who have loved him since I first told them I was pregnant, even though he might not want to be with them, I want him to see their faces. He gets the most valuable things I know through osmosis. Also he has no job, no car, and no income. He needs to remain in my good graces. While he lives at my house, he has to do things my way. And there are worse things for kids than to have to spend time with people who love God. Teenagers who do not go to church are adored by God, but they don't get to meet some of the people who love God back. And learning to love back is the hardest part of being alive.[8]

She knows God can find Sam anywhere, and she knows that her son is adored by God and Christ died for her son; but it is at church that Sam gets to see people trying to love God back—and this is not such a bad thing for a fourteen-year-old to see. She first witnessed this from the doorway of St. Andrew's—hearing it in their singing and seeing it

7. Lamott, *Plan B,* 50.
8. Ibid., 195–96.

in their gathering, as they radiated kindness and warmth to one another and anyone else who stumbled in. Sam needs to see it, be a part of it, be shaped by it, and know he has a path and a light of his own by which to be lead through him the changes and chances of this world.

WORSHIP IS SEEING PEOPLE TRY TO LOVE GOD BACK

I think Anne Lamott's answer to her son is a good working definition of worship. Worship is seeing people trying to love God back. I will use it and work through it, word by word, as a way to point out basic characteristics of Christian worship. Some points are common to many kinds of worship, but my focus here is on Christian worship, as expressed in the church, what is known as the Body of Christ, and passed down through the ages. Worship that is composed—in some combination or another—of people gathering in the name of the triune God, hearing scripture read and preached, receiving baptism, bread, and wine, responding in prayers, confessions, creeds, song, dance, and—upon leaving worship—trying to live like what they did defines them. This is what the early followers of Jesus did: "They devoted themselves to the apostles' teaching and fellowship, to the breaking of bread and the prayers" (Acts 2:42). It is what Christians still do.

Finally, I will try to answer a more important question: what happens when we worship? It is one thing to know about worship from the outside (and that only goes so far) but it is another to risk showing up again and again and joining in.

WORSHIP IS PUBLIC, SHARED, AND VISIBLE

For a thankfully brief season, a group of teenage boys in my congregation took to coming to church wearing ankle-length black trenchcoats with long silver swords in decorative sheaths strapped to their thin waistlines. They considered themselves part of the Goth culture. They were perplexed as to why I would not let them continue doing this (as it was legal in southern Colorado for teenage boys to buy and carry swords). "We won't use them," they promised. But I did not relent. Not only were they scaring the two-year-olds, but they had forgotten that church is a public place. "Anyone could come in, grab one of your swords, and do something crazy," I told them.

There is private worship to be sure, but this essay focuses on public Christian worship whenever and wherever it occurs. All are welcome—the curious, the confused, the person of another faith, along with those who have been a part of that congregation since before they were born, like Sam. All are invited to join in a shared service, even if that means hovering by the door and leaving before the sermon. We skip by this first characteristic of worship; but even this obvious description begins to tell us what is going on. All people are created in God's image. Christ died on the cross to draw the whole world to himself. Worship is public in response to God's universal reach. It is also public because that reach is available to all.

Worship is *shared* and must be shared. Why? There is no secret knowledge given to some and not to others. No secret handshakes or insider trading. The early church struggled with this in the form of gnosticism, that is, secret knowledge given to some and not others. But the church rejected this teaching, claiming instead that everything we need to know about God is passed down publicly from generation to generation, beginning with the apostles. Given that God's son died for all, anyone can come, listen to the same words, hear the same scripture, sing the same songs and hymns and, if they so choose, prepare to be baptized and receive the Eucharist. Everyone can pray in whatever words their hearts can muster or in the words of shared prayers.

This means that worship must, to some degree, be *ordered and repetitious*. It is hard for a group of people to join together in something if it changes every week. We would spend all of our time trying to figure out what is going on, rather than letting the words, rhythm and music point us toward what is beyond it. Imagine if, at the start of each Blue Jays game, *O Canada* was sung in a different rhythm. It would be interesting, perhaps. It would be novel, but it would be very hard to sing together. We would end up listening to a performance rather than joining in. It would not feel like baseball. Worship is like that.

A third characteristic of this first descriptor of worship is that it is *visible*. But that does not mean it is visible for us to observe as spectators, as we might watch that Blue Jays game or a DVD. Rather it means that our worship is a visible act in the world, in time and space, pointing to God, who is worthy of our worship. Over five hundred years ago, Martin

Luther posed this question about the church: "how can a poor, confused person tell where a Christian holy people are to be found in the world?"[9] His answer still holds today: it is where we can see it. Our worship is shared, public, and visible—so people can show up, check it out, join in, and say: "So that's what this church thing is about." A lot of time has passed since Luther asked that question and the world has yet to run out of confused people. Worship needs to be recognizable.

After Jesus's resurrection, his disciples ask him to tell them when he is going to restore the kingdom of Israel. But he says he cannot give them a timeline because that is on a need-to-know basis only. But then he tells them something else, something they have not bothered to ask about: what *their* role will be in God's need-to-know timeline: "you will receive power when the Holy Spirit has come upon you; and you will be my witnesses in Jerusalem, in all Judea and Samaria, and to the ends of the earth" (Acts 1:8). They were to witness to what they had seen, heard, and been taught; they were to share how they lived with Jesus, were loved by him, and how they were changed by him. Such witness was in their manner of living and loving, by what they said and taught, and by how they worshiped. Why? Because they were the only ones who got to do all these things with Christ and he needs them to pass it on.

Public, shared worship points to its center: God, who is invisible but has made himself visible to us in various ways, most fully and importantly in Jesus Christ. We need the world of sense, sight, and touch to point and lead to what is beyond this time-bound life: "by love made visible, we are caught up to the Invisible Love."[10] The visible, audible, tangible worship of the church is what drew in Anne Lamott, and pointed beyond itself, to what she could sense between the notes of the congregation's song: something holding her like a scared kid. Worship, public, visible and shared is seeing people try to love God back.

WORSHIP IS COMMUNAL

When are we most fully human? That is, when are we most fully the creatures God created us to be? In Genesis we read: "God created humankind in his image, in the image of God he created them; male and

---

9. Luther, "On the Councils and the Church," 148.
10. Underhill, *Worship*, 70.

female he created them" (Gen 1:27). Pay attention to the punctuation. We are most like God not when we are alone but as we struggle to be together, male and female, with people like us and driving-us-crazy different from us. We are most fully human when we are in community, with others, as difficult as that can be (which is most of the time). This passage from Genesis is a two-way street; it can be read backwards as well as forwards. If we are most like God when we are in relationship, this also means that way, way down deep God is relational. To the question, "When are we most fully human?" the church has a simple, yet hard answer: God is primarily relational, the Father loving the Son, the Holy Spirit joined to them, and thus we are created by God to find our true being in communion. Jesus says: "As the Father has loved me, so I have loved you; abide in my love." And then he adds the hardest part: "This is my commandment, that you love one another as I have loved you" (John 15:9, 12). So we worship together, across generations and cultures, with people that annoy us, do not act like us, sit in our seat, or let their kids kick the back of our pew.

Frequently it is impossible to tell that the church is supposed to be more than a group of people trying to get along. Jesus tells his disciples that others will know they are his followers by how they love one another (John 13:35). Given that most of the time we do such a bad job of loving one another, let alone our enemies, is it any wonder that most people sleep late on Sunday mornings? But the church holds onto the hope that it is more than a dysfunctional family or social group, like a knitting or investment club. The Bible describes how we are all in one big club, a club in which everyone in the world has already been invited to be a member. But that club is not a social group or twelve step program, but a living, breathing body. The Bible gives us two versions of creation, and the second one describes the deep connection between woman and man as coming from a drastic kind of operation, with God as the surgeon. God anesthetizes Adam, the human being, extracts a rib and with it forms a woman, Eve. Women and men share bone and flesh. We are stuck with each other.

Whatever you think of this description the same kind of surgery is used to describe what the church is supposed to be. God let his Son be killed on a cross, then took his broken, bleeding body and in it formed a new humanity, the one we were created for in the first place.[11] God has

---

11. See Secor, *Richard Hooker on Anglican Faith and Worship*, 212.

incorporated all of us into Christ's body. That means that Jesus is the head, bones, flesh and heart. Jesus is described in the Bible as the new Adam (among other things), that is, he is the human we were created to be. When we are in the church, his body, we are more than a club or motley group. We are part of his body. Given that he is wiser than we will ever be, despite all our impressive knowledge is it so bad that he is the head and not us? Without him we would be throwing tendons and jawbones at each other, poking out eyes and stepping on toes.

His body is also a school, a school for love. It is most like kindergarten. The church is not graduate school for the faithful: it is the place we come to when our world is a mess. It is when the person we sit next to in a bible study drives us crazy with his politics and the only alto in the choir cannot stay on pitch. It is when despite our messed up lives we get it right and love our neighbor halfway around the world. In rare moments the church witnesses to what that new humanity might look like and the hope that through being in Christ's warm, messy body we might attain it.

The book of Revelation gives a lengthy description of this new humanity, a vision which has been given to John. (If you have read it, you know he could not have made this stuff up!) Much to the disappointment of outdoor enthusiasts, the setting of our new humanity is not a pristine lake or a beautiful mountain top, where we can get away from it all and commune with our creator. God was constantly meeting the people of Israel on mountaintops. Jesus liked them too; so why not another one here? Probably because they are too high, and the oxygen is too thin, which means that only those who are in really good shape would get to commune with God. Rather the setting of the new humanity is a city, a vibrant, crowed city, where all the nations have streamed in (Rev 21:26). We will live our perfected humanity in a city, where cars, bikes, buses, skateboards, and motorized scooters all have to share the road. In a city you hear strange languages, and your neighbor invites you to a Chinese New Year dinner where you eat hoecake and see fat choy for the first time, even though you do not actually like oysters. It is difficult to avoid people in a city. It is difficult to be self-sufficient in a city. Worship is seeing people, lots of people, all different kinds, who do not get along, trying to love God—and one another—back.

IN WORSHIP CHRIST TAKES OUR EFFORTS AND MAKES THEM COMPLETE

To say that in worship we try to love God back is to begin to get to the heart of this description. There is no way that anything we could possibly do in worship is an adequate response to both God's infinite glory and God's willingness not only to stick with us but to redeem us, that is make us new through Christ's death and resurrection. Even Mont Saint-Michel in France or Handel's *Messiah*, two of the finest human responses to God, cannot come close. So we might as well not fool ourselves by saying that *we* worship God. Does that mean we do not even try? We skip worship and go out to brunch? To describe worship as trying to love God back is to acknowledge that something more is going on than our paltry or proud attempts. God came to Anne Lamott through the singing of a choir of five black women and one Amish-looking white man. Through their six voices something cradled her, held her and began to soften her so she could respond to God. Brunch can wait.

The church understands that as we try to worship God two thing are going on, both initiated from God's side, both having to do with our finite, all too sinful humanity and God's infinite, all too insistent love for us. The first is that God joins himself to our attempts to worship him. The risen Jesus reaches down, takes what we offer, and joins it to himself. Jesus is our mediator here. Jesus is the leader of our worship, its chief preacher, head choirmaster, high priest, lead prayer, and director of the Sunday school. He lifts us up out of ourselves to participate in the very life and communion of Father, Son, and Holy Spirit—the life of communion for which we were created, male and female, in his image.[12] Christ meets us in worship, as he met Lamott, and does for us what we cannot do: make an adequate response to God. This is what Jesus did on the cross and continues to do now that he sits at the right hand of the Father.

Scripture names all the things Jesus does for us so we can worship him. He is like a father who gives his child money so she can buy him a Christmas present. Who thinks that the pair of socks with reindeer on them—which he does not need and he has actually paid for—is the most wonderful thing he has ever received, simply because his daughter picked it out for him. Jesus teaches us to pray, he prays in us, and he prays on our behalf. When his disciples ask him to teach them to

---

12. Torrance, *Worship, Community & the Triune God of Grace*, 43–68.

pray, he keeps it clear and simple. He teaches them a prayer that covers all the bases and is one that they can remember. It is the Lord's Prayer and many of us know it as well. Secondly, Jesus knows far better than we do that our inability to pray to God is not primarily about lack of education. So God does our praying for us and in us. The Holy Spirit takes our "I- don't-know-what-I'm-doing-but-here-I-am" attempts to pray and makes something semi-coherent out of them (Rom 8:26–27). The Holy Spirit prays in us. Finally, Jesus prays on our behalf. After he came alive from the tomb, spent time with his disbelieving disciples, then went back to be with his Father, he has kept up his praying for the world (Rom 8:35; Heb 7:25). He does not let us go it alone. Jesus teaches us to pray, he prays in us and he prays on our behalf.

The first assistance God gives us as we try to worship him is Christ's willingness to join himself to our paltry efforts and lift them and us to participate in the very life of God, Father, Son and Holy Spirit. The second is that God provides us with the ingredients or elements, to center our worship of him around the things we lift to him, trusting that Christ will reach down to receive them. God makes it easy, very easy for they are all found in our kitchen: water for baptism, bread and wine for Communion, and oil for anointing. Joined with songs, dance and hymns, Scripture, prayers, children, teens, men and women, and maybe some candles and flowers, coffee and casseroles—everything God gives us to worship him is a part of our daily lives. Why? We are made in God's image in and through being creatures bound in time and space and not despite of or in defiance of it.[13] In worship God provides us with the means to worship him and those means come from being human beings and not disembodied spirits. But—and here is the part we do not like to admit—it is Jesus who has changed our humanity from a sinkhole in the road to worshipping him into a uncongested highway so that we can worship him completely. He can do this because Jesus, who is fully God, the creator, and not us, became fully human like us as well.

The church calls this the incarnation, i.e. in the flesh. What it means is that, because he had become a human, when Jesus died, went into the tomb, was resurrected and came out into the sunlight of Easter morning, he took us with him from death to new life, all of us, from humanity's most horrible to most noble intentions. The one who gives us life in the first place gives us a second chance at that life. But that chance is Jesus.

---

13. Underhill, *Worship*, 45.

God has made him a kind of two for one deal. If we want to become who God created us to be, people who live in communion with one another and God, then we follow Jesus. He is our path, the light at our feet. If we follow him, where does the path lead to? Surprise! It leads to him, life with God. Jesus is both the road and the destination.[14] This is true of all of life including worship. When we take the very human things we use to worship God, bread, wine, water, songs, the Bible, when Jesus receives them they become so much more. Why? Because in Christ our humanity has become so much more. Christ takes hold of, redeems, and consecrates the life God has given to us.[15]

We see this marvelous double movement each time we participate in the Eucharist or Holy Communion. In the back of the church on a table is a box of bread of some kind, some wine, and maybe some water. The bread and wine have been made with human hands from wheat and grapes from God's creation. An old man in the congregation, or maybe a parent holding his two-year-old, or a couple just married, or two self-conscious teenagers, will take these up to those setting the table in the front of the church. The table is the place where we will be told the story of the meal Jesus had with his disciples the night before he died. We tell it every week, even though we know it by heart, because we keep forgetting who we are. At that table, right before he was arrested and crucified, Jesus took bread, broke it gave it to his disciples and said: "Take, eat; this is my body." Then he took a cup of wine and said: "this is my blood" and passed it around (Matt 26:26–28). Finally, he told his disciples to continue doing it to remember him. That each time they did it he would show up. So bread and wine from our kitchens becomes his body and blood. We offer him these daily elements of our finite lives and he reaches down, receives them and in his crucified hands they become more, more than the most magnificent human effort could ever achieve. That is why we can try to love God back in worship: God makes it possible. Worship is seeing people try to love God back.

---

14. Augustine, *On Christian Teaching*, 61.
15. Underhill, *Worship*, 45.

WORSHIP IS NOT ABOUT US

The church claims that we cannot describe God without talking about love; and more importantly we only discern the true nature of love by learning about and living in God's love. The Bible defines love for us: "In this is love, not that we loved God but that he loved us and sent his Son..." (1 John 4:10). The Bible goes into more detail about the nature of love *only* after it has first established love's starting point: God loved us first and sent us his Son. In the passage from 1 Corinthians, the one we often hear at weddings, Paul writes: "Love is patient; love is kind ... it bears all things, believes all things, hopes all things, endures all things" (1 Cor 13:4, 7)—all of it is true only because God is patient, God is kind, God bears all things, hopes all things, and endures all things, including his self-satisfied children and the horrors they inflict on one another and this planet.

We are made in the image of God who is love. We are in that image only as we are in community, male and female, in order that we can learn to love. Because God is love it follows that we are most fully human, that is, most like him, when our lives are shaped by a love that bears all things, hopes all things, and endures all things. This means that our lives and our humanity are not about us. Let me repeat that: our lives and our humanity are not about us.

Likewise, worship is not about us, getting a spiritual high, or getting our tanks filled for the tough week ahead. It is certainly not about getting a little spirituality to round out our lives or securing some basic moral teaching for our children—as if that is all they need to get through life. Worship is about the action God took in light of the mess we have made of the life God gave us. It is about receiving a life preserver thrown to humanity which is sinking in the leaky vessel we have constructed to navigate this world. It is about knowing that without it we are sunk and that we are way beyond having any right to ask God for it. Worship is about God's decision to throw us this life preserver anyway: this is love, not that we loved God but that he loved us first and sent us his son. It is about saying thank you. Thank you for doing this and that, thank you for putting up with us, thank you for bothering, and I love you.

Somewhere in most churches there is a cross. If you enter a church where there is not a cross you are wise to see that as a kind of red flag: they are not telling you the whole truth, either about God or love. Love gives itself away and absorbs the costs so it can give itself away freely.

Why is this a nonnegotiable characteristic of love? Because that is what God did and God is love.

Jesus is that costly love because he was willing to go to where he didn't belong. Jesus was present at the creation of the world and yet he was willing to descend into the mess we had made of it. Jesus is eternal and yet was willing to be born of a human mother into the kind of life meant only for God's creatures. Jesus is and can only be perfect love and yet he was willing to be hated, misunderstood, gossiped about, and killed for crimes he did not commit. Why? So he could give us what God wanted us to have in the first place: life together with him. Christians have acknowledged for centuries that Jesus became what we are, so we could become what he is, life in communion with Father, Son, and Holy Spirit. He descends into this mess and throws us a life preserver, sets us on dry ground and says, "Come, follow me." The life preserver is not a principle, or a set of rules or an instruction book; it is not a technique for breathing or living simply—as if the mess we have made of this world and our lives can be straightened out with a few adjustments. We need a life preserver, not a chiropractor, and that preserver is the author of life himself—Jesus Christ. He absorbs the price of God's love so he can give it to us without charge, since we could never afford it. And thus we may become the people God created us to be in the first place.

One of the reasons Anne Lamott's story is so compelling is that we do not expect it from a person like her. She is an outside-of-the-box, countercultural artist with dreadlocks and strange friends. She swears and yells at her son. But she is also a Christian and happy to tell everyone. She is willing to talk about Jesus. She is even willing to admit that she is a Presbyterian. Being a Christian is countercultural. Our Western world wants us to believe that we are most fully human when we are in control of our lives, despite the obvious fact that we have created a world of utter and dizzying confusion. It wants us to believe that we are in control of where we are going and in control of how we are going to get there despite what life throws at us. The Christian begins with the life preserver God throws us and somehow admits that he or she needs Jesus Christ to keep from sinking. Sometimes we sink into chaos and despair, we can cry as Lamott and the psalmist did "Save me, O God, for the waters have come up to my neck" (Ps 69:1). Many of us are lucky enough not to know that kind of downward spiral. But still we are in the mud. Perhaps we do not feel as if it is literally up to our necks, but we find that we cannot wipe such persistent mud off our shoes, so we track into the kitchen, the bedroom, the political process, the economy, the rainforest, and everywhere we go. On our own we cannot love and live as we were created to do, that is, to love God and our neighbor with a costly not-about-me love. We blow it, nations blow it, and whole areas of the world blow it. And the cost is unconscionable: in sorrow, poverty, violence, greed, global warming, and war.

Many of us in the West are lucky. We have nice cars and nice kids. We are stressed but we manage. It is easy to avoid the truth that we are way off the mark from the kind of life God has in mind for us. We cannot even imagine what that life would look like and perhaps, saddest of all, is that we do not know that we cannot imagine it. Because we do not, it is harder to know how much we need Jesus. Maybe the only good thing about being a Haitian, especially after the destructive earthquake of 2010, is that they do not fool themselves into thinking that this is what God had in mind. What does this have to do with love? Because love of neighbor and love of God cannot be decoupled. Worship is trying to see what it looks like to love God back and then practicing it by loving our neighbor.

WORSHIP IS A RESPONSE TO WHAT GOD HAS DONE AND WHAT GOD IS DOING

One danger of hanging out in church a lot is that we can begin to think that God is easily available. This is similar to when people claim that they can worship God on the ski slope or couch. (There never seems to be much recognition that any effort might be involved.) If worship has to do with loving God back, that is, it is our response to what God has *first* done, we might be curious about what kind of response characterizes our worship of this kind of God. That question should begin to make us feel uneasy. The only way we can even think about worshipping God may be by remembering that the risen Jesus takes what we offer—our prayers, love, songs, our ears, hearts and minds—and does what we cannot do, which is to lift them and us into God's presence. If we acknowledge the length Christ went to save us from ourselves and the mess we have made of the world, then we must answer like this. Our response to God's complete offering of Jesus Christ for us and this world has to be as complete as we can possibly make it. By "complete" I mean that we offer the best of the human spirit, we offer the worst of the human spirit, and we offer ourselves—every bit of us. In other words, we risk losing ourselves in the costly love of God that saved us in the first place.

Christians, despite believing in miracles and an unseen God, have always been logical. If God thinks so highly of our humanity that God is willing to redeem it and Jesus is willing to put it on, then to show our appreciation we would do well to raise our estimation of it. We can begin by trusting that God wants us to respond to him through it and not in spite of it. Music, art, dance, poetry, babies, cakes, buildings, flowers, friendships, money, hospitals, clinics, soup kitchens, senior housing—since God created the world he gets to decide how it works. He created it to reflect his splendor and to be a vehicle that points beyond itself to the one who made it. So God is happy when we use all the cool stuff about being human to point to him. People used to be good at this. If they hadn't been, we would not have Michelangelo's *David* or the African American spiritual "Swing Low, Sweet Chariot." But lately it seems to cost too much in terms of time, money, creativity, or sheer effort. I never knew how to respond to a woman who explained to me that her family was too busy to spend an hour trying to love God back with others on Sunday morning and then *in the same conversation* told me that she had driven four hours to get her hair done and have lunch. We can begin to worship God by giving him some of our time simply because God is worthy of it and for no other reason. We waste time with people we love.[16] Teenagers spend hours hanging out with their friends, in their rooms, online, or at the mall. If we ask them what they did, the answer is the same in every language, "Oh, nothing." When we spend time with people we love, we do not ask what we got out of it, or whether it was meaningful. We do not keep looking at our watches. Worship is supposed to be like that.

Second, in worship we give God the worst of the human spirit. Christians call this confession. In some churches it is not very popular to get on our knees and say out loud to God, so that others can hear us, that we spoiled everything he gave us. Somehow it is not affirming—as if all we need is a little boost to our self-esteem. One reason we do not want to confess our sins—things done and left undone—is that we do not want

16. Marva Dawn develops a liturgical theology of "waste" in Dawn, *A Royal Waste of Time.*

God nosing around our lives. We do not want the church or anyone handing us a ruler and saying "Here, measure your life by this." But is that so odd? I am sure Anne Lamott did not say to herself as a child, "When I grow up, I want to be drunk and pregnant without wanting to raise a child." Or how many of us thought when we were kids, "When I grow up, I want the U.S. to enter an economic meltdown so I can lose my job in Halifax." Or, "When I grow up, I think it would be all right if a million people in Haiti spent over a year living in crummy tents while I enjoy my three-car garage." If we do not want these things, is it such a stretch to acknowledge that God does not want them either? Sin is missing the mark on what God wants for the world he created: life in union with him and each other. We miss that mark every day, and the world suffers for it. Why would we want to keep the hardest parts of our lives to ourselves? To respond to God's self-offering is to respond as completely as we can. This means confession through giving up the game, telling God that we blew it by his measure, not just ours, so he can give us a full measure of his mercy. Do not worry, Jesus says, I already know what to do with this mess. (But try not to do it again.)

Third, and this is the hardest, we respond to what God has done by offering ourselves as completely as we can. Here I am, God; use me. Maybe this only makes sense if we believe that God has something he is doing, which he can plug us into as the world keeps on acting as if we were in charge. If Jesus throws us a life preserver, sets us on dry ground, and then says, "Come, follow me," we can be pretty sure he is going somewhere. But where? The church describes this as mission: what God is doing in the world now, right now. Paul explains this plan in surprisingly clear language in his letter to the Ephesians. God is continuing to gather up the whole world—planets, people, plants, animals, in the outstretched arms of Jesus Christ. Somehow it all fits, and that is partly because he has transplanted all of us to his body. At the end of worship services churches say in some way or another, "Go in peace to love and serve the Lord." Or in other words, the worship has ended, now get to work.

I know people who are afraid to come to church because they worry that if they do, God will send them to Africa or make them become a nun. That could happen, but it is more likely that God will ask us to complain less, because we are really very blessed. Or show some patience with the person in line in front of us at the grocery store.

A student came to me to complain about being a Christian. "There are a lot of days I wish I wasn't," she said, "because then I wouldn't have to forgive my mother." This will be no easy task. When she was ten, her mother inexplicably resigned from doing what mothers or fathers are supposed to do. She stopped cooking dinner or going shopping. So my student picked up the reins as mom lay on the couch. For the next eight years, each evening she made a dinner of sorts for her family of six, and in the morning she packed her little brothers' lunches. Now, my student cannot forgive her mother yet, and who knows if she will ever be able? But—and this is what it means to follow Jesus—she knows that she cannot explain herself out of the need to. In other words, she cannot justify herself. What she can do and is doing is to continue to let Jesus love her, even though she does not feel very lovable, and continue to let him recreate her day by day into a new person and continue to follow him, even though she wishes she could skip the hard parts.

In response to what God has done for us and what is God is still doing in the world, we offer him ourselves as completely as possible. Here I am; use me. Not just when we have a crisis (as if God were some kind of emergency room), not when it is convenient and fits into our schedule. These days there are not many spare hours in our week, are there? But true worship means that God gets first dibs. We give him the fanciest fruit, the cream off the top, and not just the leftovers in the back of the fridge.

WORSHIP IS EASY. LOVING IS HARD

An obvious omission of this essay so far is this simple fact: church is often lousy, both the worship services and the people. Although worship is my oxygen, this truth has not eluded me or my family. My kids have been dealt two parents who are both clergy, and their childhood has been church and more church. One afternoon when our son was about seven and still too small to sit in the front seat of the car, a hesitant voice came from the back as we drove: "Mom, I don't want to hurt your feelings, but if it wasn't for you and Dad, I wouldn't spend nearly so much time in church." Church services can seem boring or irrelevant, and people wonder what they are supposed to get out of them. Church is filled with people just like us, who are petty, jealous, and stingy; they argue with each other and are oblivious to God's incredible splendor and mercy that spills out everywhere. "Isaac," I told my son, "I feel the same way a lot of the time." There is a lot to be said about these complaints. It is incredibly easy to justify showing up just at Christmas and Easter or not at all.

But such complaints do not get us off the hook. The point is that coming to church is relatively easy—the problem is that we do not want to, cannot be bothered, or do not think it is worth it. All this would be all right if life was not hard, or if learning to love was not hard, or if we could learn to love on our own, without God, without Jesus, and without our fumbling churches—these schools of love filled with sinners just like us, who make a mess of things. Getting to church and learning to be a part of a flawed community is the easy part. It is learning to love that is hard and we need to accept whatever help we can find, even if it's a mixed bag. I have a friend whose twenty-one-year-old son just lost both legs after stepping on an explosive in Afghanistan. That is hard. Forgiving a spouse who has betrayed you—that is hard. Trying to raise children in a world that has told them they have to begin to get everything right at kindergarten if they want to get ahead—that is hard if you are a parent, and even harder if you are a child.

Churches, big and small, for their human failings and shortcomings, are schools of love, where Christ is the teacher. Granted most of us seem to be flunking out, but at least we know we need to be there and have not come close to graduating. As Anne Lamott told her son, we need to be surrounded by people who are trying to love God back by loving one another. We need to see it when we have no idea how to do it in our own lives, let alone in the world. We need to know that Christ has already done it for us and knows the way. Actually getting to church is the easy part.

WHAT HAPPENS WHEN WE WORSHIP?

My favorite part of a worship service is watching people come forward to receive the blessed bread and wine. Since I usually help to lead a church service I am lucky enough to get a front row seat. Everyone comes up to the rail that surrounds the table: little kids in parents' arms, teenagers who wish they were someplace else, single mothers, couples that have been married for sixty years, and people with walkers or electric wheelchairs. Into all those outstretched hands, big, small, weathered, trembling, somebody offers blessed bread and a cup of blessed wine and with them come words that declare what they are giving them. Sometimes the words are a simple as, "The body of Christ, the bread of heaven" or, "The cup of salvation given for you." My favorite words are those attributed to Saint Augustine, which express this sense of growing into what Christ has already made us: "Become what you receive: the body of Christ, given for the world." Everyone is fed with bread, wine, or a blessing.

When we worship, we become the Body of Christ, no longer isolated individuals but cells in a warm, living body. This is a body that exists not for itself but for the world that Christ is gathering to himself. It is a body where the head and heart are thankfully not our own. What happens when we worship is that over time we become the people Jesus has already made us to be in his death and resurrection. It does not happen overnight and it probably will not happen before we die. But if we keep showing up we will get somewhere. We can hope that through the motley collection of cells God has gathered in his son's magnificent and crucified body, we become more like him.

WHAT HAPPENS IF WE DO NOT WORSHIP?

We do not get to see what trying to love God back looks like. It is not something we are probably going to recognize on our own, and it does not come naturally, like learning to sit up. We need to see it and to have it embodied so we can try to imitate it. If we do not worship we most likely will not get to see what loving God back looks like and we will not get to see what we can look like.

I heard a story on radio about a woman who came to the United States from South Korea as a young woman.[17] Her adult daughter asked her how she came to have an atypical marriage by Korean standards. By that she meant that her parents showed affection for each other. Her mother, Hee-Sook Lee, explained that in typical Korean marriages no affection is shown between husband and wife. Husband and wife do not kiss good morning or goodnight; they do not hold hands or embrace; a man will never tell his wife, "I love you." The tenderness that softens our

---

17. "Hee-Sook and Joyce Kim Lee," *StoryCorps*.

days and cements daily love does not exist. But when she came to the U.S. in 1960 as a young, single woman, she met a missionary couple, Bob and Allen Pingston, and she started going to church with them. They were in their sixties, but she could tell they were very happy. They began English-language Bible classes in their home, which Hee-Sook attended, and there *she observed their life together.* They would say, "I love you" to one another, or "Thank you," or "I'm sorry." When Barb washed dishes, her husband would stand next to her and dry them. They were smiling and happy. Hee-Sook said to herself, "I want a marriage like that." She had never heard her own father say thank you to her mother, or "I love you," or hold her mother's hand.

Hee-Sook met a young Korean man, and in 1963 they married. She said he was a typical Korean man, who expected her to treat him like he was king. He would sit in the living room, reading the paper, expecting her to bring him tea or a meal. This she did but would add, "I love you." At first he would just grunt from behind his paper, but she kept it up, and after a while he would say, "Okay." She kept practicing it and would say lovingly to her husband, "Can't you say, 'I love you too'?" After a while he did say, "I love you. I love you too." They kept practicing—hugs, kisses on the check, showing love and appreciation, and they were happy.

We need to see people trying to love God back. We need to see what it looks like, to practice it and be a part of it. As Anne Lamott told her son: "There are worse things for us to do than spend time with people who are trying to love God back." Jesus has been saying, "I love you" to us while we hide behind our laptops and expect God to fix all the problems in our life. Or, at the least, hope he will leave us alone. But God keeps it up because he loved us first and sent us his Son. He knows firsthand what he can make of us if given half a chance. That is, if we worship together, stick with it, and make it a habit. Maybe we too will learn to show appreciation and say thank you. And be happy.

13

Pastoral Perplexity

Paul Friesen

THIS SHORT ESSAY WAS invited as a pastoral perspective on Christian perplexity, especially on the other essays of this volume, essays that address the perplexities of faithful Christians. Faithful Christians are those who worship the risen Lord in the company of the rest of the saints. So this volume is not directed to those who have washed their hands of the church, or to those who are interested in Christianity as a "system" of religious ideas, or to the halfhearted.

On the one hand, the pastors and their faithful who will benefit from this book have no unique sociological profile; they have neither a standardized education nor a particular ethnic background nor a particular level in society or skill set for life. Nor are they assumed to have come from any one Christian tradition or body of churches. The faithful, on the other hand, do have a hearty and persistent desire as expressed by Saint Paul. He said, "For now we see in a mirror, dimly, but then we will see face to face. Now I know only in part; then I will know fully, even as I have been fully known" (1 Cor 13:12). In other words, "to know and be known" by Christ (a most splendid divine mystery) and by Christ's body (the greatest of human mysteries) is the goal of what we might call a "fruitful perplexity." This is also where this genuine perplexity must begin, and be nurtured. Those who learn to have their perplexities resolved by fast and easy answers are simply swerving away from Christ in the opposite direction from those who time and again claim their "perplexities" will not allow them to make any confessions of faith at all.

So what about the authentic perplexity of the faithful? At least since the twelfth century, when the Hispanic Jewish scholar Moses Maimonides first penned his Arabic *Guide for the Perplexed*, the most helpful replies that religious perplexity has evoked (in any language) have not simply offered more information. When it comes to theology (that is, the language of faith), information can do little more than fill the minds of the curious or the otherwise bored.

Knowledge in place of information is a step up. But perhaps it is true that a little knowledge is a dangerous thing. In any case, a little perplexity is most certainly not. This leads to pastoral observations about the goodness of perplexity and the offerings of those who have thought out loud about it for the benefit of those who will read this book.

This is the first observation: these essays have not been written to dispatch irksome mental distractions or to solve inconvenient intellectual problems or trivia-themed inquiries so that pastors can get bothersome laypeople off their backs and *get on* with real parish *business*. Additionally, they were not written to stare down venerable perplexities like enemies and "shoot them down with the gospel gun" (in the words of the old spiritual). To put it another way, this *Guide* is completely unlike *The Complete Idiot's Guides* or the similarly titled *For Dummies* series.

The second observation is that this *Guide* was written to honor the spiritual intentions of those in any flock who are heartily perplexed and desire illumination, and to aid their pastors to aid them. These essays were not written to declare intellectual foreclosure on dangerous thoughts. Rather, the very real and sad problem is that there are far too many comfortable conclusions—and that there is far too little perplexity—among those who confess the orthodox faith.

The virtues of perplexity are widely underrated in parish life. I am not speaking of recreational uncertainty, of those "always being instructed and can never arrive at a knowledge of the truth" (2 Tim 3:7), rightly castigated by Saint Paul. Nor am I extolling the virtues of being "confounded," something rightly dreaded in the ancient hymn we call the *Te Deum Laudamus*.[1] Nor am I speaking of the kind of belligerent bewilderment Jesus addresses all too often before and after his parables—a bewilderment that flows out of a "hardened heart," as he regularly put it.

A better picture of true perplexity is Jesus's encounter with the man immortalized as the rich young ruler, who asked about the road to eter-

---

1. Anglican Church of Canada, *The Book of Common Prayer*, 9.

nal life. When he pressed Jesus a second time, he heard that it meant selling all his possessions, giving them to the poor, and following Jesus. Many of us might recall the result in the words, "But when he heard this, he became sad, for he was very rich" (Luke 18:23). Luke feels no compulsion to satisfy our curiosity about what eventually happened to the young heir in the wake of this exchange. But the evangelist was in no doubt that the inquirer had genuine perplexity at the outset, or that the perplexed actually "got it" in the end—leading, he suggested, to further fruitful perplexity about what he ought to do once he had made a choice.

This evolution of a fruitful perplexity, through the working of the Holy Spirit, is certainly the story of the disciples as Jesus's death turned to his absence, and his absence to his resurrection, and his resurrection to his ascension, and his ascension to the birth of the church.

Genuine perplexity is ever fruitful; and so it is that as the next generations of the church passed on the faith, they passed on a hearty perplexity through the great creeds. Even after the councils of Nicaea and Constantinople the church confessed—as we still do—that the best resolution of our perplexity about Jesus being both a member of the godhead and a member of the human race was to regularly say (or better yet, sing) the poetry of the great confession—"God from God, Light from Light, true God from true God, begotten, not made . . ." What church, afraid of further perplexity (the gateway into divine mystery), would ever commit itself to such a confession?

It was the gnostics, as Rowan Williams has reminded us, who had the tighter, more insular doctrinal definitions and in the end were the less tolerant of perplexity. The catholic "family," the truly faithful, lived together and argued together on the edge of fruitful perplexity as a matter of course.[2]

This, of course, was quite a different dynamic from the one sparked by the disciples in their worst moments, and spread by the cynical inquiries of certain religious leaders, scholars, and theologians who tried to "catch Jesus in his words"; to discredit his messianic mission with cheap debating tricks. Indeed, some of these sorts of cynics are described by the authors of this collection of essays; these cynics have in fact had all the perplexity sucked out of their minds and hearts and are worse off for it. These sorts Jesus dispatched sometimes with palpable anger and sometimes by toying with the "questioners" (the insincerely perplexed)

---

2. Williams, "Does It Make Sense to Speak of Pre-Nicene Orthodoxy?" 13–15.

to the delight of the crowds. But for the truly perplexed, Jesus had plenty of time. And so do our essayists.

The key to a pastoral response to perplexity is (not surprisingly) the pastors themselves. There are several ways for us to serve the faithful with these essays; I would say the best road into the perplexity of the faithful is to consider our own perplexities first by the reading of this book. Few essays will hold thoughts most pastors have not already considered (if only in passing) at some point in their formal theological studies. But to simply sit and read and meditate upon these offerings is a wonderful way to reenter the fruitful perplexity one entered during seminary studies. It is easy to forget what a wonderfully perplexing thing faith is when honestly considered for the first time or the seventh time. Recalling this perplexity ourselves is one of the best ways we can fit ourselves for the good of our congregations, whether it is the wonderfully perplexed or the dangerously unperplexed and overperplexed in their midst.

As one reads these essays, they fall naturally into clusters. If they do not fall into precisely the same clusters for all of us, I think the clusters I propose will make some sense as pastoral starting points. It seems to me that the first cluster has to do with the heart of our tradition, the Scriptures; the second has to do with the Christian identity of faithful communities; and the third blossoms out into our various engagements with the world for which we exist as Christ's witnesses. I would suggest that the best pastoral response would be to recommend their reading in this order. On the other hand, any one of them read on its own will reward its readers.

SHOULD WE NOT SHUN PERPLEXITY WHEN WE ARE SO CLOSE TO HOME AS OUR SCRIPTURES?

Certainly we should shun unfaithfulness to our first witnesses to God our Father, our Lord Jesus Christ, and the Holy Spirit. But we should learn—or learn again—to embrace rather than circumvent what makes our scriptures the antitheses of the self-help book they are, sadly, often made out to be. The scriptures cannot be captured or boxed or labeled and dismissed; in fact they are not first the chapters of a "book" called the Bible, unless they are a book that can be eaten and drunk and lit as a torch in the dark—as the first generation of Anglican pastors and parishioners learned in the first edition (1547) of the first homily in the *First Book of Homilies*, entitled "A Fruitfull Exhortation to the reading and knowledge of holy Scripture." It goes this way:

> And there is no trueth nor doctrine necessarie for our iustification and euerlasting saluation, but that is (or may bee) drawne out of that fountaine and Well of trueth . . . And as drinke is pleasant to them that bee drie, and meate to them that be hungrie: so is the reading, hearing, searching, and studying of holy Scripture, to them that bee desirous to know GOD or themselues, and to doe his will . . . For the Scripture of GOD is the heauenly meat of our soules (Matthew 4:4), the hearing and keeping of it maketh vs blessed (Luke 11:28), sanctifieth vs (John 17:17), and maketh vs holy, it turneth our soules (Psalm 19:7–10), it is a light lanterne to our feet (Psalm 119:105), it is a sure, stedfast, and euerlasting instrument of saluation, it giueth wisedome to the humble and lowly hearts . . ."[3]

We should not shun perplexity when it comes to what the scriptures are.

Our guides in Terry Donaldson, Glen Taylor, and Ann Jervis, who pick up on the perplexity of the faithful who search the scriptures, are imbued with this very spirit. It is true, without a doubt, that there is plenty in their essays to aid pastors and those in their spiritual care when it comes to moving through initial perplexities, comprehending what the words of the witnesses said in their own days, and what they certainly still say, or seem to say, or most definitely do not say about Jesus and his words, about the "God of the Old Testament and the God of the New," and about suffering in its kinds.

But the further aid these Wycliffe faculty members provide us in our perplexity is to remind us is that they are no more mechanics than we are their apprentices and the Bible is an automobile manual. They remind us that there is such a thing as eagerly, intelligently, faithfully eating or drinking—or wilfully or opportunistically or vengefully refusing to eat or drink—our witnesses to the incarnate Christ, and through him our witnesses to the blessed and holy Trinity.

What a hearty antidote to the fundamentalisms of the right and left these three essays are! What a helpful alternative to dead conformity, on the one hand, and (on the other hand) to well-meaning Christian

---

3. Text available online: http://www.anglicanlibrary.org/homilies/bk1hom01.htm.

"strategies," "models," and "tools" that halt the best kind of perplexity in its tracks and offer mere palliatives to perplexity in place of the faithful cultivation of further fruitful perplexity. When it comes to the fundamentals of our faith that feed our souls (instead of the "systems" that starve our souls), fruitful perplexity recovers the Christian hope—not first of individual Christians, but of parishes, churches, and communities of faith. Pastors will be refreshed and their flocks fed by these essays.

WHAT SHOULD PASTORS DO WITH PERPLEXITIES AS THEY ARISE AROUND AND ABOUT OUR IDENTITY AS CHRIST'S FAITHFUL COMMUNITY?

To be sure, our identity is found in our collective relationship to Christ—the only Christ to whom the Scriptures genuinely, authoritatively, and uniquely witness. Yet the same Christ, the head of our Christian body, is best apprehended through the church, by the church, with the same fruitful perplexity that the church carries to its contemplation of the Scriptures. This is the path along which Annette Brownlee steps out along with the banner of worship, which with all its perplexities surely marks out the pilgrimage of the body of Christ as nothing else can.

In fact, given how closely intertwined worship is with the meaning of the church for her, Brownlee's chapter might just as well be called, "Why Bother with the Church?" For there really is no such thing as Christianity, one might even say—only the church. The question of the worshipping church is in fact one of the most perplexing of questions that pastors repeatedly confront. The response Brownlee offers in her wonderful reflection is perplexing itself, though genuinely so. It promises to open out into genuine spiritual growth for pastors and their churches.

It is the "glorious noise" Brownlee describes as coming from the motley crew called the church that says out loud (earnestly, not flippantly), "to hell with sociology"—says it not to sociology as a body of knowledge or a form of self-criticism, but says it to sociologically contrived, homogenous-unit Christian clubs, which take the easy way in the place of the churches about which Saint Paul enthuses. It is out of the contradictory shape of compressed humanity—complicated by antithetical cultures and genders and ages and more—worshipping in one place at one time (i.e., being loved by God and loving God in response) that fruitful perplexity draws us into communion with our maker and redeemer and with each other. It is the tragic flaw of communities bound only by affinity or blood or class that fruitful perplexity is only drained away and mystical communion rationalized.

It is out of this authentically "perplexed worship"—rather than in spite of it—that the community of faithful shapes its pilgrimage and clothes itself with doctrine, evangelism, and interreligious dialogue, as the essays of Joseph Mangina, John Bowen, and George Sumner express it.

What is doctrine, asks Joseph Mangina, but the authoritative signpost or pattern or memory of the worshipping church? Doctrine is not at all like the discipline of reciting the theorems of a science textbook, meant to be memorized for a lower-level exam. Doctrine is most certainly the action of confessing truth about God and about ourselves, but not in a way that prohibits further rewarding perplexities that come to the faithful in pursuit of divine truth. What a relief; what a liberating invitation to any pastor's congregation! An authoritative signpost, a pattern, a memory point us ahead as much as they help us comprehend our past. That doctrines do not provide tight and immediate answers and pop-up, street-view perspectives is a backhanded compliment to their salutary perplexity.

Something similar might be said about evangelism, the most battered and shamed face of the worshipping church. To give over evangelism for "use" as a technical skill or a method or a strategy for a few diocesan public-relations experts would be the easiest response to the infamous legacy of coercion and manipulation that many parishes still recall. For John Bowen, the greatest problem, in fact, has been our lack of perplexity about sharing the love of the God whose Trinitarian mystery is the hope of all evangelism. To enter into this mystery is to not close down evangelistic conversation but to open it up.

For how could the exploration and enjoyment and sharing of the mystery of the love among Father, Son, and Holy Spirit close down rather than open up the invitation of the church to those outside it? What has been so often missing, Bowen reminds us, is the notion of joy, the joy of the dance with which our maker and redeemer invites those outside of the company of the faithful into the divine life. There is no flowchart, no boxes to tick, no evangelistic tools or technologies to manage in this joyful perplexity. It is not a church with a "plan," but a church enjoying being a church.

There is in this kind of properly perplexed evangelism, a true openness to the work of God through the Holy Spirit that arises in such a community, a work rooted in the incarnation of God in the life of Jesus Christ. It is a "work" (if that is the best word for it) that does not throw up walls between the church and the rest of the world but opens up all forms of communication; a church that invites others (of whatever distinctive character or history or belief) into the joy of its company to hear its story.

But surely many will say that perplexity ends at the frontier between what we call Christianity and what we call world religions. Must truth either be anxiously enforced or shrugged off as secondary or tertiary, perhaps? This is precisely what George Sumner takes up. Is there room for genuine perplexity somewhere between genuine charity and genuine truth? This is the invitation: not a compromise between politeness and bullishness, but a full embrace of both charity and truth. It is the more fruitful, if messy way.

This way does not simplify enlightenment, but it learns to make distinctions between God's work through creation among all religions on the one hand, and the uniqueness of the universal work of Christ on the other hand. This way learns to veer away from "religious consumer purchases" made from among more or less similar "religious products," at the same time as this way is not afraid to embrace hearty statements for its singular hope in Christ in the midst of the "blessed collisions" of Christian confession with all other sorts of confession. This way recognizes that Christian confession cannot be reduced to one simple summary, not to one configuration of culture and ethics, but can be summed up in one person: Jesus Christ. This begets the very best kind of perplexity when Christianity is "compared" with other "religions," and it is the most helpful thing for pastors to recommend to their congregations.

Christian identity is too precious to let go with a sigh; Christian identity is too precious to be left uncontested and unexamined; too life giving to be stuffed into tidy little phrases lobbed at the enemy.

SURROUNDING OUR COMMUNAL IDENTITY ARE OUR VARIOUS ENGAGEMENTS WITH THE WORLD FOR WHICH WE EXIST AS CHRIST'S WITNESSES

It is inevitable that these would elicit the most disagreements and the most possibilities among Christian communities, given the derivative nature of these engagements, with their distance from our Scriptures and our identity in Christ—atheism (Ephraim Radner), spirituality (Merv Mercer), Celtic Christianity (Tom Power), international development (David Kupp), and, of course, sexuality (David Reed). There could be, of course, a long list of others to add to them, though these are certainly well chosen.

It is these issues or felt perplexities that are often the starting place of sustained reflection for those communities for whom pastors are responsible. That they are derivative does not make them unimportant but locates them in the deeper perplexities of the church.

Atheism, of all things, given its claims and the militancy of its contemporary exponents, might be seen as an open and shut case for the perplexed Christian. But that is not quite good enough for Radner, nor should it be good enough for pastors and their people. The best known of these atheists have been properly savaged for their lack of philosophical, literary, and theological intelligence by some who are perceptive, though no friends of the church.[4] But that is no reason to dismiss atheists without some perplexity of our own. In fact atheists do us a favour by making us let go of our very lack of perplexity.

This consideration begins *not* in fighting fire with fire (that is, not fighting the mindset of Enlightenment atheism with the adoption of Enlightenment Christianity—if there really could be such a thing). This consideration does begin, on the other hand, with the acceptance that God *is* and so the ordering of our experience—wounds and all—by our ad hoc "unveiling" of his character. That God is unveiled by Christ, and Christ by the Scriptures is not a claim for any one method of knowledge, nor is it a claim for a silver bullet to save us from the atheist hounds at our heels. Indeed, this "unveiling" should lead us to contemplate the incomprehensibility of God, but not the illogicality of God or the con-

---

4. See, for instance, Terry Eagleton's rollicking (and scathing) set of lectures published as *Reason, Faith & Revolution*.

clusion that *God* can mean anything. This is a fruitful beginning to the challenge of what calls itself atheism.

The turn to "spirituality" in the last few decades of Eurocentric life would seem to offer the opposite challenge; what could be more perplexing than the maze of "spiritual" rabbit trails, the murmur of unintelligible dialects before the faithful ever open their mouths? Yet Merv Mercer neither leads us on a militaristic sally into the ranks of the incoherent pagans, nor closes down the life of the spirit in favor of "objectivity." But he does offer great hope to legions of pastors weary of "Christians" who seem to know an awful lot more about, say, Buddhist forms of consciousness than about the deep and ancient streams of Christian spirituality that are their inheritance. In offering hope to pastors, he offers hope to their people.

Mercer does it by returning the life of the spirit to the life of corporate worship and confession, rather than sketching in a sort of spiritual self-fulfilment course for Christians. It is the "rhythm of redemption" he offers the perplexed, a life that radiates from the life and death and resurrection of the incarnate Christ, that catches up the truly faithful in its rhythms. It is entry into the shared life of the blessed Trinity that he offers the truly faithful. It is the Father's welcome he offers the faithful, the ones who know they are wayward children. It is a "spirituality" that restores communion with God and within the Body of Christ, and that offers healing to the world. There is nothing cut and dried about this, no dead ends or box canyons. There is no end to the joyous perplexity that such spirituality will work in the church.

Is, then, Celtic Christianity to be left in the New Age shop with crystals and dream-weavers and "Arthur and Guinevere" T-shirts? Tom Power is not in the least bit unwilling to enter the shop; to embrace the topical, one might say, in the spirit of Saint Patrick himself. He is not in the least bit unwilling to say, "yes, but," once inside, to Christians and enthusiasts gathered in odd corners of the country to remember something lost about "the God of nature and nature's God." In fact, Power reminds us that the Celtic revival reveals our losses more than it reveals the genius of the Celtic spirit. It reveals our dissatisfaction with systemic rationalism, with mass society clogging concrete highways, with "planned" journeys that are not journeys at all, with isolation in the midst of mobs, and with systems of dominance.

What then is there to say? To begin with, here is the need to say, "Thank you. We were forgetting something." To begin with, there is, actually, listening and remembering an older faith, an older faithfulness and an older church that has always been in our gift. Because wholeness, and divine immanence, and genuine, flexible communality, and the embrace of both love and sacrifice in the death and resurrection of Christ for us are precisely what we need at the tattered end of modernity. These give birth to a rather different perplexity than one meets in the faces of those who wander the streets of Glastonbury; a perplexity that leads instead into a deeper faith and faithfulness. The whole act of remembering offers a fruitful path when we are reminded by other contemporary movements about mystical truths that rouse hopes of other things increasingly forgotten.

In all our perplexity, perhaps we can at least avoid talking about sexuality? Pastors and congregations know how fruitless most exchanges on the topic are. We groan (at best) when a new horror is described, when a new survey, a new discussion guide, or a new diocesan resolution arrives—or when a complex history of exchanges on the topic is reviewed and we find that nothing whatsoever has been clarified while infinitely more passions have only been stirred. Discerning minds and charitable hearts seldom seem simultaneously to inhabit the same pastor or the same flock. We need help untangling things, not complicating things, we beg to say.

Yet David Reed (quite rightly) does not spare us knowledge of the consequences of an age of radical experimentation with sexual identities, or of things tastefully (or carelessly) left unsaid; nor does he shoot them down with a quiver full of barbed biblical texts. Instead he takes us on a tour of modern human sexuality and interprets it for us through lenses formed by faith and invites us into the reclaiming of a Christian perspective. This is no simple task as even the most conservative of Christian minds has been shaped by some of the very things it purports to reject about modern experimentation. The perplexing way is not the easiest but it is the best.

Reed takes us by the arm and steps us back to comprehend with what great things sexuality is enmeshed—personhood in the image of God (rather than personality with detachable and interchangeable components), genuine intimacy (not a technique-driven leisure activity), and community (both in present intention and future hope). That is to say, sex education resources that sound like nothing more than biological plumbing manuals are no more useful than actual plumbing manuals to those perplexed about the meaning of sexuality. The answer to the numbing of our "sexual nerves" is not highly polemical chastity rallies (which have been shown in any case to produce ephemeral results) but the reforming of our humanity in the wonderfully complex image of God.

Finally, could it be that international development has topical urgency? Certainly, it is never more the case than when highly advertised Christian charities employ public strategies indistinguishable from those of scores of free-market agencies working for the public good, in which end and means seem to have become bewilderingly detached from each other.

David Kupp gets us past the usual platitudes and rebuttals into perplexities that offer enlightenment, and with enlightenment the chance of our becoming participants in genuine international development. He unfolds for us (like a set of Russian *matryoshka* dolls) complexities within complexities: differing histories of international inequity, different stages of economic evolution, different stages of urbanization, differing models of international development, and different theological commitments when it comes to the environment. It need not immobilize the faithful, but such thoughtfulness will invite the church into greater faithfulness to its witness to the kingdom of God.

Is there a pastoral perspective on Christian perplexity? I have argued that there certainly is, and that the essays of this volume embrace it not by getting through or around perplexity so much as embracing true Christian perplexity, the clearheaded, largehearted confessional gateway into the mystery of the divine Trinity. It is this that the church, the community of the faithful, is offered. It is an invitation worth taking up.

14

Pew Perplexity

Karen Stiller

I AM A PERPLEXED CHRISTIAN. Big questions— with occasional bouts of flat-out incredulity— have been my faithful companions in faith. I do believe. With my heart. And with a pretty good part of my soul. It is my mind that has presented the occasional problem.

I am a lazy Christian. I have not wrestled enough. I have inwardly digested only so far. It has been easier to read Max Lucado than Dietrich Bonhoeffer and more cozy to curl up with a novel at the end of the day than the Thirty-Nine Articles of Religion. I had four or five false starts with C. S. Lewis's *Mere Christianity* before I finally ploughed through it—mostly to prove to my husband, an Anglican priest, that I could. He has been inching Dallas Willard's books towards me for years, but the sad truth is that theology can put me to sleep. At the urging of a scholar I respect, I gamely set out to read Leslie Newbigin's *The Gospel in a Pluralist Society*, but faltered by page thirty. It sits within sight as I write, condemning me for my neglect. I will read it though, because, as I struggled with yet another paragraph for the second time, I realized that I have been feeding my theological mind the equivalent of marshmallow fluff. Here I was grappling with prime rib and finding myself hardly up for the task.

I feel free to be so honest, because I am convinced that I am not alone in my sporadic Bible reading, my aborted attempts to read rigorous theology, and my general devotional sloppiness. It is like going to the gym. I know the benefits; I see the proof as the flab shrinks away or piles back on, but up to the very moment I turn the doorknob to walk in, I can still be talked out of it and go grab a coffee instead.

A Gallup poll of Americans—instructive because it has been one of the churchiest of countries out there—revealed fourteen percent of respondents belonged to a bible study group; and only sixteen percent of Americans said that they read the bible each day. In bible study groups I attend, we inevitably have cautious new members who have attended church for years, but do not own a bible—or if they do, they rarely read it. They slowly reveal their questions about everything from the nature of the Trinity, to why such awful things happen to nice Christian families, to why God seems like he is in such a bad mood each and every day of the Old Testament. A Canadian Ipsos-Reid poll in 2006 revealed that one in four Canadians attend church weekly. One can speculate, and I can confirm this anecdotally because I sit there too, that the majority of our Canadian church pews are filled— or depressingly half empty— with people who want to believe even more and who may or may not believe that the Bible or reading theology is relevant to that quest.

The introduction to this book issues us with the following challenge: "Reading the Bible well, therefore, requires disciplined, critically aware, and discerning interpretation." As I inwardly digested that line, I outwardly groaned. Many of us in the pew fall far short of that ideal. This is the audience for which *Guide for the Christian Perplexed* is written.

It may be something about being in my forties, but I feel like the suffering of friends and family is increasing exponentially. Cancer is diagnosed, marriages are crumbling, jobs are being lost left right and center, or so it seems. I eagerly read Ann Jervis on "The Challenge of Suffering" because suffering *is* such a huge faith challenge. If there is one question that all the Christian perplexed out there surely must ask, it is about suffering. The most mature believer among us can still bawl "Why?" to the heavens when catastrophe strikes our world, our family, or even, embarrassingly enough, our plans for the day.

It is true that to be like Christ is to eventually suffer, because any genuine attempt to do that will, at some point, cost you something. It is usually in the paying that we find pain. "Loyalty to Jesus," writes Jervis, "is at the same time disloyalty to many of society's most dearly held values."

You may find your suffering in the passing up of a questionable opportunity to make quick money because you are such a goody two shoes; it might be the invitation to a party you never receive because people think you are boring and churchy and yucky; or it might be when you die saving someone else's life because the opportunity to do so very inconveniently presents itself and you know you can do no other.

"In other words," says Jervis, "the society of those who follow Jesus does not provide for social ladder climbing, with all its material and ego benefits." No kidding. It is hard to believe that the seductive health and wealth gospel— and which of us has not wished, even for a second, that health and wealth were just around the corner— can spring from the same Bible where Jesus says, "If any want to become my followers, let them deny themselves and take up their cross and follow me" (Mark 8:34). There is a comfort in Jervis's reminder that even the earliest Christian writers "wrestled with the continued presence of suffering." After all, we wrestle yet today. Jesus is healer, but healer to a people and a world in which suffering was, and is, alive and well.

In my work as a Christian journalist, I have the privilege of hearing and telling often astonishing and moving stories. When Glenn Penner, chief executive officer of the Voice of the Martyrs, was dying of cancer, he allowed me to interview him about suffering and dying. I stood on holy ground—and then got to write about it.

Penner, whose ministry had been devoted to those who suffer for their faith all around the world— "suffering that accompanies belief in Jesus," as Jervis writes— was living in, and dying from "the sufferings that all humans know." His knowledge of suffering straddled both of Jervis's categories of suffering, and tears the walls down between the two in a powerful way.

"One of the things that has helped me through this has been working with a ministry that deals with suffering and death on a daily basis. It's a rare privilege," said Penner. His work with Christians suffering for their faith helped him cope with his suffering in his body in his dying days. He told me that he had said to God: "If those people can stay faithful to you, so can I. Help me not to dishonor you through this." Penner held on to that prayer, as he struggled to breathe, as he let go of his never-to-be-finished projects, as he sifted through his life's accomplishments and regrets. "One of the great joys for me is having people around the world who are being persecuted praying for me too. I've had the honor of meeting them. It's the fellowship of suffering," he said. Penner died just months after our interview at forty-eight years of age. It *is* a fellowship of suffering, and as Jervis points out, and as Glenn Penner lived out, "through handling in faith an experience of pain and loss we may, in fact, be being conformed to the image of Christ."

Even sex can lead to suffering. Sex is a complicated subject, as David Reed quickly points out in his chapter, "Let's Talk about Sex." It is "a complex social reality" with which "Christianity has had a checkered career." Reed outlines some of that history for us. "The Puritan bed," he writes, "achieved a surprisingly high degree of sexual intimacy and mutuality." Who knew? Being surprised by an active Puritan sex life goes to prove Reed's point that we tend to divide sex from God, when Paul—and God of course—clearly did not intend that to be the case. "For Christians," writes Reed, "sexual acts are not extraneous to one's relationship with God." I have a friend, in fact, who suggests that Christian couples pray together before they have sex, committing the act to God's glory. Honestly, I cannot picture it. But, underneath her earnest idea is something beautiful.

Reed talks about the "spheres of life," each claiming authority within "its own orbit, but cannot impose that authority beyond its own boundary." Here, I found myself dealing with marshmallow-fluff brain once again, struggling to bring the academic down to the everyday— a struggle I faced often working through this book. What I did understand was that the community of one's church can help an individual make good and healthy decisions about things like sex—but not unless that church is willing to talk about it in an open way.

One Sunday, my husband preached a sermon called "The Joy of Sex is God's Idea." There was tittering in the pews. But it was an honest sermon about the fact that we are all sexually broken and that our sex life, as part of the whole of our lives, is in need of redemption. Sex is powerful, never casual, and there are always strings attached, often invisible in the moment. But they show up later. As a mother of three growing kids, I want them to hear that.

I recently interviewed a woman who had been prostituted for many years. When I spoke with Katarina, she had been out of the life for just over two years, and carried the heavy burden with her still of the ten thousand men or so she estimated had bought her for a time. She was slowly rebuilding her life, working to help rescue victims of human trafficking, speaking in Toronto area schools in graphic language and hardcore detail so that girls and boys alike would understand what that life is really like.

Prostitution is at the far end of any talk about sex, because, of course, the experts say it has more to do with power than intercourse. But Kat said something interesting to me about her final days as a prostituted woman: "I felt that everybody had put a piece of themselves on me, and that Kat didn't even exist." Whether you sleep with three women, too many, or thousands of men, there is a little piece of you gone each time, because we are body and spirit—and we are God's. Shame shows up eventually. But thankfully, God can rebuild us. Sex is for the Christian, as Reed says "a moral and spiritual matter." I like that Reed calls the church to embody both "judgement and mercy." Maybe the judgement is for those who would hurt the most vulnerable among us with something meant to be beautiful, made careless and cruel. The mercy must be for those coming home to be restored after the damage has been done.

Redemption is, after all, what the church does best. As George Sumner points out in "Does God Condemn Non-Christians?" redemption in Jesus Christ is what sets us apart from other religions. "Christians have no reason to fear," writes Sumner, "or resist these moments of religion side by side in the bazaar: they underline the distinctiveness of the gospel offer and the accompanying need for conversion, a decisive turning of heart and mind." But for those of us who can get confused in the crowded bazaar, lured by the seductiveness of not being viewed as a narrow-minded blockhead for rattling on that Christianity is the only way, it can get confusing.

Sumner defines where the world's religions intersect, and where Christianity breaks off on a new path, the redemptive path of Jesus Christ, the One and Only. "But when we come to the point of redemption, and here alone, Christianity is in a unique position, precisely because redemption entails and requires the specific Redeemer, Jesus Christ."

My friend Kat, the former prostitute, was speaking to her daughter, a committed Christian, one day on the phone, shortly after she had escaped her life. "I didn't have a word for what I received until my daughter said, 'Mom, it's grace!'" She said to her daughter that day, "That's it!" The word *grace* became her fifty-ninth and final tattoo. Maybe we should all get the word *grace* tattooed on our necks like Kat did, because that is the distinctive, utterly unique thing that has saved our necks. "For this reason alone, and not for any virtue in us, Christianity is incomparable, and by being so, it is unique," writes Sumner.

That is fine for us, but what about everybody else? That is what most of us ordinary Christians hear, when we clumsily share that we believe Jesus is the way, if we ever do work up the nerve to actually say those words to someone who does not already believe them too. Sumner gives an answer that was new for me. That the end times—another Christian topic that us ordinary pew dwellers would rather stick needles in our eyes than talk about over coffee at work—has something to say about this. Eschatology, "the thought that these events in Jesus's life usher in the end of all things, lies not at the periphery, but at the very heart of the New Testament message. If this is so," writes Sumner, "then it follows that the claim made by Jesus must have the same universal reach for all persons, in all cultures, in all places and times. To believe that Jesus is who he claims to be is to believe that he by rights makes that same claim on all the people of the earth." To say that Jesus is not for everyone, because that is way more comfortable, is not to *give* freedom, but to deny others the unique freedom that Jesus has to offer.

Maybe I can be an evangelist after all—which seems to be what John Bowen would have me believe. "Evangelism is God's invitation for people to join the eternal dance of joy. It is as simple as that," writes Bowen. To invite someone to join in a dance is a warm and loving thing. Bowen positions evangelism for we ordinary folks as a message that takes place within the context of a respectful relationship that grows over time, based on speaking, but also listening. Ultimately it is not about my stunning unpacking of the Trinity, but about God at work and me having the occasional privilege to join in.

Once, in Saskatchewan, a new friend said to me: "If I was religious I would want to be like you. Because it doesn't show." I think that actually may have been one of the best compliments I have received—because she knew I did *not* have it all together. I was honest with her.

Years ago, my husband took a course on evangelism. The instructor, a prominent evangelist, told the class that whenever he went to the dentist, he wore a big smile on his face and was cheery with the receptionist. If she ever asked why he was so different from the subdued patients, he could tell her about Jesus. My husband, a rabble-rouser, asked "But, what if you hate going to the dentist?" Back and forth they went, all semester long. My husband received a poor grade in the course.

Some of us have believed that evangelism is like going grinning to the dentist. Bowen, with his conversations over coffee emerging naturally from growing friendships, tells a different story. The "this-is-what-I-know" story frees ordinary believers who have been touched and changed by their relationship with Jesus to speak about it.

We are a people who forget, so we need to remember the times we have felt God's presence like a friend in the room, the days when we have experienced church as a rescue crew, the moments in which we have known faith as certainty. Remembering why and how we first came to believe is a powerful bit of good news to share, after we have listened and it is our turn to speak.

But of course, the conversation we might have will probably lead to questions about Jesus, or so we might hope. At this point, we might flounder. In Terence L. Donaldson's chapter "What Can We Know of Jesus?" we find some answers.

Donaldson graciously concedes this is potentially confusing material, as he unstrings the beads of the Jesus Seminar and then unpacks, not so much what we learn about Jesus in the gospels, but how the gospels can be read, in order to learn as much as we can.

I found myself feeling, at times, the same way I do when someone rattles off the ingredients from the side of the granola box. I do not need to know about the triticale and the evaporated cane juice. I just want it to nourish me, and I want to be able to trust it. I wish it could be that easy with reading the Bible. I find the *Q*s, and now *X*s, both fascinating and troubling. I long for the ease with which some of my more confident Christian friends declare that every word, every jot and tittle is the undisputed, all-time Word of God. And if it is in red, you will want to read it twice.

But as Donaldson rightly points out, there are shelves full of books challenging the church's claim that Jesus was more than a carpenter. We need to respond intelligently. The question of how Jesus perceived himself—when did he know he was the son of God, the third person of the Trinity?—actually comes up now and then in the Bible study I am currently in. When people muster up the courage to ask these questions, it is reassuring to know there are scholars holed up somewhere trying to figure it out. But I think my Bible study friends would be even more perplexed if they read that it is possible Jesus did not perceive himself as such at all. It is not that we think he was laying in the manger, plotting his next move. But there is something about him *not* knowing, that feels off too.

Donaldson writes: "It is not necessary to assume, for example, out of a misguided loyalty to orthodox tradition, that it was part of Jesus's self-conscious agenda to generate a church that would endure for centuries after his death and resurrection, founded on the belief that he himself was 'true God from true God, begotten not made . . .'" But Donaldson also points out that the opposite is true, out of loyalty to critical scholarship, we do not need to avoid the "possibility that Jesus understood his person and mission in ways that might, under the influence of the Easter experience, have produced the kind of faith that is presupposed by the New Testament accounts as a whole." Easter always changes everything including how the gospel writers wrote their accounts. Donaldson's work reminds me that our faith need not be blind, but it might take some work to see.

Years ago, I decided to be "reconfirmed" in the United Church in which I grew up. I remember thrusting my hand up in the air when my minister at the time asked us which part of the Bible was the most important, the New or the Old Testament. "The New!" I blurted out, so sure of myself. But it was a trick question. A trick question in confirmation class!

For many of us, the Old Testament can feel like one long, awful drag, full of blood and guts and rules and rape and anger and a really irritable God. In his chapter, Glen Taylor names the difficulty many of us have reconciling the two parts of the Bible, that mean Father/nice Son dichotomy. I have never heard this disconnect framed as a potential for anti-Semitism, but it is an incredible loss to the faith story when we forget or neglect the soil from which the New Testament slowly grew.

I think this is truly a question that perplexes many Christians. Did God get a makeover between testaments? Taylor presents the Old Testament as much more than the before of a dramatic before-and-after story. It presents "what we find distasteful about ourselves and about God, things we might otherwise choose to ignore or hide." Bring on the Psalms with their misery and bewilderment, anger and pain and, eventually, worship! I find myself in them every week and am grateful to be in a liturgical tradition that forces one on me every Sunday. There is nothing like reading Ecclesiastes on a rainy Monday to know you are not alone.

Most of us have, perhaps, not wished to dash someone's head against a rock—or maybe we have. I like that Taylor does not back away from the darkest verses. His admonition to have a mind open to the "writer's agenda" and not the reader's as in the example of Micaiah, may be his most helpful point to me, the perplexed in the pew. We read to get something out of it, but Taylor reminds us to also read asking what the writer was putting into it. That takes practice. What I have come to see in the Old Testament, and what I share with my Bible study group who misguidedly look to me as a leader, is a loving God calling his people home, again and again and again. What I see in the New is the way made very clear once and for all.

Ephraim Radner's essay on "God Bless the Atheists: Faith and Antifaith Today" made me reflect on the brushes I have had with atheists, almost atheists, and the occasional atheist. None of them, thankfully, approached their arguments with the finesse of the four famous contemporary atheists Radner writes about.

At first, reading Radner's conclusion that "the main answer to modern rationalistic arguments against the Christian God, I would insist, is that of Christian *experience*," I felt let down. I wanted him to decimate Dawkins and Dennett, and halt Hitchens and Harris in their tracks. I wanted smart-sounding stuff to quote, of which there is an abundance. What Radner does, in the end, is encourage Christians to do exactly what I have done in my conversations with people who did not believe there is a God and found me perplexing for thinking otherwise. That is to speak out of my own experience with God.

Radner lays out some of the issues atheists throw at Christians to disprove their idea of a loving God, things like suffering, genocide, disasters, and so on. Then he uses the Christian's stubborn and biblical persistence in belief through it all as proof that God is real after all. Christians, "no less open to the realities of human existence—its brutalities as well as its glories—as anyone else," bring to the anguish and beauty of life, the reality of God itself.

In my work as a journalist I have interviewed believers who have gone through more than I can ever imagine and emerged with a faith stronger than I have. God showed up, and their faith was more essential than a crutch—that favorite image of faith thrown around as being only for the weak who cannot hobble through life without it. To my friends who have lost so much, it was not a crutch. It was oxygen. That is not the weakness of believing, it is the strength.

Tom Power's essay on "Celtic Christianity and the Postmodern Spiritual Quest" presents the interest of our contemporary culture with all things Celtic. In fact, the self-respecting agnostic is sometimes more comfortable with the Christianity of the ancient past than of the present. The jewelry is certainly cool. The music and dance is infectious. Who does not want to step-dance?

Power contends that even while traditional religion is rejected, there is ongoing searching for the sacred that might find a resting place in the Celtic tradition, with its perceived emphasis on wholeness and harmony, and a spirituality that is not overly doctrinal or theological, but rather earthy, even environmental.

Of course, those who reach that far back into history are always at risk of romanticizing what they see from such a far distance. Power points out that the church then did not shrink away from taking on the powers that be, even (and maybe *especially*) if they were the powers of darkness. Celtic Christianity, with its feet firmly in the ground of the culture in which it was planted, provides some kind of model for the contemporary church to engage with its own culture, and to engage with God in devotional practices that are rich and fertile. I am not sure whether identifying the roots of the interest in Celtic Christianity is a perplexing question for most people. Its appeal is clear. Power argues well that we need to dig deeper.

In "Who is My Neighbor? The Perplexities of International Development for Communities of Faith" we find another topic where we would do well to dig deeper. I am happy to say I found immediate application in this chapter for an international development project our church is mulling over. We, in the church, often fall too easily into the category of the "amateur innovators of aid projects," that David Kupp writes about. He provides an excellent framework for critical thinking on even the best intentioned projects.

A few summers ago my husband and I took our three children to live on the island of Roatan, Honduras, for six weeks. He worked alongside Anglican clergy there, helping to establish and teach at a satellite seminary. It was a good project. The kids and I fumbled our way through an English class for the forgiving and often amused crowd that gathered once a week in a neighborhood school room. It was a questionable project, but we all became good friends. I took the time to interview a Canadian woman who had lived in Roatan for years, running an outreach to women living with HIV and AIDS. There are many such women in Roatan. She told me that all Christians seem to want to do on the island is build orphanages. "Church people *love* orphanages," she said with barely concealed disgust. There are, in fact, plenty of extended families to take in children orphaned by HIV and AIDS, and this extended family reality is part of the backbone of Honduran society. Kupp uses the same example in his chapter of good ideas gone wrong.

We tend to do projects that we want to do, that fit with what we want to offer and that make us feel very good inside, instead of asking and listening to what local people want, need, and can help deliver to their own communities. Being the lazy and busy people we are, we do not want to make changes in our own lives which might make us uncomfortable, like reducing our private consumption and our ecological footprint, as Kupp explains so clearly. As he also points out, starting locally and asking the question, "Who in our neighborhoods is not experiencing the fullness of life for which Jesus came?" is a great starting place.

Years ago, I entered an International Development degree in Dalhousie University fresh from a few months in Colombia with a youth exchange program. Going in, I had all the answers. I graduated with none. Years of writing for relief and development agencies and a few eye-opening trips overseas have shown me that responding effectively to issues of poverty and oppression is perplexing indeed. Perplexing, but possible, and completely imperative.

Joseph Mangina's chapter, "Signposts in a Strange Land: Doctrine, Memory, and Christian Life 'On the Way,'" is about how we believe, more than what we believe. Doctrine, or even worse, dogma have become bad words, associated with almost legal requirements to be a Christian. I like that Mangina points out that Christianity is not alone in asserting that it contains teachings that Christians believe to be uniquely true. Go ahead and claim to have the truth, as most every other self-respecting religion does. It is a bit silly not to. Mangina helped me understand why doctrine is important and healthy—the church's living memory — that invite us all into a deeper relationship with the Jesus we know to be more than a mystery man.

Once I sat in a cafe debating the Trinity with a recent convert to the Jehovah's Witnesses. I quickly realized I was way out of my depth. My friend must have attended "How to Debunk the Trinity" classes, for she knew my doctrine far better than I did. She did not challenge my faith that day, but she did challenge my confidence in knowing why I believe what I believe, and being able to wrap words around it. Knowing even basic Christian doctrine brings us out of the warm and fuzzy, or cold and shivery, experiential side of Christianity that some of us cling to as proof of faith and into our heads a bit more—which does not make it as dry as Melba toast.

I have gradually come to view the Nicene Creed as I recite it almost every Sunday, as a joyful invitation to believe. It is not a dry husk of faith, rather it is a vessel *for* faith. Mangina's image of doctrine as a "signpost" of a Christian life carried out in community, but no substitute for actually embarking on "the Way," rings true for this traveller.

Merv Mercer's piece on "Why Christian Spirituality?" tackles one of the most pressing issues for any church today, the idea that we have bought into that church and spirituality are all about us, and not all about God. This reminds me of missional writer Alan Hirsch's observation that the church does not have a mission, but that God's mission has a church. It takes what we have become quite comfortable thinking, that it is about our comfort, our growth, our experience, and turns it and us on our heads. Mercer writes, "Each stage of a Christian's spiritual development incorporates some measure of self-emptying, a death in order that he or she be more filled and sustained by the heartbeat of God."

Most of us are not thrilled with this idea. We would prefer one big death at the end, instead of a bunch of little ones along the way. It is more comfortable to think that life in the church, for example, is about the kind of coffee I want to drink at fellowship hour, the songs I prefer to sing (and in which order), and how I feel about last week's sermon. Christian spirituality, however, moves us from selfishness to selflessness and does it out of a love for God and an experience of being loved by God and embraced and restored by his son. Standing at the cross, our heads are yanked out of our bellybuttons once and for all and then, later, when we forget again and again. "Having Jesus's work on the cross as our referential truth lifts us beyond our individualistic delusions and incorporates us into the cosmic story that is afoot." We move from isolation to community.

Community will lead us to "Is Worship a Waste of a Good Sunday Morning? " by Annette Brownlee. Referring to one of my favorite writers, Anne Lamott, Brownlee defines worship as "seeing people trying to love God back." As such, it is inherently communal, "shared and must be shared."

Brownlee names the church for what it is, warts and all, an imperfect group of people trying to love each other—like each other even!—and trying to love God. Of course, it would all be easier to just sleep in one Sunday after another than to join in this "warm, messy body." God gives us the place to worship, the desire to worship, and more than enough reason to worship. Our job is to show up. In communion, we meet at a table to hear the story of how he lived, died, and rose again for us. "We tell it every week, even though we know it by heart, because we keep forgetting who we are." We are a forgetful people who need to be brought back home. "Worship is about the action God took in light of the mess we have made of the life God gave us," writes Brownlee.

In worship, we confess, receive, are restored, and then head back out. The community is flawed, the music might stink, the preaching might be boring and sometimes way too long, and there is occasionally someone sitting beside me who smells funny. I do not like them there. But that is church. It is about saying I am sorry and thank you and use me and hearing I love you. Brownlee's chapter can re-anchor the Christian floating away from the discipline and joy of weekly worship. It anchors them well.

I know I am not alone, sitting perplexed in the pew. If those sitting beside me there dig deep enough and are, at times, able to translate the language of the academy (at times perplexing in itself!) into their own experiential awareness, they will find some answers to their perplexing questions in this volume. They should keep reading. I know I will. The theologians and scholars who are attempting to be relevant to the perplexed Christian in the pew should definitely keep writing.

15

Study Guide

J. Andrew Edwards

INTRODUCTION

As seminary students often learn during their first semester, reading theology is not a simple matter of following words on a page and soaking in raw information by osmosis. Instead, discussion is necessary to tease out various thoughts. Lectures are coupled with tutorial sessions, in order to make the material "one's own" through discussion and debate.

This is not to say that every idea about God is as good as the other. In recent years, some theologians have asserted that theological studies should be taken no less seriously than medical studies, in order to ensure *spiritual* health and well-being. It is indeed tempting, however, for the theological student to approach his or her studies with the underlying assumption that, in the final analysis, one's ideas about God are just as good as another. You have your God, I have mine and, by sharing our ideas, we may indeed develop those ideas but without challenging them. The problem with such an assumption is that it restricts theological discussion by asserting that any theological statement, as merely a subjective expression of religious "taste," does not *ultimately* matter.

For instance, it often amazes students when they hear that, for years, they have subscribed to a particular "heresy," regarding a construal of the Trinity or whether it is proper to describe Mary as the "Mother of

God." Of course, due to history's treatment of heretics, learning that one qualifies as one is a potentially threatening thought. Some respond to this discovery by minimizing the category, perceiving it as a laughable fiction from a time before the advent of modern religious toleration. Others respond with less humor (but no less of a dismissal) by countering the Christian tradition, arguing that they alone are correct and that it is an unfortunate incident of history, politics, and patriarchy that has tainted Christian "orthodoxy" into falsehoods and error. Yet both dismissals of the distinction between orthodoxy and heresy, by either lightheartedness or a hardhearted opposition, fail to acknowledge the accumulated wisdom of the centuries in which the church has grappled with the mystery of Christ and its proclamation.

Another possible response to theological discussion is its absence: complete silence. Born of a fear of being deemed "heretical," some students attempt to perform a complete abstinence from theological claims. While such a response may be appropriate in a preliminary setting (indeed it is often wiser to listen than to speak), one must eventually speak in order to make a particular claim one's own. If such issues are too great—too *perplexing*—to assert anything with finality or certainty, then we may as well avoid them altogether. In such a scenario, it is perhaps best to look at a third category between orthodoxy and heresy: heterodoxy.

It would be wrong to presume that heterodoxy must always be nothing more than a flirtation with heresy. In many cases, a postulation of heterodox belief is necessary in order to tease out the possibilities or ramifications of a certain line of thought. Given that the mystery of the triune God's revelation in Christ may not be fully comprehended *anywhere* on this side of eternity, it is a testament to that mystery that we should "test the waters" by advancing constructive claims and test their validity and coherence with our peers in the Christian body.

In many instances, heterodoxy may be perceived as a type of doctrinal purgatory, a way station through which one must travel in order to arrive back at orthodoxy itself. In other instances, one may wish to remain heterodox on issues that are legitimately up for debate. For instance, a Presbyterian may decide to hold to the traditionally Lutheran concept of the *communicatio idiomatum*, the idea that there is a full and open sharing of attributes among the divine and human natures of Christ. Such an issue does not make the Presbyterian any less of a

Christian, despite the more heterodox position within that particular tradition. Of course, such denominational heterodoxy may be construed as just another form of the temporary way station, as we work toward reconciliation of our denominational disunities here on earth and await the full and final disclosure of God's mysteries in heaven.

Ever since the Council of Jerusalem (see Acts 15 and Galatians 2), Christians have conferred together to make judgments regarding true belief and right action. Jesus himself authorizes such practice in the gospel of Matthew, asserting God's presence wherever "two or three are gathered" (Matt 18:20). It must not be overlooked that the proper context of that statement (Matt 18:15–20) has to do with practical discernment and right judgment within the Christian community.

Such is the basis for the early Christian councils, in which classic doctrinal formulations were written, such as the Nicene Creed (at the Councils of Nicaea and Constantinople in 325 and 381, respectively). Such councils are often called "ecumenical" because they involved the *whole* church, with bishops present from every region. As the church began to split, however, such ecumenism broke down and councils increasingly represented smaller constituencies with more specialized and localized interests. Yet the principle of plurality continues to entail God's presence all the way down to wherever "two or three are gathered."

Among the numerous methods for evangelical spiritual renewal proposed by the Anglican priest, John Wesley, was Christian conferencing. As one of six "means of grace," Wesley held that meeting together with fellow Christians is one of the primary ways in which God works to bring about holiness of heart and mind. Early Methodist "societies" met on a weekly basis in order to pray, study, and hold each other accountable.

It is with such a vision that this study guide has been prepared. Through prayer, study, and honest discussion with our fellow members in the body of Christ, God may indeed draw forth in us both true faith and holy living.

Paul Tillich is often quoted by marital specialists as having said that "the first duty of love is to listen." Yet the larger context of his statement provides a deeper grounding than this pithy statement alone. Listening is but the *first* task, to be followed by both self-sacrifice and forgiveness. These three elements of love are, for Tillich, what unify love with justice. In other words, in order to become right with one another and with

God, we must truly listen to one another, make ourselves vulnerable to criticism, and grant forgiveness.[1]

Therefore, as you gather with fellow Christians to discuss the chapters in this book, the following method of discussion is recommended.

First, begin with prayer. The Veni Sancte Spiritus is particularly appropriate: "Come Holy Spirit, fill the hearts of your faithful and kindle in us the fire of your love. Send forth your Spirit, and we shall be created. And, you shall renew the face of the earth. O God, who by the light of the Holy Spirit did instruct the hearts of the faithful, grant that by the same Holy Spirit we may be truly wise and ever enjoy your consolations. Through Christ our Lord. Amen."

Second, group members may get "on the same page" by answering a few preliminary questions at a basic descriptive level. Here evaluative statements may be suspended for the moment, if only to arrive at basic agreement regarding what the essay says. If evaluative statements do arise, simply take note of them and return to them later in the discussion.

Third, read the recommended passage of Scripture together. By attending to a single passage, participants may continue getting "on the same page" by looking to God's Word. Another question or two about the scripture passage will help center the group around the prophetic and apostolic witness to God in Christ.

Fourth, the group may now turn to evaluation of the essay under consideration. Questions are included here, but the group may also choose to return to observations as discussed previously under the "descriptive" rubric. The goal here is to assess the extent to and manner in which members agree with the essay. Of course, agreement is not mandatory. But the ability to listen, sacrifice one's own ego, and forgive others (as well as oneself) is paramount.

Finally, several "praxis" questions will bring the discussion to the practical level of everyday life. Such questions are by no means less serious or more relevant. On the contrary, such questions simply place a different lens on the same issue, albeit one that may be more familiar in the realm of personal and community experience.

---

1. See Tillich, *Love, Power, and Justice*, 82–86. It should be noted that the author of this study guide has some significant methodological differences with the theology of Paul Tillich. Yet the vision of Christian conferencing outlined here demands that one must even be willing to quote those theologians with whom one disagrees.

In order to make the best use of everyone's time, the group may wish to appoint a scribe whose task is to take notes throughout the session. At the close of each session, the scribe may read over those notes in order to provide a review of the territory crossed and milestones achieved. Such a record of discussion may also serve as a means for achieving consensus, although minority reports are certainly allowed. It may be best to alternate this role among the participants.

CHAPTER 1: WHAT CAN WE KNOW OF JESUS?

Description

Describe the disjunction between the Jesus of history and the Christ of faith.

Scripture: Mark 8:27–30

If someone asked you who Jesus was, what would you say? Where would you begin? Where would you end?

Evaluation

Is it necessary to get beyond what the author calls "the dark ages of theological inquiry"? Why or why not?

In his concluding remarks, Donaldson states that he has examined the historiographical process itself more than any particular portrait of Jesus. Is such attention to process important? Why or why not?

Where do you find yourself on the spectrum between minimalist (i.e., Bultmann) and inclusivist (i.e., Wright) approaches to knowledge regarding the historical Jesus?

Praxis

Among the various types of historical sources for information regarding Jesus—canonical gospel accounts, noncanonical gospels (Q, *Gospel of Thomas*), historical chronicles (Suetonius, Josephus)—how should each inform the quest to understand who Jesus was or is?

What does Jesus's identity have to do with the Christian life—from the big picture down to everyday circumstances?

CHAPTER 2: HOW CAN THE WRATHFUL GOD OF THE OLD TESTAMENT BE RECONCILED WITH THE GRACIOUS LORD OF THE NEW TESTAMENT?

Description

Who was Marcion, and why is his continuing influence problematic for Christian approaches to scripture?

Scripture: John 6:40–51

How many references to the Old Testament can you identify in this passage?

If the Father to whom Jesus refers is the same God of the Old Testament, how does one learn from this Father, as described in v. 45?

Evaluation

The author names several possible explanations of Psalm 137:9. Which explanations seem most plausible? Do either of these fall short in any way? Can you think of any additional responses to such a difficult passage?

Praxis

What passages have you found offensive in the Old Testament? How may they be considered reflective of nature and experience? Where is the good news in your response to them?

Think of a particularly "brutal" experience, whether it be your own or that of someone else. How might the Old Testament's combination of brutality and beauty help to transform your understanding of such an experience?

CHAPTER 3: THE CHALLENGE OF SUFFERING

Description

How do you understand the Pauline perspective that Christians suffer *with* or *in* Christ's suffering?

Scripture: Mark 14:3–9

Combining the simultaneous optimism and realism of the New Testament view of the world's "groaning," how then may we read Jesus's response to his disciples in this passage?

Does Jesus's response here undercut our attempts to alleviate poverty? Why or why not?

Evaluation

When has your own experience of suffering been "the inevitable accompaniment to the task of extending the reign of God"? Were you aware of this at the time? If so, did such awareness help? If not, would it have helped?

Have you ever been embarrassed by good health and happiness? Did you come to a point where you could accept it?

Praxis

Imagine a suffering that has not happened to you but could. Without minimizing its seriousness, how could you respond in a way that would be neither self-focused nor depressive? In other words, how could you respond with hope, productivity, and purpose?

How may you assist others in your faith community to discern the proper response to suffering?

CHAPTER 4: SIGNPOSTS IN A STRANGE LAND: DOCTRINE, MEMORY, AND CHRISTIAN LIFE "ON THE WAY"

Description

Why does the author spend so much time emphasizing the particularity of Israel's history and the historical person of Jesus of Nazareth?

Scripture: Jude 1:20–21

How is one's relationship to the members of the Trinity characterized in this passage? Do you find that such a characterization gets deeper as you ponder it further? Or does it become an intractable problem?

Evaluation

If the Apostles' and Nicene Creeds are maps for an adventure, where might one go? What might one encounter on such a journey? Who might journey with you?

Praxis

What doctrines are essential to your faith? Are these defined by the church or your own personal preference? Identify some practical implications of these doctrines.

Does your particular church have its own doctrinal core? What distinguishes it from other churches in your community? How does it provide witness to those beliefs? How are such doctrines reflected in worship? How does your church receive the witness of other churches in the community?

CHAPTER 5: GOD BLESS THE ATHEISTS: FAITH AND ANTIFAITH TODAY

Description

What differences are there (if any) between religious and atheistic violence?

Scripture: John 12:37–43

This passage describes how such inequity (noted earlier in Isaiah) still demands human responsibility, despite being part of the divine will. Is this fair?

Evaluation

Do you find the experience of God to be "self-authenticating"?

Through his essay, Radner performs a deconstruction of atheism, where the demand for "fairness" and a universality of knowledge of God "grasps after faith." Is this a fair portrayal of the position of atheists that you know? Can you think of any other atheistic arguments that reveal underlying Christian values or beliefs?

Praxis

What would it look like for forgiveness to be an integral part of rational discourse and public deliberation?

In conclusion, Radner discusses the "inequitably distributed experience" of God's action and presence in the world. How, where and when have you witnessed such inequity of experience?

CHAPTER 6: DOES GOD CONDEMN NON-CHRISTIANS?

Description

What components make up the series of beliefs that are distinctive to the Christian faith?

How does the author relate each of these components to non-Christians?

Scripture: John 1:1–18

What does it mean for the goal of all history and creation to be Christ and Christ alone?

Evaluation

Sumner defers the task of answering the title question of his essay, arguing that it is the wrong question to ask. Do you agree?

What is the effect on the believer of reducing faith to a consumer choice?

Praxis

How do various Christian beliefs (creation, sin, redemption, church) impact your relationship with your neighbors? Do your neighbors' beliefs impact that relationship as well (i.e. whether they are Christian or not)?

Imagine a missionary coming into your neighborhood with the good news of redemption through Christ. What habits and practices of your community would have to be rejected, retained, or transformed in order to "localize" this new religion?

CHAPTER 7: WHY EVANGELISM? BEING CAUGHT UP IN THE SWOOP OF GRACE

Description

What is the "swoop of grace"? What difference does it make to view evangelism within a "swoop of grace"?

Scripture: John 4:38

If evangelism is like farming, at what stage of the process do you see your own practice? Do you stay at the same stage with everyone? Or is your work spread out?

Evaluation

Review the questions presented in the section, "What should I say?" Which of these questions are most helpful for you in terms of evangelism?

Praxis

Are your thoughts about God the most important thing about you?

A vulnerability emerges whenever one offers to strangers an intimate look at one's personal beliefs. How may such vulnerability be seen through a distinctly Christian lens?

Where does evangelism end and discipleship begin?

Is talking the walk more difficult than walking the talk? Why or why not?

Does your church plan social events where nonmembers (or even nonbelievers) would be welcome? Does your church plan events that would appeal to nonbelievers? Do you and/or your church participate in ministries that would appeal to nonbelievers?

CHAPTER 8: WHO IS MY NEIGHBOR? THE PERPLEXITIES OF INTERNATIONAL DEVELOPMENT FOR COMMUNITIES OF FAITH

Description

What are the differences between a development worker as a "technician" and as a "facilitator"? To which model have you typically adhered?

What are some of the many variables in understanding poverty?

What are "participatory poverty assessments"?

Scripture: Matthew 7:7–12

How do you see your role in the Father's gifting of good things to his children?

Evaluation

Why is local participation and ownership of development initiatives so important?

Is the Christian tradition to blame for Western environmental complacency, as Lynn White asserts? Explain.

Praxis

How sustainable are the regular practices of your household and/or church community?

How does your congregation approach local and international missions? Is there local participation and ownership?

Do you consider the development initiatives of your church community the work of amateurs or professionals? Does this matter? What might the alternative look like?

If you could choose your own "pet project" to address one issue in your community, what would it be? How could you tackle such a problem in a way that is consistent with Kupp's vision here?

CHAPTER 9 LET'S TALK ABOUT SEX

Description

How is procreation a "symbol" of Christian hope?

What does the author mean when he states that sex is also about the people with whom we *don't* engage in intercourse?

What does the author mean when he states that mutual submission is a virtue that requires years of practice?

Scripture: Genesis 2:21–24, and Ephesians 5:21–33

What difference does it make that Eve was made of the same flesh?

Evaluation

Is the "ethic of intimacy" sufficient to guide sexual practices? Why or why not?

The author states that even sexual relationships outside the marriage norm have "limited benefits." Name some of these benefits, as well as some of the ways in which such relationships fall short.

Praxis

Name some effects of the sanitization of sexual vocabulary.

Name several groups of persons with whom the church should have a wider conversation regarding sexual practices.

How does the sexual revolution's move from moralism to morality help the church's conversation regarding sex?

CHAPTER 10: WHY CHRISTIAN SPIRITUALITY?

Description

Describe the three spiritual "movements" that Mercer describes in the last section of his essay. How have you encountered these movements in your own spiritual journey?

Scripture: John 14:16-17, 25-26; 15:26-27; 16:7-15

What is the role of the Holy Spirit in John's "Paraclete" passages?

Evaluation

Read T. S. Eliot's *Choruses from "The Rock"* (see bibliography). Does Eliot's sense of the descent of culture resonate with your own perceptions?

Eliot addresses the paradox that modern culture rejects the notion of divinity in theory, while functionally substituting "gods" (such as money or power) in God's place. Where do you see this paradox today?

Praxis

Consider the history of your faith community. Does that history play a role in its present? Is that history generally held within its memory?

Speak with those members of your faith community who can remember and tell its stories. How has your community transformed over time? What has remained constant? How may these stories shape its future?

CHAPTER 11: THE CELTIC TRADITION AND THE CONTEMPORARY SPIRITUAL QUEST

Description

What aspects of the Celtic world are appealing to postmodern sensibilities?

Scripture: Acts 2:1–21

Having read the account of the Holy Spirit among the early church at Pentecost, compare and contrast the wild goose and the dove as images of the Holy Spirit. Does one of these images speak to you more than the other? How may each image be considered scriptural?

Evaluation

The author concludes his essay with the observation that contemporary Christians must be open to Celtic spirituality while avoiding a romantic idealism. Why should such idealism be avoided? What is the value of historical realism in Christian spirituality?

How do you see the Celtic tradition's emphasis on God's presence in nature? Do you receive such an emphasis in terms gleaned from scripture, contemporary culture, or both?

Praxis

By what practices may your church community utilize the Celtic tradition to evangelize a postmodern world?

By what practices may your church community utilize the Celtic tradition to grow in discipleship and holiness?

CHAPTER 12: IS WORSHIP A WASTE OF A GOOD SUNDAY MORNING?

Description

What does Brownlee mean by saying that worship is, by and large, about seeing other Christians *try* to love God?

Why should worship be ordered and repetitious?

Scripture: Revelation 21:1–8

Which of the many images described in this passage (bride of Christ, wiping away tears, water of life, and the like) resonates with your experience of worship? Which images challenge your understanding of worship?

Evaluation

The author states that worship is easy but loving is hard. Do you agree?

How do we become the Body of Christ in and through worship? Do you understand this as an occasional event of manifestation, i.e. in the service itself, or as a process over time?

Praxis

Was there a time when you shifted from being *taken* to church by others to going on your own volition? Explain.

How may the importance of worship be shared with those who would not go otherwise?

Review the elements of your church community's worship. How does God take each effort and make it complete?

Bibliography

Achtemeier, Elizabeth. *Preaching from the Old Testament*. Louisville: Westminster John Knox, 1989.

———. *The Old Testament and the Proclamation of the Gospel*. Louisville: Westminster John Knox, 1973.

Adam, Peter. "The Trinity and Human Community." In *Grace and Truth in the Secular Age*, edited by Timothy Bradshaw, 52–65. Grand Rapids: Eerdmans, 1998.

Adams, Douglas. *The Ultimate Hitchhiker's Guide*. New York: Wings, 1996.

Algoso, Dave. "Don't Try This Abroad." *Foreign Policy*. 26 October 2010. Online: http://www.foreignpolicy.com/articles/2010/10/26/dont_try_this_abroad.

Allegro, John M. *The Sacred Mushroom and the Cross : A Study of the Nature and Origins of Christianity within the Fertility Cults of the Ancient Near East*. London: Hodder & Stoughton, 1970.

Anderson, Ray S., and Dennis B. Guernsey. *On Being Family: A Social Theology of the Family*. Grand Rapids: Eerdmans, 1985.

Anglican Church of Canada. *The Book of Common Prayer*. Toronto: Anglican Book Centre, 1962.

Atheist Bus Campaign. Website. Online: http://www.atheistbus.org.uk.

Augustine, Saint. *On Christian Teaching*. Oxford's World's Classics. Oxford: Oxford University Press, 1999.

Ayittey, George B. N. *Africa in Chaos*. New York: St. Martin's, 1998.

Barth, Karl. *Evangelical Theology: An Introduction*. Grand Rapids: Eerdmans, 1963.

———. "The Strange New World Within the Bible." In *The Word of God and the Word of Man*, 28–50. New York: Harper & Row, 1957.

Beaudoin, Tom. *Virtual Faith: The Irreverent Spiritual Quest of Generation X*. San Francisco: Jossey-Bass, 1998.

Berman, David. *A History of Atheism in Britain: From Hobbes to Russell*. London: Routledge, 1990.

Berry, Wendell. "A Secular Pilgrimage." In *Western Man and Environmental Ethics: Attitudes toward Nature and Technology*, compiled by Ian Barbour, 132–55. Addison-Wesley Series in History. Reading, MA: Addison-Wesley, 1973.

Bhatia, Pooja. "Haiti's Angry God." *New York Times*, January 14, 2010.

Bitel, Lisa M. *Isle of the Saints: Monastic Settlement in Early Ireland*. Ithaca, NY: Cornell University Press, 1990.

Bouma-Prediger, Steven. *The Greening of Theology: The Ecological Models of Rosemary Radford Ruether, Joseph Sittler, and Jürgen Moltmann*. American Academy of Religion Academy Series. Atlanta: Scholars, 1995.

Bowen, John P. *Evangelism for "Normal" People: Good News for Those Looking for a Fresh Approach*. Minneapolis: Augsburg Fortress, 2002.
Brown, Peter. *The Body and Society: Men, Women, and Sexual Renunciation in Early Christianity*. New York: Columbia University Press, 1988.
Bultmann, Rudolf. *Jesus and the Word*. New York: Scribner, 1934.
Bunting, Madeleine. "The New Atheists Loathe Religion Far Too Much to Plausibly Challenge It." *The Guardian*, May 7, 2007.
Butler, Katy. "Sex in a New Age Guise." *The Globe and Mail*, March 9, 1994.
Chambers, Robert. *Whose Reality Counts? Putting the First Last*. London: Intermediate Technology, 1997.
———. *Ideas for Development*. London: Earthscan, 2005.
Christian, Jayakumar. *God of the Empty-Handed: Poverty, Power and the Kingdom of God*. Monrovia, CA: MARC, 1999.
Christian, William A., Sr. *Doctrines of Religious Communities: A Philosophical Study*. New Haven: Yale University Press, 1987.
Clapp, Rodney. *Families at the Crossroads: Beyond Traditional and Modern Options*. Downers Grove, IL: InterVarsity, 1993.
Cobb, John B., Jr. *The Earthist Challenge to Economism: A Theological Critique of the World Bank*. Basingstoke, UK: Macmillan, 1999.
Crickmore, Mary. "Bread, Stone, or Snake? How Globalization Has Complicated the Golden Rule." *The Banner*, November 2006, 34–48.
Crossan, John Dominic. *The Historical Jesus: The Life of a Mediterranean Jewish Peasant*. San Francisco: HarperSanFrancisco, 1991.
Cunningham, Lawrence S., and Keith J. Egan, *Christian Spirituality: Themes from the Tradition*. New York: Paulist, 1996.
Dawkins, Richard. *The God Delusion*. Boston: Houghton Mifflin, 2008.
Dawn, Marva. *A Royal Waste of Time: The Splendor of Worshiping God and Being Church for the World*. Grand Rapids: Eerdmans, 1999.
Dennett, Daniel C. *Breaking the Spell: Religion as a Natural Phenomenon*. New York: Viking, 2006.
DeWitt, Calvin B. *Caring for Creation: Responsible Stewardship of God's Handiwork*. Edited by James W. Skillen and Luis E. Lugo. Grand Rapids: Baker, 1998.
Durning, Alan. "Asking How Much Is Enough." In *State of the World: 1991*, edited by Lester Brown et al, 153–69. State of the World Library. New York: Norton, 1991.
Dyrness, William A. *A Primer on Christian Worship: Where We've Been, Where We Are, Where We Can Go*. The Calvin Institute of Christian Worship Liturgical Studies Series. Grand Rapids: Eerdmans, 2009.
———. *The Earth Is God's: A Theology of American Culture*. Faith and Cultures Series. Maryknoll, NY: Orbis, 1997.
Eagleton, Terry. *Reason, Faith & Revolution: Reflections on the God Debate*. New Haven: Yale University Press, 2009.
Eden, Martyn, and David F. Wells. *The Gospel in the Modern World: A Tribute to John Stott*. Leicester, UK: Inter-Varsity, 1991.
Eliot, T. S. *Choruses from "The Rock."* In *The Complete Poems and Plays, 1909–1950*, 96–116. New York: Harcourt, Brace, 1952.
Ellis, Roger, and Chris Seton. *New Celts: Following Jesus into Millennium 3*. Eastbourne, UK: Kingsway, 1998.

Febvre, Lucien. *The Problem of Unbelief in the Sixteenth Century: The Religion of Rabelais.* Translated by Beatrice Gottlieb. Cambridge: Harvard University Press, 1985.

Fiddes, Paul S. "On Theology." In *The Cambridge Companion to C. S. Lewis,* edited by Robert MacSwain and Michael Ward, 89–104. Cambridge Companions to Religion. Cambridge: Cambridge University Press, 2010.

———. *Participating in God: A Pastoral Doctrine of the Trinity.* Louisville: Westminster John Knox, 2001.

Fields, Suzanne. "Chaste Chase." *The Washington Times* January 17, 2000.

Fletcher, Joseph. *Situation Ethics: The New Morality.* Philadelphia: Westminster, 1966.

Flew, Anthony. *God and Philosophy.* New York: Prometheus, 2005.

Force, James E., and Richard H. Popkin. *Essays on the Context, Nature, and Influence of Isaac Newton's Theology.* International Archives of the History of Ideas 129. Dordrecht: Kluwer Academic, 1990.

Fowler, Alan. *Striking a Balance: A Guide to Enhancing the Effectiveness of Non-Governmental Organisations in International Development.* London: Earthscan, 1997.

Freire, Paulo. *Pedagogy of the Oppressed.* New rev. 20th anniversary ed. New York: Continuum, 1993.

Funk, Robert W. *Honest to Jesus: Jesus for a New Millennium.* San Francisco: HarperCollins, 1996.

Funk, Robert W., Roy W. Hoover, and the Jesus Seminar, editors. *The Five Gospels: The Search for the Authentic Words of Jesus.* New York: Macmillan, 1993.

Funk, Robert W., and the Jesus Seminar, editors. *The Acts of Jesus: The Search for the Authentic Deeds of Jesus.* San Francisco: HarperSanFrancisco, 1998.

Global Footprint Network. Website. Online: http://www.footprintnetwork.org.

The Global Rich List. Online: http://www.globalrichlist.com.

Gornik, Mark R. *To Live in Peace: Biblical Faith and the Changing Inner City.* Grand Rapids: Eerdmans, 2002.

Grenz, Stanley J. *A Primer on Postmodernism.* Grand Rapids: Eerdmans, 1996.

———. *Sexual Ethics: An Evangelical Perspective.* Louisville: Westminster John Knox, 1997.

Gunton, Colin. *The One, the Three and the Many: God, Creation and the Culture of Modernity.* Cambridge : Cambridge University Press, 1993.

Hamer, Dean H. *The God Gene: How Faith Is Hardwired into Our Genes.* New York: Doubleday, 2004.

Harris, Sam. *Letter to a Christian Nation.* New York: Knopf, 2006.

———. *The End of Faith: Religion, Terror, and the Future of Reason.* New York: Norton, 2005.

Harris, Sam, and Andrew Sullivan. "Is Religion 'Built Upon Lies'?" Online: http://www.beliefnet.com/Faiths/Secular-Philosophies/Is-Religion-Built-Upon-Lies.aspx.

Hart, David Bentley. *Atheist Delusions: The Christian Revolution and its Fashionable Enemies.* New Haven: Yale University Press, 2010.

Haslam, Paul, Jessica Schafer, and Pierre Beaudet. *Introduction to International Development: Approaches, Actors and Issues.* Don Mills: Oxford University Press Canada, 2009.

Hatchett, Marion. *Sanctifying Life, Time and Space: An Introduction to Liturgical Study.* New York: Seabury,1976.

Bibliography

Hauerwas, Stanley. "Christianity: It's Not a Religion, It's an Adventure." In *The Hauerwas Reader*, edited by John Berkman and William T. Cavanaugh, 522–36. Durham, NC: Duke University Press, 2001.

"Hee-Sook and Joyce Kim Lee." *StoryCorps*. Online: http://www.storycorps.org/listen/stories/hee-sook-and-joyce-kim-lee.

Hitchens, Christopher. *God Is Not Great: How Religion Poisons Everything*. New York: Twelve, Hachette, Warner, 2007.

Houston, James M. *The Heart's Desire: Satisfying the Hunger of the Soul*. Colorado Springs: NavPress, 1996.

Hunter, George G., III. *The Celtic Way of Evangelism: How Christianity Can Reach the West . . . Again*. Nashville: Abingdon, 2000.

Israel, Jonathan I. *Radical Enlightenment: Philosophy and the Making of Modernity, 1650–1750*. New York: Oxford University Press, 2002.

Izzo, Kim, and Ceri Marsh. "Modern Manners for the Morning After." *The Globe and Mail*, June 10, 2000, R3.

Jenson, Robert W. *Canon and Creed*: Interpretation: Resources for the Use of Scripture in the Church. Resources for the Use of Scripture in the Church. Louisville: Westminster John Knox, 2010.

———. *Systematic Theology*, Vol. 2, *The Works of God*. New York: Oxford University Press, 1999.

Jervis, L. Ann. *At the Heart of the Gospel: Suffering in the Earliest Christian Message*. Grand Rapids: Eerdmans, 2007.

———. "Accepting Affliction: Paul's Preaching on Suffering." In *Character and Scripture: Moral Formation, Community, and Biblical Interpretation*, edited by William P. Brown, 290–316. Grand Rapids: Eerdmans, 2002.

———. "Suffering in the Reign of God: The Persecution of Disciples in Q." *Novum Testamentum* 44 (2001) 3–20.

Johnson, Luke T. *Faith's Freedom: A Classic Spirituality for Contemporary Christians*. Minneapolis: Fortress, 1990.

Kierkegaard, Søren. *Philosophical Fragments; Johannes Climacus*. Edited and translated by Howard V. Hong and Edna H. Hong. Kierkegaard's Writings 7. Princeton: Princeton University Press, 1985.

Kluckhohn, Clyde. *The Navaho*. Cambridge: Harvard University Press, 1948.

Korten, David. "Civil Engagement in Creating Future Cities." *Environment and Urbanization* 8 (1996) 35–49.

———. *Getting to the 21st Century: Voluntary Action and the Global Agenda*. West Hartford, CT: Kumarian, 1997.

Kristof, Nicholas D. "D.I.Y. Foreign-Aid Revolution." *New York Times*, October 24, 2010.

Lamott, Anne. *Plan B: Further Thoughts on Faith*. New York: Riverhead, 2005.

———. *Traveling Mercies: Some Thoughts on Faith*. New York: Anchor, 2000.

Lewis, C. S. *The Cosmic Trilogy*. London: Bodley Head, 1990.

———. "The Weight of Glory." In *Screwtape Proposes a Toast and Other Pieces*, 94–110. London: Collins Fontana, 1965.

Lubac, Henri de. *Medieval Exegesis: The Four Senses of Scripture*. Translated by Mark Sebanc and Edward Macierowski. 3 vols. Grand Rapids: Eerdmans, 1998–2000.

Luther, Martin. "On the Councils and the Church." In *Luther's Works 41: Church and Ministry III*, 9–178. Philadelphia: Fortress, 1996.

Lyne, Adrian, director. *Indecent Proposal.* Produced by Sherry Lansing. Screenplay by Amy Holden Jones. 1993. Widescreen DVD Collection. United States: Paramount Home Entertainment, 2002. DVD.
Mace, David, and Vera Mace. *The Sacred Fire: Christian Marriage through the Ages.* Nashville: Abingdon, 1986.
Márkus, G. "Rooted in the Tradition." *Christian History* 60 (Nov.1998) 19–21.
McFague, Sally. *Models of God.* Philadelphia: Fortress, 1987.
McGrath, Alistair. *The Twilight of Atheism: The Rise and Fall of Disbelief in the Modern World.* New York: Galilee/Doubleday, 2006.
———. *Christian Spirituality: An Introduction.* London: Blackwell, 1999.
———. *Understanding the Trinity.* Eastbourne, UK: Kingsway, 1987.
McKibben, Bill. "Climate Change and the Unraveling of Creation." *Christian Century* 116/34 (December 8, 1999) 1196–99.
McLaren, Brian D. *A New Kind of Christian: A Tale of Two Friends on a Spiritual Journey.* San Francisco: Jossey-Bass, 2001.
Meier, John P. *A Marginal Jew: Rethinking the Historical Jesus.* Vol. 1, *The Roots of the Problem and the Person.* Anchor Bible Reference Library. New York: Doubleday, 1991.
Meilaender, Gilbert. "Sexuality." In *New Dictionary of Christian Ethics and Pastoral Theology,* 71–78, edited by David J. Atkinson et al. Downers Grove, IL: InterVarsity, 1995.
Milanovic, Branko. *Worlds Apart: Measuring International and Global Inequality.* Princeton: Princeton University Press, 2005.
Montaigne, Michel de. "Of Cannibals." In *The Complete Essays of Montaigne,* translated by Donald M. Frame, 150–58. Stanford: Stanford University Press, 1958.
Mungello, D. E. *Curious Land: Jesuit Accommodation and the Origins of Sinology.* Honolulu: University of Honolulu Press, 1989.
Myers, Bryant L. *Walking with the Poor: Principles and Practices of Transformational Development.* Maryknoll, NY: Orbis, 1999.
The New Atheism. Website. Online: http://newatheism.org.
Niebuhr, Reinhold. *The Nature and Destiny of Man.* Vol. 2, *Human Destiny.* New York: Scribner 1943.
Onfray, Michel. *Atheist Manifesto: The Case against Christianity, Judaism, and Islam.* New York; Arcade, 2008.
Osmer, Richard R., and Friedrich Schweitzer. *Religious Education between Modernization and Globalization—New Perspectives on the United States and Germany.* Studies in Practical Theology. Grand Rapids: Eerdmans, 2003.
Percy, Harold. *Good News People: An Introduction to Evangelism for Tongue-Tied Christians.* Toronto: Anglican Book Centre, 1996.
Percy, Walker. *Signposts in a Strange Land.* Edited with an introduction by Patrick Samway. New York: Farrar, Straus and Giroux, 1991.
———. "Notes for a Novel about the End of the World." In *The Message in the Bottle,* 101–18. New York: Farrar, Straus and Giroux, 1975.
Phillips, D. Z. *Religion without Explanation.* Oxford: Blackwell, 1976.
Placher, William C. *Unapologetic Theology: A Christian Voice in a Pluralistic Conversation.* Louisville: Westminster John Knox, 1989.
Plantinga, Alvin, and Nicholas Wolterstorff, editors. *Faith and Rationality: Reason and Belief in God.* 3rd ed. Notre Dame: University of Notre Dame Press, 1991.

Pohl, Christine D. *Making Room: Recovering Hospitality as a Christian Tradition*. Grand Rapids: Eerdmans, 1999.
Pollard, Duncan, editor. *Living Planet Report 2010: Biodiversity, Biocapacity and Development*. Gland, Switzerland: World Wildlife Fund, 2010.
Popenoe, David. "The Top Ten Myths of Marriage." Online: http://www.catholiceducation.org/articles/marriage/mf0043.html.
Popkin, Richard. *The History of Scepticism: From Savonarola to Bayle*. Rev. ed. New York: Oxford University Press, 2003.
Ramsey, Paul. "A Christian Approach to the Question of Sexual Relations Outside of Marriage." *Journal of Religion* 45 (1965) 100–18.
Rinehart, Paula. "Losing Our Promiscuity." *Christianity Today* 44/8, July 10, 2000, 32.
Robinson, Marilynne. *The Death of Adam: Essays on Modern Thought*. Boston: Houghton Mifflin, 1998.
Ruether, Rosemary Radford. *Sexism and God-Talk: Toward a Feminist Theology*. Boston: Beacon, 1983.
Sachs, Jeffrey D. *The End of Poverty: Economic Possibilities for Our Time*. New York: Penguin, 2005.
Sacks, Oliver. *Musicophilia: Tales of Music and the Brain*. New York: Knopf, 2007.
Saliers, Don E. *Worship and Spirituality*. Philadelphia: Westminster, 1984.
Sayers, Dorothy L. *Creed or Chaos?* New York: Harcourt, Brace, and Company, 1957.
Schemo, Diane Jean. "Virginity Pledges by Teenagers Can Be Highly Effective, Federal Study Finds." *New York Times*, January 4, 2001.
Secor, Philip. *Richard Hooker on Anglican Faith and Worship: Of the Laws of Ecclesiastical Polity, Book V—A Modern Edition*. London: SPCK, 2003.
Shalit, Wendy. *A Return to Modesty: Discovering the Lost Virtue*. New York: Free Press, 1999.
Sheldrake, Philip. *Living between Worlds: Place and Journey in Celtic Spirituality*. London: Darton, Longman & Todd, 1995.
Shweder, Richard. "Santa Claus on the Cross." In *The Truth about Truth: De-confusing and Re-constructing the Postmodern World*, edited by Walter Truett Anderson, 72–78. New York: Putnam, 1995.
Smart Marriages. Website. Online: http://www.smartmarriages.com.
Smedes, Lewis B. *Sex for Christians: The Limits and Liberties of Sexual Living*. Grand Rapids: Eerdmans, 1989.
Stackhouse, Max. *Covenant and Commitments: Faith, Family, and Economic Life*. Family, Religion, and Culture. Louisville: Westminster John Knox, 1997.
Stafford, Tim. *The Sexual Christian*. Wheaton, IL: Victor, 1989.
———. "Intimacy: Our Latest Sexual Fantasy." *Christianity Today*, January 16, 1987, 25.
Straus, Jillian. *Unhooked Generation: The Truth about Why We're Still Single*. New York: Hyperion, 2006.
Stringfellow, William. *The Politics of Spirituality*. 1984. The William Stringfellow Library: The Dissent Trilogy. Eugene, OR: Wipf & Stock, 2006.
Taylor, Michael J. *The Sacred and the Secular*. Englewood Cliffs, NJ: Prentice-Hall, 1968.
Thiessen, Elmer John. *The Ethics of Evangelism: A Philosophical Defense of Ethical Proselytizing and Persuasion*. Downers Grove, IL: IVP Academic, 2011.
Tillich, Paul. *Love, Power, and Justice*. New York: Oxford University Press, 1954.
Torrance, James B. *Worship, Community & the Triune God of Grace*. Downers Grove, IL: InterVarsity, 1996.

Toynbee, Arnold. "The Religious Background of the Present Environmental Crisis." In *Ecology and Religion in History*, edited by David and Eileen Spring, 137–49. New York: Harper & Row, 1974.
Tozer, A.W. *The Knowledge of the Holy: The Attributes of God; Their Meaning in the Christian Life*. New York: Harper & Row, 1961.
Turner, Philip. "Sex and the Single Life." *First Things* 33/5(May 1993) 15–21.
———. *Sexual Ethics and the Attack on Traditional Morality*. Cincinnati: Forward Movement, 1988.
Underhill, Evelyn. *Worship*. New York: Harper, 1937.
United Nations Millennium Development Goals. Online: http://www.un.org/millenniumgoals.
Vovelle, Michel. *The Revolution against the Church: From Reason to the Supreme Being*. Columbus: Ohio State University Press, 1992.
Wainwright, Geoffrey et al., editors. *The Oxford History of Christian Worship*. Oxford: Oxford University Press, 2006.
Walsh, Brian. "The Church in a Postmodern Age: Ten Things You Need to Know." *Good Idea* 3/4 (Winter 1996) 1–5.
Weil, Simone. "The Love of God and Affliction." In *The Simone Weil Reader*, edited by George A. Panichas, 439–68. New York: McKay, 1977.
Weinberg, Steven. *Lake Views: This World and the Universe*. Cambridge: Belknap, 2009.
Wenham, John W. *The Goodness of God*. London: Inter-Varsity, 1974.
West, Diane. "Generation XXX." *The Washington Times*, April 7, 2000.
White, Lynn, Jr. "The Historical Roots of our Ecologic Crisis." *Science* 155 (1967) 1203–7.
Wilkinson, Loren. "The Bewitching Charms of Neo-paganism." *Christianity Today*, November 15, 1999, 58–63.
Williams, Rowan. *Christian Spirituality: A Theological History from the New Testament to Luther and St. John of the Cross*. Atlanta: John Knox, 1980.
———. "Does It Make Sense to Speak of Pre-Nicene Orthodoxy?" In *The Making of Orthodoxy: Essays in Honour of Henry Chadwick*, edited by Rowan Williams, 1–23. Cambridge: Cambridge University Press, 1989.
Wilson, David Sloan. *Darwin's Cathedral: Evolution, Religion, and the Nature of Society*. Chicago: University of Chicago Press, 2002.
Winner, Lauren. *Real Sex: The Naked Truth about Chastity*. Grand Rapids: Brazos, 2005.
Wright, N. T. *Jesus and the Victory of God*. Christian Origins and the Question of God 2. Minneapolis: Fortress, 1996.
———. *The Resurrection of the Son of God*. Christian Origins and the Question of God 3. Minneapolis: Fortress, 2003.
Wright, Ronald. *A Short History of Progress*. Toronto: House of Anansi, 2004.
Wuthnow, Robert. "Small Groups Forge New Notions of Community and the Sacred." *Christian Century* 110, December 8, 1993, 1236–40.
Yoder, Richard et al. *Development to a Different Drummer: Anabaptist/Mennonite Experiences and Perspectives*. Intercourse, PA: Good Books, 2004.

www.ingramcontent.com/pod-product-compliance
Lightning Source LLC
Chambersburg PA
CBHW071243230426
43668CB00011B/1559